DAVIES THE OCEAN *Railway King and Coal Tycoon*

David Davies on the steps of his mansion at Broneirion, with his spaniel, Midge.

DAVIES THE OCEAN
Railway King and Coal Tycoon

HERBERT WILLIAMS

UNIVERSITY OF WALES PRESS
CARDIFF
1991

British Library Cataloguing in Publication Data

Williams, Herbert, 1932–
  Davies the ocean: railway king and coal tycoon.
  I. Title
  385.092

  ISBN 0–7083–1116–4

Jacket design by Ruth Dineen

Typeset by Action Typesetting Limited, Gloucester
Printed at Biddles Limited, Guildford

FOR DOROTHY

'Whatsoever thy hand findeth to do, do it with thy might'

Contents

Illustrations

Preface

David Davies of Llandinam was a man revered in Welsh cottages in Victorian times as a symbol of success. This one-time sawyer was reputedly the first Welsh businessman to attain millionaire status, and what endeared him to the *gwerin* — the ordinary people of Wales who often have such extraordinary gifts — was that he appeared to be still one of them at heart. He continued to live in his native village of Llandinam in Montgomeryshire, even when the hub of his business empire was in the Rhondda Valley, and to worship in chapel every Sunday with the people he had known all his life.

Even in his lifetime, however, there were many who saw David Davies in a different light, and a century after his death he has become a distant figure. He is confused, very often, with his grandson, the first Lord Davies of Llandinam. David Davies, founder of the family fortune, was a Liberal MP for some time, but he never achieved the grandeur of a peerage. He was also far from being a plaster saint. In this book I try to show how Davies the millionaire was, in my view, a lesser man in some respects than Davies the sawyer, but for all his faults he continues to fascinate me. I first made his acquaintance through Ivor Thomas's biography *Top Sawyer*, a work which has deservedly won an honoured place in Welsh biography. While acknowledging my debt to Mr Thomas for firing my interest in the subject, I have felt for many years that the time had come for a fresh look at David Davies, as every age has its own perspective on the past. Naturally, my view of David Davies differs in important respects from Ivor Thomas's, and I have been obliged here and there to correct statements about Davies's family background which have now turned out to be false. I hope I have done so without arrogance, for there is no final word on any subject and we all work within the limits of the information available to us.

Readers should note that the names of railway stations and collieries are spelt as they were in Victorian times.

In writing this book I have been fortunate to receive the help of people whose interest in David Davies has almost equalled my own. My special thanks are due to my brother and sister-in-law, Victor and Shirley Williams, whose patient examination of census returns, tithe maps and bishops' transcripts has led to a much greater understanding of Davies's family background. My other brother, Richard Williams, was good enough to help me with my researches at the Public Record Office at Kew; my sister Lilian translated one Welsh text and moral support came from my other sister, Kate Hughes. In Cardiff, Kevin Burt was a diligent and enthusiastic researcher.

The staff of the National Library of Wales have been unfailingly helpful and I am particularly grateful to Dafydd Ifans and Hefin Williams. Mr Ifans dug out the William Richard Jones diary and very kindly translated several articles into English, and Mr Williams listed all the collections in which I might find source material. In the Cardiff Central Library, Bryn Jones and other members of staff were of great assistance. I was also fortunate in being able to look up works in the university college library in Cardiff and in the South Wales Miners' Library in University College, Swansea.

No praise would be too high for the staff of the Welsh Industrial and Maritime Museum in Cardiff, whose enthusiasm for this project has been a delight. An especially warm 'thank you' to Dr W.D. (Bill) Jones, who not only checked my chapters dealing with the coal industry but provided me with expert and good-humoured guidance. His colleague Dr David Jenkins also gave me valuable advice and the museum's Keeper, Dr E.S. Owen-Jones, was an unfailing source of encouragement and wisdom.

Howell and Iona Edwards in Cardiff and Aled Llyr of the TV company Delta.translated several texts. The late T. Mervyn Jones — a worthy son of Llandinam — was kind enough to lend me notes of his own researches into the Davies family, and his interest in the book was such that it is sad that he did not live to see its publication. My thanks are due also to Dr John Cule of the University of Wales College of Medicine, Dr E.L. Ellis of Aberystwyth, Owen Gibbs of the Institute of Civil Engineers, Michael Meredith of British Coal, J.P. Cunnane of Rhondda Borough Council, Dr Glyn Tegai Hughes and Eleonora Bowen Davies. Revd Professor S.I. Enoch and Professor Ronald Feuerhahn were my friendly guides through the maze of Calvinistic Methodism. I am grateful to David Rowlands of Grants Photographics in Newtown and John Idris Jones for taking photographs and to Richard Jones for his active interest and encouragement,

The village of Llandinam itself has obviously been a focal point of my researches, and the lively interest in David Davies still shown there has been a boon. The local historian supreme, Miss Lucy Waite, is an oracle to whom I have turned time and again, and I am grateful for her guidance and forbearance. Miss Maureen Cullen, Guider-in-Charge of Broneirion, now the Guides Cymru Training Centre, kindly allowed me to wander around the house and grounds. My thanks, too, to Mr and Mrs Reg Francis of Draintewion, Mrs Jean Naish of The Old Station and Mrs Ann Brown of Gwerneirion for allowing me on to their property; to Johnny Griffiths and to Peter Garbett-Edwards for his local knowledge and keen interest.

Lord and Lady Davies of Plas Dinam have been most co-operative, not least in allowing copies to be made of photographs in their possession. In addition, it has been my good fortune to receive the full support of the surviving sons and daughters of the first Lord Davies: the Hon Edward Davies, the Hon Mrs Mary Noble, the Hon Islwyn Davies and the Hon Mrs Jean Cormack. My sincere thanks to them all.

I have happy memories of the HTV/Delta television drama-documentary *Davies the Ocean*, which I scripted. My thanks to all concerned, especially executive producer Martyn Williams, producer/director Dennis Pritchard Jones and the actor who gave us such a memorable portrayal of David Davies, Dafydd Hywel. I should also like to express my gratitude to those who have followed the David Davies trail before me: Goronwy Jones, who − lucky man − was able to talk to people who had known Davies personally; Ivor Thomas, author of *Top Sawyer*; and two men whose research notes still lie in the National Library of Wales archives, T. Hughes Jones and Vyrnwy J. Lewis.

I wish to acknowledge the generous award of a bursary from the Welsh Arts Council to assist in the writing of this book; their faith in me, and in the work, is much appreciated. The then Literature Director of the Welsh Arts Council, Meic Stephens, was also good enough to send me the rumbustious verses on Barry Docks by George Fardo which I would otherwise have missed.

In addition, I should like to thank Ned Thomas and Liz Powell of the University of Wales Press for their careful and considerate editing of my manuscript.

My wife Dorothy has once again turned up trumps, helping out with the research and providing unstinting support and encouragement. Without her, I doubt if I would have stayed the course.

The last acknowledgement has, I fear, some sadness in it. It was Lynn Hughes who commissioned this biography in the early years of his publishing house, Golden Grove. Sadly, in spite of all his efforts the firm went under at a time of high interest rates, and I am grateful to the University of Wales Press for rescuing my manuscript.

Acknowledgements

The author and publishers wish to thank the following for kind permission to reproduce photographic material:

Lord Davies and Grants Photographics of Newtown: David Davies at Broneirion (frontispiece), Talerddig cutting (p.61), ceremonial trowels (p.139) Davies at Broneirion (p.178).

John Idris Jones: bridge and statue at Llandinam (p.15), Broneirion (p.84), statue of Davies (p.227).

Llanidloes Museum: commemorative medal (p.24).

The National Library of Wales: letter to Ann Warburton Owen (p.58), opening ceremony at Machynlleth (p.81), advertisement (p.128), hand-bill (p.210).

Welsh Industrial and Maritime Museum: General Wood locomotive (p.120), Barry Docks (p.195).

All maps of Davies's railways were drawn for this publication by Victor Williams.

1 The Navvy's Shirt

On a summer day in 1886, election fever ran high in the seaside town of Aberystwyth. A bitter campaign had been fought, and now the result was eagerly awaited.

One of the candidates was a stocky man in his late sixties, with a clean-shaven upper lip and straggling whiskers. The windows of his committee rooms above the town's roller-skating rink in Queen's Square, opposite the site of the present Town Hall, were plastered with telegrams sent from polling stations throughout Cardiganshire, conveying encouraging news of how the cause was progressing.[1]

The candidate was the legendary David Davies, the sitting member — a man famed throughout Wales as 'Davies the Ocean' or 'Davies Llandinam'. His opponent, eighteen years younger, was Bowen Rowlands QC, who for all his virtues was little known outside the south Wales circuit where he practised as a barrister.

For Davies, this was far more than an electoral battle. It was a test of his credibility as a public figure, for he had staked all on his personal standing in a county which only a year before had been regarded as his fief. He was one of the richest men in Wales, a wealth derived not from inheritance but from unremitting personal effort; and he had given unstintingly of that wealth, not least to help establish the 'college by the sea', the founding college of the University of Wales, in a bizarre mock-Gothic agglomeration of towers and turrets half a mile away.

He believed that personal regard and gratitude would be enough to take him back to Parliament, but he was to be disappointed. At a quarter to five on the afternoon of Saturday 10 July, a telegram was delivered to the Liberal Club with a three-word message, 'You are in'. Exultantly the supporters of Bowen Rowlands swept to the Belle Vue Hotel on the promenade to give him the news.[2]

Rowlands, the official 'Gladstonian' candidate, was in by nine votes. Davies, standing as a Liberal Unionist in defiance of Gladstone's policy of Home Rule for Ireland, was out in the cold.

The born winner had become a loser.

Before we look closer at this extraordinary man, let us go forward fifty-eight years to catch a glimpse of a patient propped up on pillows in Sully Hospital, just outside Penarth in what is now the county of South Glamorgan. He has a room to himself, his importance being such that the nurses' sick bay has been temporarily given over to his exclusive use, and on this balmy afternoon in the spring of 1944 he is gazing over the Bristol Channel. The coast of Somerset is clearly visible, but his inward eye looks beyond that to occupied Europe. He is being tended by a young nurse, Eleonora Bowen Davies, who during his brief time as a cancer patient in her care has come to admire his courage and humour. He makes an unexpected remark that, years afterwards, stays fresh in her memory. 'Just think, nurse,' he says. 'A lovely day like this, and our boys are fighting a war. If the League of Nations had worked, it need never have happened.'[3]

He, too, is a David Davies, and he too has suffered a defeat and had to reconcile himself to the fact that his crusade for a better world order, a crusade into which he has poured much of his inherited wealth, has come to nothing.

Over a hundred miles away, in that same year of 1944, two unmarried sisters are walking through the wooded grounds of their country mansion in Montgomeryshire. They are Gwendoline and Margaret (Daisy) Davies, and their mansion is Gregynog. Ten years earlier, the place had been an enchantment of music and verse. Their festivals brought world-famous poets and musicians to Gregynog, and their private press was synonymous with excellence. But in 1944 the press is idle, and the hall is filled not with stiff and starched patrons of the arts but by wounded soldiers, sailors and airmen. Gregynog has been turned into a Red Cross hospital. Gwennie and Daisy are doing their bit.

Davies, the dying patient in Sully, is better known as the first Lord Davies, the baronetcy having been created in 1932. He is the brother of Gwendoline and Margaret, and the grandson of the man who lost the Cardiganshire election to Bowen Rowlands.

But there is another link between the generations. It is money.

At the outbreak of the Second World War, the Davies family of Llandinam and Gregynog was one of the richest in Wales, noted not only for its wealth but for its good works. Its philanthropy seemed limitless; it had funded an all-Wales campaign against the scourge of tuberculosis, established the world's first Chair of International Politics in Aberystwyth, bequeathed a priceless collection of French Impressionist paintings to the National Museum of Wales, provided the first pithead baths in Wales for miners, restored Owain Glyndŵr's Parliament House in Machynlleth, built garden villages and had poured money into a variety of religious and charitable causes. In the gathering gloom of the 1930s Lord Davies had campaigned vigorously, almost frenziedly, for a new international machinery which would make war obsolete, and had raised a Temple of Peace in Cardiff to give physical expression to his ideals. None of this would have been possible had not his grandsire, the loser in Aberystwyth, been born with the strength of an ox and an indomitable will to succeed.

The founder of the dynasty was called Davies the Ocean after his Ocean group of collieries in the Rhondda and neighbouring valleys, and Davies Llandinam after the tiny Montgomeryshire village which he made a synonym for success. But he was also known by another name, Davies Top Sawyer, for at an early age his muscles were being hardened in the saw-pit on his father's hillside smallholding in Llandinam. When he died in 1890 his personal estate was valued at £404,424. 10s. 1d.[4] He would have considered the penny important.

David Davies was regarded as a giant in his own generation and the next, but with the replacement of Liberalism by Socialism – or rather Labourism – as the dominant political force in Wales in the first half of the twentieth century his reputation inevitably suffered. When he was thought of at all, he tended to be dismissed as just another blood-sucking capitalist boss, an exploiter rather than a giver. Capitalist he certainly was, but to view people as stereotypes is to see through a glass darkly. David Davies was in the true sense an original, who in his prime commanded an admiration amounting to hero-worship. 'Everywhere in Wales his name is mentioned with pride,' enthused some 1870s copywriters in a newspaper advertisement. He had just become an MP, and a 'Life-like Portrait' of him was on sale for five shillings.[5] For Goronwy Jones, writing in 1913, he was 'one of the morning stars, an exceptional instance of keen insight, of a powerful will, of indomitable perseverance, who surmounted untold difficulties.' While gathering material for the first full-scale biography of David Davies, Jones had interviewed people who had known him well and would sigh, 'Eh but he was a wonderful man, we shall ne'er see his like again.'[6]

What had he done to deserve such adulation? The fact that the question needs to be posed, a century after his death, might be held to be proof of the vanity of the human endeavour which Davies rated so highly. Yet there is no doubt that the Wales of 1890 was vastly different from that of 1818, and that a significant part of this change was directly due to his efforts. He pioneered railways in mid Wales, ushered in a new era in the Rhondda by successfully gambling on finding rich seams of steam coal there, and finally confounded the powerful Bute family in Cardiff Castle by spearheading the outrageously bold plan to provide a brand-new port at Barry.

Impressive as they were, however, it was not so much his deeds that stirred the pulse as the manner of the man. He had a charisma that marked him out as something special, a gusto and self-belief that fired the imagination. Above all, he proved that a boy born in Wales to parents with very little money, and who worked like a slave in adolescence to put bread in the mouths of his younger brothers and sisters, could earn the respect, not only of the highest in the land, but of foreign potentates.

The words on his tombstone in Llandinam churchyard are taken from the ninth chapter of the Book of Ecclesiastes: 'Whatsoever thy hand findeth to do, do it with thy might; for there is no work, nor device, nor knowledge, nor wisdom, in the grave, whither thou goest.'

They are singularly well chosen, for never did an epitaph more truly reflect the philosophy of the person whose remains lie beneath it.

David Davies had the reputation of being the first Welsh millionaire, and although this may be open to argument there is no doubt that the wealth at his disposal was colossal. At the time of his death the London *Star* reported that 'he told the writer in 1873 that his annual share of the profits [of the Ocean Coal Company] was then £95,000 and that he had refused an offer of £375,000 for his interest'.[7] When questioned about the cost of the Barry Dock and Railway scheme he declared, with jaunty self-assurance, 'If the public will not come forward I will find the whole of the money myself.'[8] Nothing seemed beyond him; until well into the twentieth century, the words 'Davies Llandinam' signified boundless wealth.

It was not only the amassing of a fortune but the use he made of it that won David Davies respect. While suffering no qualms of conscience about wealth which he would have claimed to be earned honestly, he felt — as his grandchildren were to feel — that riches resulting from communal effort should be returned in some measure to the community. Thus we find him putting thousands of pounds alongside the 'pennies of the poor' to enable the first Welsh university college to be established in Aberystwyth, and donating generously to other causes. (He was said to be the first Welshman to contribute in sums of four figures.)[9] Once he was asked how much he gave to religious charities in a year and replied that it was probably around £10,000, although he 'never troubled to keep account of such gifts'.[10] The first Baron Davies of Llandinam believed his grandfather acted on the principle of giving one-tenth of his income to philanthropic causes, thus following the scriptural precept on the payment of tithes.[11] In the exceptionally prosperous year of 1873 his gifts were said to total £16,000.[12] Yet the circumspection which tempered the boldness of his business dealings also influenced his charitable bequests. When a new Calvinistic Methodist chapel was proposed for Llandinam he provided most of the money but not all of it, 'so that no one can say it was David Davies's chapel.'[13]

In many ways Davies the Ocean embodied the beliefs and attitudes of his contemporaries in Wales. He was Nonconformist in religion, Liberal in politics and empirical in his approach to the Welsh language. (He spoke it fluently, but acknowledged English to be the language of commerce and for 'getting on' in the world.) One of his obituarists, however, believed that certain newspapers had committed a 'great error' in seeing him as a 'typical' Welshman: he was far too exceptional to be a representative figure.[14]

David Davies was, without doubt, one of the most colourful characters ever to bestride the public stage in Wales. He was boastful and overbearing at times and touchingly humble at others. His pride in his great wealth, a pride he never concealed, never degenerated into snobbery. He might lecture his workmen on the virtues of thrift, but he did not treat them as social inferiors. When bad weather brought his railway works in mid Wales to a temporary halt, he would go into the shed where his navvies were sheltering and engage in wrestling bouts and other feats of strength with them to pass the time.[15] In his prime he was a man of powerful physique who could do anything he asked of his workmen. At the opening of the Tenby and Whitland Railway in 1866, a few months short of his forty-eighth birthday, he boasted of being able to do

> ... all that was required to make a railway with his own hands. He could use a pick and shovel and show the men how to do it. He could cut down trees for sleepers and fencing, and saw them up and fix them. He could drive an engine, take it to pieces and put it together again. He could show the traffic manager how to make rates and arrange traffic, and although a Lord was a great fellow he felt better than a Lord for he believed the working man to be the finest fellow in the land, for he was his own master and independent of everybody.[16]

All this might be true, but it made the sophisticated cringe. Davies, however, was not a sophisticated man and did not pretend to be one. 'It is a great honour to be able to wear a navvy's shirt and command £100,000,' he would say,[17] and when he reached Parliament he brought to the Commons a trenchant and demotic style of address which had the momentum and power of one of his locomotives. Within three months of his election as Member for Cardigan Boroughs in 1874, he startled the House with a maiden speech short on measured phrases and oratorical flourishes but full of fire, fury and the kind of rugged humour that rarely found expression there. It was hailed by the press as a speech of fervour and vigour which 'tickled the ear' with its 'broad vernacular'[18] and 'kept the House in a roar of laughter'.[19] In the words of the *Liverpool Daily Post*

> There was something grotesque in his manner, in his words, and in his phrases ... To hear an honourable Member allude to another

honourable Member as 'Our friend across there' is as exhilarating as it is unusual.[20]

There were those, though, for whom Davies the Ocean was anathema, and some were coal-owners like himself. During the great Parliamentary battle over the Barry Dock scheme, Alfred Tylor, who gave his name to Tylorstown in the Rhondda, went before a Select Committee of the Lords to rail against 'great capitalists like Mr David Davies', who 'had all the plums' while less fortunate employers bore 'all the discomfort and loss'.[21] More predictably, during the bitter coalfield dispute of 1875 he found himself categorized as a man who, in common with the other 'masters', would 'crush the men down to the dust.'[22] He could endure the accusations of his fellow-capitalists much easier than the taunts of those who claimed to represent the workers, for he was ever proud – even boastful – of the fact that he had sprung from the ranks of working men. 'It is hard, just before I am going into the grave, to have such an accusation made against me,' he said,[23] and the fact that the grave was still fifteen years distant does not make his protest any the less plaintive.

The story of David Davies, the country boy who rose from rags to riches, thrilled the people of his generation, yet he has a much wider significance. In many ways he was a bridge: between the peasantry and the moneyed classes, the old Wales of scattered farmsteads and the new Wales of the industrial valleys, the old politics of the squires and the new politics of the bright young radicals. His obstinacy was sometimes rooted more in self-interest or vanity than high principle, and his political career ended in tragi-comedy, but he is an important figure in modern Wales, and by the sweat of his brow and the boldness of his ambition he founded a family dynasty.

2 *Peasants of the Better Class*

'It is I should think an almost unique condition of things for so large a fortune to go to what is absolutely still a family of peasants of the better class.'[1]

This very superior sentiment sprang from the pen of the Liberal MP for Montgomery, Arthur Charles Humphreys-Owen, on 12 January 1898, six days after the funeral of Edward Davies of Plas Dinam. He was writing to Lord Rendel, who had held the seat before him – the first Liberal to do so.

Edward Davies, the only son of David Davies and his wife Margaret – there were no other children of the marriage – had died at the age of forty-five, leaving £1,206,311.[2] There is no questioning the size of the fortune, though whether he was a peasant, of a better class or otherwise, is a matter of opinion. He would certainly have been grossly offended to hear himself described thus, for the wealth he had inherited gave him such lofty ideas that less than two years before his death he expressed the view that the lack of honesty in politics was due to the extension of the franchise to those who had never enjoyed the benefits of a good sound education.[3]

It is doubtful, however, whether Humphreys-Owen was alone in thinking of the Davies family of Llandinam in such disdainful terms. There were people still living at the end of the century who remembered the days when the originator of the family fortune had been fed on evil-smelling bread, bread so repulsive that it made him cry when forced to eat it.[4] Little wonder that such a simple thing as wholesome bread held, for David Davies, a significance which later ages would find hard to understand. He once conjured up a vision of the good life with the immortal words, 'If you are content with brown bread, you may of course remain where you are; but if you wish to enjoy the luxuries of life, with white bread to boot, then the way to do so is by the acquisition of English.'[5] The fact that he was speaking on the National Eisteddfod platform tells us as much about the cultural climate of the time as it does about the importance of bread. The world into which David Davies was born in 1818, the eldest of ten children (not nine, as hitherto supposed),[6] was one in which to be poor and Welsh was a twin disability that needed great strength of will to overcome. The days when the Welsh gentry had trooped off to London to jostle for places in the Tudor court, confident that Wales had at last come into her own, had long gone. Wales was commonly regarded, at best, as a rather quaint appendage to

England, with a backward population which insisted on speaking an incomprehensible tongue. The very idea of Wales, as a distinct country rather than a mere region, was held in question throughout the century; even in the 1880s, a Welsh bishop was able to argue that the term 'Wales' was 'merely a geographical expression'.[7]

There is no doubt that David Davies was born in Llandinam, a village of no pretensions in the upper Severn Valley between Llanidloes and Newtown, but there are some intriguing puzzles surrounding his birth. He enjoyed saying that 'My age is three eighteens', and gave his date of birth as 18 December 1818,[8] but this is clearly incorrect as the Llandinam parish records show that he was baptized on 20 November 1818 by the vicar, John Tilsley.[9]

A more intriguing question still is how the story originated that his parents came from Cardiganshire, when all the evidence points to the fact that they were Montgomeryshire folk, born and bred. The census returns for 1841, unavailable in detail to earlier biographers, show David and Elizabeth Davies of 'Neuoddvach', Llandinam − the parents of David Davies − answering 'Yes' when asked if they had been born in the county of Montgomery.[10] This was the first census in which the occupants of properties were actually named; before this there were only head counts. David Davies the elder had died by the time of the next census in 1851, but Elizabeth gave her place of birth as Llandinam[11] and did so again in the census return of 1861, nine years before her death.[12]

It would have been strange had she not done so, because until her marriage she was Elizabeth Reynallt or Reynolds, living in Cwm, a small farmhouse half a mile from the village of Llandinam, where she 'kept house for her father and grandmother'.[13] Confirmation of her maiden name is to be found in the 1861 census, which records that her brother, Richard Reynolds, a railway labourer, was then living at Neuaddfach with her and two of her children.[14]

Clearly, then, the notion advanced by Ivor Thomas in *Top Sawyer* that she was one Elizabeth Felix of Lledrod, who 'crossed the hills from Cardiganshire to Montgomeryshire' with her husband after their marriage in Lledrod, was mistaken.[15] Intriguingly, though, there is some evidence to suggest that David Davies's paternal *grandfather* may have come from Cardiganshire. On 26 October 1937, before the publication of *Top Sawyer*, Ivor Thomas wrote to the first Lord Davies (David Davies's grandson), saying:

I had Dr W. Ll. Davies [then librarian of the National Library of Wales] to lunch here today ... He says he heard from an old woman of 80, who died about 20 years ago, that David Davies's grandfather and a brother came from Pontrhydfendigaid to

Montgomeryshire, that the grandfather settled in Llandinam and the brother set up a corn mill at Trefeglwys, which still flourishes there.[16]

Thomas asked Lord Davies if he could 'throw light on the generation in which this migration from Cardiganshire to Montgomeryshire took place', but Lord Davies replied that he had 'no knowledge' of his great-grandfather's birthplace.

> Honestly, I did not know until I read it in the book [a MS copy of *Top Sawyer*] that he was supposed to have emigrated from Cardiganshire to Montgomeryshire, and it is news to me that his brother settled at Trefeglwys.[17]

The information (which we now know to be incorrect) on which Ivor Thomas eventually relied was presumably that contained in notes on David Davies's life made by Edwin Jones, headmaster of Llandinam Board School from 1889 to 1907, who says at one point that David Davies senior 'was born in Llanilar in 1795' and at another that he was 'born in Lledrod or Llanilar', providing no evidence for either of these claims.[18] It is only fair to add that the information contained in the census returns of 1841–61, quoted above, would have been unavailable to Thomas when writing *Top Sawyer*, as such personal details remain confidential for 100 years.

The Bishop's Transcripts for the parish of Llandinam record the baptism on 2 January 1788 of David, 'son of David Davies and Mary his wife a Popor [pauper]'.[19] This could conceivably have been the baptism of David Davies's father. If it were, it would show that the subject of this biography had been given the Christian name not only of his father but of his grandfather. There is no ambiguity in a later entry, which reveals the marriage on 2 June 1818 of Davies the Ocean's parents, David Davies and Elizabeth Reynolds, 'both of this parish, by banns', the ceremony being conducted by John Tilsley, vicar, with David Reynolds and Maurice Davies as witnesses.[20] The fact that their eldest son was baptized only five and a half months later, on 20 November, proves that Elizabeth was many weeks pregnant when she went to the altar.[21] Why David Davies should give 18 December as his date of birth when he must have been born at least a month earlier remains a mystery; it could not have been to conceal the fact of his mother's pregnancy, because this would still have left only six months between her marriage and his birth.

The house in which David Davies first saw light of day was ominously called Draintewion, 'the place of the thick brambles'. A traditional Welsh long house standing on the lower slopes of Yr Allt Gethin, which rises to a height just short of 1,500ft above the village of Llandinam, it had timber walls and a thatched roof at the time of his birth. Cowshed, pigsty and barn were under the same roof as the living quarters.[22] The house, much altered and modernized but still bearing its original name, was the home of Mr Reg Francis late in the 1980s. He had been born there and, a carpenter by trade, had carried out a radical reconstruction in 1951, when he replaced the timbered walls with concrete blocks.[23] The original massive oak timbers of the roof remained untouched by this alteration, but the saw-pit had long since disappeared.

Draintewion was not so much a hill farm as a smallholding, and David and Elizabeth Davies knew that any comforts they obtained there would not be won easily. The hillside above the house rose steeply to the table-top summit so typical of hills in the vicinity, and there was no farm machinery to lighten their labour. It was a long walk along the rough track to and from the village, but such rigours were an accepted part of life. They were sustained by their religion, for they were staunch Calvinistic Methodists who worshipped in the meeting house which had been built twenty years before in Llandinam on a plot of land known as 'William Breese's garden'.[24]

Scriptural texts came to David Davies with his mother's milk. He had the breadth of imagination that might have made him a poet, had he not been gifted with the strength and practical genius that took him in other directions. The very situation of Draintewion might have had a formative influence on him, for the spaciousness of the view over the valley would have a powerful effect on a boy encouraged to feed on the symbolism and poetry of the Bible. He may not quite have seen the Promised Land beckoning, but he would certainly have been alive to its possibility. In later life quasi-biblical phrases were to run trippingly off his tongue. 'I often feared this would be the rock of my destruction,' he would say portentously of one of his greatest engineering feats, the Talerddig cutting, 'but instead it has proved the rock of my salvation'.[25]

The community into which David Davies was born was one in which self-help was allied to a spirit of neighbourly obligation. Sheep were brought down from the hills to a common fold for shearing, and the men would perform the work in groups.[26] Davy — as he was known as a boy — quickly learned the harsh realities of life, for he had to trample in the oat seed scattered by his mother, and to climb the steep hill in all weathers to tend the sheep and lambs. The diet was plain and unrelenting — rough rye bread for the most part, bread made often from mouldy corn, a pasty, ill-smelling substance he had to stuff in his mouth like a penance.[27]

Life at Draintewion was governed by the seasons. Few people travelled far from their own parish, for practically all the business of life was enacted close to home. The old order was, however, about to pass away, and David Davies was to be one of the instruments of that change. He was in his seventh year when the Stockton and Darlington Railway brought the first steam rail passenger service to Britain, but at the time the boy's parents would probably have regarded this as no more than a distant and irrelevant sensation.

Llandinam was seen in idyllic terms by the few visitors who frequented this out-of-the-way spot. It was 'a quiet little village close upon the river', with half-timbered whitewashed cottages and 'a grassy knoll on which stands the village church with its wooden tower and its peal of silvery bells'.[28] The picture is less idyllic, however, when one considers how often those bells tolled for the young.

Although agriculture was the chief concern, the cottage industry of weaving had made its appearance in the locality. There were weaving lofts in nearby Newtown and these occupied the entire upper storey of many houses in the town, particularly north of the River Severn.[29] Llanidloes was another focal point for the county's developing woollen and flannel industry. In due course Newtown would become known as 'the Leeds of Wales',[30] but this applied only after the introduction of powered looms, which did not exist in the town in any numbers until the 1870s.[31]

As the pace of economic change quickened, the social and political forces that were to transform society gathered momentum. Before David Davies reached manhood the Reform Bill of 1832 had been passed, and seven years later there were Chartist riots in Llanidloes several months before the great march on Newport. Within the timbered walls of Draintewion, however, the political pamphleteers were of less account than the prophets of Israel. Davy's mother, robust in body and mind, was regarded as an authority on theological questions by those of like persuasion, the discussions often turning on what now seems the decidedly esoteric matter of the Five Points: The Election of Grace, Redemption, Free Will, The Effectual Call and Perseverance in Grace.[32] Davy had a healthy interest in the rough pursuits of childhood, but whatever impatience he may have felt from time to time with the religiosity surrounding him did not lead to any serious alienation. On the contrary, his faith never appears to have faltered. Even at the busiest periods of his life he continued to take a Sunday school class in Llandinam,[33] Sunday schools in those days being for the mature as well as the callow. 'The Bible was sacred to him, he read it like a little child,' wrote Daniel Rowlands at the end of Davies's life. 'Frequently while listening intently to the words of the Gospel, tears would come to his eyes and run down his cheek.'[34] Even after making allowance for the zeal of the obituarist, it is clear that the chapel was a cornerstone of David Davies's existence. It symbolized spiritual probity, and he believed it should stand for financial rectitude also. A debt on a chapel, he would say, was like a devil on the roof.[35]

One of the central facts of David Davies's life is that he had scarcely any formal education. He is supposed to have attended the local voluntary school up to the age of eleven — a makeshift affair held in the fusty gallery of St Llonio's — but for all he learned there he might as well have stayed away, for in all probability he remained semi-literate until his thirties.[36] While saying very little about his early studies he was never ashamed to admit that he had 'not been properly educated'.[37] He would certainly have been of far more practical use to his father at Draintewion than in trying to play the little scholar. Davies senior was a sawyer as well as a farmer, felling trees on commission. Davy worked alongside him in the saw-pit as soon as he was able to handle the long saw and by the age of fifteen he was doing a man's job: indeed, his father would say he was worth a sovereign a day to him in the timber season.[38] This suggests that by the mid-1830s the family was achieving a modest prosperity, no small part of this success being due to young Davy's prodigious strength and enthusiasm. His father's own enterprise, however, must not be discounted: he worked up a lively trade with carpenters in neighbouring Cardiganshire, where farmers' daughters often received a three-cornered cupboard (*cwpwrdd tridarn*) on their betrothal. Montgomeryshire oak was in big demand, and Davy and his father provided it. The story goes that Davy was known as the hardest worker for miles around, barely stopping for meals. He also had the extraordinary ability of being able to gauge the amount of timber in a tree at a glance.[39]

Since the saw-pit was central to David Davies's youth, it is not surprising that it provided him with one of his liveliest sayings in later life: 'Find a rest for a lever and you could lift the world'. Lifting timbers with levers was part of the sawyer's craft, and even in the saw-pit there was a basic inequality which Davies cunningly turned to advantage in the days of his prosperity. There were always two men at work in the saw-pit, the bottom sawyer grasping one end of the saw with the top sawyer standing above him. When taunted with being 'only a sawyer' he would exclaim triumphantly, 'Aye, but I was always top sawyer, wasn't I?'[40]

The saw-pit naturally held a fascination for the children of Llandinam, and many of their games took place in or around it. One of them reflected the religious obsessions of the age, for mock preaching meetings would be staged, with the 'preacher' on the beam that straddled the top of the pit, the 'deacons' on either side and the 'congregation' at the bottom. There were more vigorous pursuits such as hunting the squirrel to death, David Davies's boyhood friend Matthew Humphreys recalling how young Davy 'would not be beaten but would persistently follow the squirrell (*sic*) climbing tree after tree with unwearied patience. The principle was, as it were, inate (*sic*) in him, & to all his companions in the years of child and boyhood he was known by all to be possessed of this quality.'[41] No doubt the will to win appeared more admirable in retrospect than it did at the time.

The brutal game of hunt-the-squirrel would not have unduly offended the sensibilities of the age. A diary kept in Llandinam in 1855 records the setting of steel traps not only for marauding foxes but for rooks guilty of 'pulling the thatch off the corn ricks', and the casual beating to death with a broomstick of a blackbird which 'came to look for meat in the back kitchen'.[42]

In the autumn of 1821, a second child was born at Draintewion. The first of David Davies's siblings was christened Thomas at Bethel Calvinistic Methodist Church, Llandinam, on 28 October that year, but beyond this nothing is known about him whatever.[43] He is not included in the census returns for the parish of Llandinam mentioned above, so it is possible that he died in infancy. John, the third child of David and Elizabeth Davies, was born in 1823, Edward in 1826, Richard in 1827, Mary on Christmas Day 1830, Joseph in 1833, Sarah in 1835, Elizabeth in 1838 and Jane in 1840.[44]

By the time of the 1841 census the Davieses were no longer to be found at Draintewion; they had packed their possessions and moved downhill to Neuaddfach, a larger holding on lower ground near the turnpike road between Llanidloes and Newtown, with a wood-and-plaster farmhouse. Davy was then in his twenty-third year and had suffered a reverse. An anonymous note in the Llandinam Papers says he had 'nursed a fondness for a charming young neighbour, a Miss D ... of Creigfryn', and was so confident of winning her that he even bought the ring. Alas for his hopes; he was rejected because her parents 'would not entrust the future of their child to him'.[45] Easy to laugh at them now; but how could they have known that young Davies, a lad with few prospects, would become one of the richest men in Wales?

It is likely that this disappointment in love spurred David Davies on to even greater efforts to prove his worth and the validity of his ambitions. Now, early in the 1840s, his thoughts began to reach beyond the farm and the saw-pit to contemplate wider prospects not as some future dream but as an immediate possibility. He knew he could work anyone into the ground; when the strength of others gave out he was able to keep on labouring at his task, seemingly as fresh as at the day's beginning. He also knew his own ability to handle money; his avoidance of the tavern was due, perhaps, as much to his reluctance to spend as the Calvinistic aversion to alcohol he shared with his parents. He gained a reputation for being tight-fisted,[46] given to bouts of generosity only within the confines of the chapel; here he gave on a scale which astonished other members of the congregation. When money was required to repair the building he pledged five pounds, a sum so large that people doubted his ability to pay, but when the time came to honour the pledges a year later he produced not five pounds but ten,[47] to the chagrin of those who would have gained much more satisfaction from seeing him taken down a peg or two. He was fortunate in possessing not merely strength and intelligence but the ability to arrive instantly at a decision which others reached only after much agonizing. He had a kind of intuitive insight which he learned to trust; he came to say that he made mistakes only when he took the advice of others. 'He often spoke,' wrote Goronwy Jones, 'as one seeing the invisible.'

His first chance to distinguish himself came in 1846, when he was twenty-seven. The county surveyor for Montgomeryshire and Denbighshire, Thomas Penson, was looking for a reliable contractor for an important job in Llandinam. He was throwing an iron bridge across the Severn and needed someone to lay its foundations and make the approach road. Penson was a remarkable man who, since his appointment in 1819,[48] had brought about immense improvements to the roads and bridges in the two counties. He was a notoriously hard taskmaster[49] with a low opinion of the local contractors and scant sympathy with those driven to the wall by the severity of his methods. Word reached him of the young Llandinam farmer who was busily improving Neuaddfach and after inspecting his work at first hand, he offered him the contract. The excitement which this caused in the Davies household can be imagined, but the sibling rivalry between David and his younger brother Richard — whom he employed as a waggoner on the site — gave rise to a day of high drama during the construction work. Nineteen-year-old Richard was late turning up for work one morning and David was none too pleased. 'Where has te' been all day, mon?' he demanded, to which Richard belligerently replied, 'I'll warm thee before night, don't thee mind.' As the brothers frenziedly tried to prove who was the more vigorous worker, they 'warmed' not only themselves but poor Matthew Humphreys, now working for his friend Davy as a labourer. Humphreys would ruefully recall in his old age how he and 'Mr D.D.' loaded no fewer than eighty tons of gravel from the river bed that day, 'this being as much as four of the best men of the present day can perform'. Had Humphreys been on piecework it would have been some consolation, but all he received was his usual day wage of eighteen pence.[50]

The handsome single-arch bridge, cast in Hawarden, bears the date of its construction, 1846. It was the first cast-iron bridge in Montgomeryshire, with a span of ninety feet,[51] and Penson's satisfaction was such that he

*The building of this single-arch bridge across the Severn at Llandinam in 1846
provided the young David Davies with his first major contract. To the right is a
statue of the rich and successful Davies, and in the distance a local symbol of his
wealth and social standing — his mansion at Broneirion.*

awarded David Davies fifteen pounds over and above the agreed fee,[52]
an unheard-of act of generosity. The acceptance of this commission by
Davies was of vital importance, for it provided the springboard for his
later triumphs.

Unhappily the celebrations at Neuaddfach were short-lived, for on 28
September 1846 David Davies senior died at the age of fifty-nine. He had
been ill for years with the wasting disease then rife in rural Wales, an
affliction known by many names: consumption, phthisis, the white
scourge, tuberculosis (TB), or simply — and perhaps most luridly — 'the
decline'. This is the word that appears on the death certificate issued on
30 September by Thomas Davies, registrar. The cause of death of David
Davies, farmer, of Neuaddfach, Llandinam, is given as 'Decline', and the
next column, reserved for the 'signature, description and residence of
informant', bears the words: 'The Mark X of David Davies Present at the
Death Neuaddfach Llandinam.'[53] Eight weeks later he made his mark a
second time, as witness to the death of his brother Edward. Five years
were to pass before he carefully wrote his name on his marriage

certificate[54] — the first extant example of David Davies's handwriting.

The cause of Edward's death on 23 November, six weeks short of his twenty-first birthday, appears as 'Ruptured a blood vessel',[55] which might indicate a stroke from a brain haemorrhage or bleeding from a stomach haemorrhage. It could also indicate a lung haemorrhage resulting from pulmonary tuberculosis,[56] and given Edward's age this is, perhaps, the most likely explanation. It would have been a frightening sight, the young man drenched in the blood coughed up from lungs destroyed by the deadly bacilli. He was buried in the grave where his father had so lately been taken, at the lower end of St Llonio's churchyard, not far from the spot where the lich-gate now stands. Less than five months later, in the spring of 1847, there was another death in the family: that of John, aged twenty-three. The word 'Decline' on his death certificate tells us everything.[57]

The fact that David Davies's father and at least one of his brothers succumbed to this highly contagious disease gives added significance to the bold and far-sighted campaign which his grandchildren waged against it in the early part of the twentieth century. When Lord Davies and the Gregynog sisters set up the Welsh National Memorial Association in 1912, TB was the commonest single cause of death in Wales.[58] It was akin to war in the toll it took of young lives; there were many who believed its curse would never be lifted. Yet the Association's declared aim was not simply to treat tuberculosis, but to 'eradicate' it.[59] That one word speaks volumes for a commitment and breadth of vision rarely encountered.

For David Davies, work was the answer to grief; he applied himself to it more vigorously than ever. Most of his earnings came the hard way, but he was also discovering the delight of making a quick profit. There was the day the squire of Llandinam, John Offley Crewe-Read of Llandinam Hall, offered him the job of removing an oak tree near the hall; it was his for £5, promised the squire, if he would chop the tree down and cart the timber away. Davies readily agreed, and made an £80 profit; such decisions came easily to a man who had only to look at a hog or a bullock to be able to judge its weight with surprising accuracy.[60] Luck was also on his side; when ten trees were up for sale near Neuaddfach, he chose five and a man from Newtown the others. When the trees were sawn up, the timber yielded by David Davies's trees was found to be excellent, whereas the other man's timber was worthless.[61]

John's death was a blow in more ways than one. Until weakened by illness he had been of great assistance to his eldest brother, helping him saw wood into beams. Now he was no longer there, David could not manage alone and employed men to saw for him.[62] The Montgomeryshire tithe maps for 1845 give us an insight into the family concerns at the time. They show David Davies to be the occupier not only of the 158 acres of 'Neuodd Fach' (*sic*) but of the 215 acres of Tyn-y-maen, which became the home farm of Plas Dinam when the mansion was built in 1873. He was renting both holdings; the owner of 'Neuodd Fach' was given as John Osley (*sic*) Crewe-Read, while ownership of Tyn-y-maen was shared by H. Selleck Brome and J.O. Crewe-Read. Both farms consisted predominantly of pasture, with a small amount of arable land; Tyn-y-maen had a 100-acre sheepwalk, while the sixty-two acres of 'Eskern wen bank' provided most of the pasture at Neuaddfach.[63] The names of the fields were written on David Davies's heart: Cae Ffynnon, Cae Glas, Cae Tan y Ffordd, Cwm Mawr, Erw Ucha, Erw Isa, Cae Domen. English names mingle with the Welsh on the tithe maps: at Tyn-y-maen we find Lower Cae Bedw and The Four Acres (which turn out to be two acres and twenty-seven perches!).

It is impossible, at this distance, to trace the exact sequence of events. According to Matthew Humphreys, David Davies moved to Tyn-y-maen 'with his mother and all his brothers and sisters',[64] implying that this followed his father's death. As we know from the tithe maps, however, the farm was already being rented by David Davies at least a year earlier. Humphreys is our best guide to this period, as he was employed at Tyn-y-maen as a farm labourer. In his recollections of David Davies, he emphasizes the part religion played in day-to-day life on the farm. There were family prayers night and morning and Bible readings. Humphreys was called on to lead in prayer in the morning, and no one working on the farm escaped this daily dose of religion. There were grumbles that 'the boss and Matt think they can transform us with all this praying', but Humphreys assures us that 'nothing disheartened Mr Davies. He had decided upon the path he would follow, and no smile nor scorn would deflect him from it.' His view of David Davies was of a man who had made a compact with God: 'He believed that God never forsook anyone who had put his trust in Him and he never undertook any project without first consulting his Creator.'[65]

Humphreys went on to draw what might seem a somewhat strained analogy between David Davies and the Biblical figure of Solomon:

God asked Solomon, 'Ask what I shall give to thee?' and Solomon answered, 'Give thy servant a wise heart.' He not only gave him 'a wise heart' but God provided Solomon with a great deal of riches on top of it. It was the same with Mr Davies. He always asked for Divine guidance and he was blessed with a strong intellect and much riches.[66]

Whatever we may feel about this implied relationship between God and Mammon, an acknowledgement of the depth of David Davies's religious faith is essential to our understanding of him. Outwardly it expressed itself in attendance at chapel three times every Sunday when at home in Llandinam, and a strict Sabbatarianism which continued into his years of prosperity.

> He would not receive from the Post Office any business letters on Sundays ... Neither he nor Mrs Davies ... would ever make use of their carriage and horses to drive to their Sunday services in the chapel. They invariably, while their health was maintained, walked from their mansion ... associating freely with the ordinary country folk on the same errand. Their numerous servants had the fullest liberty, and were always relieved of every form of unnecessary work on Sundays.[67]

The story most often told to illustrate this unyielding Sabbatarianism is of the time a county official turned up in Llandinam one Sunday morning, after travelling all the way from Welshpool on what he regarded as urgent business relating to David Davies's highway contracts. Finding Davies at chapel, he sent word inside that he was waiting to see him. The firm reply he received was: 'Tell him to come back tomorrow'.[68] It is easy to overlook the strength of character displayed in this incident by a young man still making his way in life, and dependent on the good will and patronage of people of influence.

Whether the county official was Thomas Penson himself or a subordinate we have no means of telling, but this firm attachment to principle evidently did David Davies no harm, as the late 1840s saw him building on his initial success as a contractor. He was awarded several other contracts for bridge construction in the county. According to Matthew Humphreys, he built bridges at Pontdolgoch, Llangurig, Nantyfilltir, Montgomery and Buttington. He also built one at Llanfair Caereinion, and it was in the course of constructing this that he met his wife-to-be.[69]

By this time the Davies family had moved yet again. They were no longer to be found at Tyn-y-maen, for in 1850 David Davies struck his biggest bargain to date with the squire, John Offley Crewe-Read: to rent Gwernerin, a 240-acre farm at the foot of the hill fort of Cefn Carnedd. This was indubitably a step up the ladder: Gwernerin (later known as Gwerneirin) was prime land on the far side of the river, approached by means of the iron bridge he had helped to construct. Tyn-y-maen then passed to Samuel Breeze, but David Davies continued to rent Neuaddfach. No longer did he farm it himself, however; that task fell on brother Joe, although he was only eighteen when the Government enumerator entered him as head of the household in the 1851 census, his sister Mary — the only other occupant — being marked down as 'housekeeper'.[70]

The rest of the family, Richard apart — his whereabouts at this time are a mystery — had by then moved to Gwernerin. Apart from David and his mother there were the three younger daughters, Sarah, Elizabeth and Jane. Sarah, aged fifteen, was helping her mother to keep house, Elizabeth was learning dressmaking, while the 'baby' of the family, eleven-year-old Jane, was going to school. David Davies was becoming a man of substance, able to afford hired hands who lived in as well as those who went back to their homes in Llandinam of an evening. The 1851 census tells us their names and status:

> Margaret Davies, house servant, unmarried, age 17.
> Davied [*sic*] Evans, agricultural labourer, married, 40.
> Richard Morris, agricultural labourer, married, 26.
> James Jones, agricultural labourer, unmarried, 23.
> Rhees [*sic*] Morris, agricultural labourer, unmarried, 18.
> David Evans, agricultural labourer, unmarried, 13.

David Davies, the head of the household, 'age 32, farmer, 240 acres, employing labour,' was unmarried when the census was taken, but by the summer he was a bachelor no longer. His bride was Margaret Jones, youngest daughter of Edward Jones, a farmer living in The Wern, Llanfair Caereinion. It was what the worldly would have called 'a good marriage' for someone as ambitious as Davies, as the Joneses of The Wern were known as a 'highly-respected Montgomeryshire family,' but once again, parental opposition had to be overcome.[71] Margaret was, however, a woman of independent mind who had flown in the face of her father's wishes by joining the Methodists: the Joneses were staunch Anglicans. At twenty-seven she was far more mature than 'Miss D of Creigfryn' had been when David had first sought a bride, and her character was such that she would have appealed to his head as well as his heart. She was said to possess 'high intellectual and moral powers', with a piety which equalled his — no small matter — and a memory acute enough to enable her to learn substantial parts of the Bible by heart. In time her husband came to speak of her as 'God's most precious temporal gift',[72] the most high-flown of his tributes to a woman whose support appears to have wavered only when she feared he might overreach himself. She hated the thought of his failing at anything; in her eyes, he was a man born to succeed.

They were married at Capel Isaf, Llanfair Caereinion, on 7 May 1851, 'according to the Rites and Ceremonies of the Calvinistic Methodists'. The witnesses were Evan Jones, Christopher Jones and Richard Jones, and the registrar was Evan Evans.[73] In the great romantic tradition this was love at first sight — or pretty near it — as they had met only the previous winter, while David Davies had been building temporary wooden bridges to replace those swept away by floods.[74] The help he had acquired at the farm was essential, as Llanfair is nearly twenty miles from Llandinam: a considerable distance in an age when the only horsepower was provided by horses. His journeys around the county as a contractor were not only increasing his bank balance but broadening his mind; at Llanfair he found himself in a small, old-world town where anglers fished in the River Banwy and the stage coach from Shrewsbury clattered over the cobbles on its way to Aberystwyth. Davies's most important job in the vicinity entailed the building of Neuadd bridge across the river a mile or so out of Llanfair,[75] all these contracts coming his way through the good offices of Thomas Penson. Davies had, in fact, won the contract for building Oswestry's new smithfield in 1850 as a result of some blatant favouritism on the part of Penson. Asked to prepare a quotation, he had provided one in five minutes, scribbling a series of figures on the back of an envelope. They totalled £553. 7s. 6d., the famous 'five-minute contract'. Perhaps infamous might have been a better word for it, as long after Penson's death − and just before his own − Davies revealed that Penson, the architect for the scheme, had allowed him to steal a march on his rivals by showing him the plans and specifications beforehand and telling him exactly what the job was worth.[76]

It was while building the smithfield that David Davies first met Thomas Savin. The meeting appears to have been arranged by George Owen, a man of Kent from Tunbridge Wells who had begun his business career in Montgomery with Charles Mickleburgh, land surveyor and enclosure commissioner.[77] Owen and Savin were both ambitious, and they saw in Davies a man of ability and energy who could prove useful to them. At twenty-four, Savin was already in business as a mercer (draper) in his native Oswestry, partnering Edward Morris. Even then, he aimed high; instead of being content to sell flannel shirts to farmers he was out to lure the gentry into his emporium. Within a few years he and Morris would be advertising winter cloaks and 'jacquettes' which aped the newest Paris fashions, and exhibiting opera cloaks and lace head-dresses in a heavily curtained room lit with gas in broad daylight 'to show the effect of the articles worn at night.'[78]

It was not the frills and fopperies of high fashion that Savin had in mind when he first shook David Davies's hand in a room above a tobacconist's, however, but something much more basic: railways.[79] Everyone knew they must some day come to Montgomeryshire; the question was when. The iron road was in the process of transforming society, expanding markets and giving people a new concept of distance: towns which for practical purposes might have been continents apart when the only means of communication was the lumbering stage-coach were now within a few hours' journey of each other.

By this time, the 'Railway Mania' of 1845 had come and gone, with nothing achieved in the county. A scheme had been put forward for the conversion of the Montgomeryshire Canal into a railway, but it had proved impractical because of the meandering route the canal followed.[80] The riot of speculative schemes spawned in the frenzy of the mid-1840s had ruined many investors and introduced a much-needed note of caution to the railway business, but the general advance was irresistible: by 1850 there were 6,000 miles of railways in operation in England and Wales, and the spirit of the age was personified by such men as the financier George Hudson, the Railway King, and Isambard Kingdom Brunel, the engineering genius known as The Little Giant.

To our knowledge, Owen and Savin had no immediate proposition to put to Davies, but in years to come all three would have important roles to play in the development of railways in mid Wales: Davies and Savin as partners in a series of pioneering enterprises, and Owen as engineer of the combine which was to result from their efforts — the Cambrian Railways.

3 Contract Won

The bride whom David Davies took back to Llandinam from Llanfair Caereinion found herself living in a much smaller community where her husband was fast becoming – might, indeed, already have become – the dominant secular figure outside the ranks of the gentry. There were, however, other people of ideas in the locality, and one was David Kinsey, who had become the village schoolmaster in 1847, instructing his pupils in the church gallery. His credentials for assuming the role of pedagogue were based not on strong educational qualifications but on enthusiasm supported by a lively intelligence and knowledge of the world: probably as good a foundation for teaching as any. Kinsey had left home at twelve to work in a grocery shop for three years, before learning the craft of bookbinding in Newtown. He was also a shoemaker, and was to become the village postmaster and parish clerk, as well as a stone mason of distinction.[1]

This man of many talents, who was said to be as capable of making a mark in the world as David Davies himself,[2] kept a diary for more than forty years in which he made terse but often revealing notes on the happenings in the locality. He was a man gifted with humour and cursed by human frailties (notably a weakness for the comforts of the tavern) and thanks to him, vivid cameos of village life are rescued from oblivion. We are thus able to relish the grotesque blunder of old Edward Benbow who, when marrying Sarah Woosnam on New Year's Eve in 1852, said 'plight thee my cock' instead of 'plight thee my troth', and for good measure uttered the memorable promise, 'Aye, aye, I'll buy Sarah a cow,' in place of the far more mundane 'With all my worldly goods I thee endow'.

It is thanks to Kinsey that we know it was only eight and a half months before this that a mail coach began running through Caersws,[3] a fact which illustrates how isolated such communities remained on the very brink of the railway age. He also recorded the severe winter of 1855, when six weeks of pitiless cold and deep snow were followed by a sudden thaw and swollen rivers. A bridge at Dolwen was swept away and in the last week of February the ever-willing David Davies of Gwernerin began putting up a new one for £45.[4] He was still hard at it at the beginning of May, when a bitingly cold day brought a heavy fall of snow and the east wind was so cruel that even he had to admit defeat and send the men home at midday.[5]

The experience of those bitter months, when cut bread glistened with the ice that was in it and urine froze at night in the chamber pots under beds,[6] must have served to harden David Davies's ambition. He did not yearn for the soft sheets of luxury, but there were better ways of living than this. As the year progressed, the talk was all of railways. Various schemes had been projected for Montgomeryshire, and now at last there was action: on Friday, 28 September 1855, the *Shrewsbury Chronicle* carried on its front page an inch-deep advertisement inviting 'Excavators and Railway Contractors' to tender for the construction of the first portion of the Llanidloes and Newtown Railway. They were requested 'to meet Mr R. Hopkins, the company's engineer' at eleven o'clock the following Tuesday morning at the company's offices in Llanidloes, when 'the plans, sections and specifications may be inspected and the line will be afterwards pointed out.' The notice, signed by company secretary Thomas Hayward, continued: 'Any contractor possessing a small quantity of materials may undertake the contract, as the works are to be paid for in cash, by monthly instalments.'

It seemed an invitation especially designed for such as David Davies and one can imagine him, brisk and businesslike, scrutinizing those plans acutely on that October morning. He needed to bring all his powers of quick calculation into play, for the tenders had to be submitted to the directors by seven o'clock that very evening, but no doubt he had spent the weekend pondering the line of country he knew so well and making provisional estimates. For at least a month he would have had a pretty shrewd idea what the job might be worth, as newspaper accounts of the company's half-yearly meeting towards the end of August had reported the engineer, Rice Hopkins, as saying that he estimated the cost of the construction work as £48,000, or 'only £4,000 a mile, including bridges, stations etc'.[7] Seven tenders were received, the company's minute book naming them as Messrs Dickson & Co, Wellington; G.C. Panting, Egremont; Joseph Holmes, Shrewsbury; James Holmes, Shrewsbury; Colin McKensie (*sic*), Wellington; Daniel C. and E. Davies, Shrewsbury and London; and David Davies, Gwernerin. Davies's tender was the lowest − even below the engineer's estimate[8] − and although it was a remarkable coup, the fact is that Davies of Gwernerin was no unknown quantity but a contractor of repute in the locality. He was known to *The Times* as 'a contractor for county works in Montgomeryshire,'[9] while the *Shrewsbury Chronicle* quoted Rice Hopkins as saying that 'as he had had great experience in making roads and bridges in this county and elsewhere, there was every reason to believe that he would satisfactorily complete the contract'.[10]

Whatever celebrations there were at Gwernerin that night would have been unlikely to result in any hangovers, as through his entire life David Davies scorned alcohol as he scorned debt. He went against Montgomeryshire tradition by refusing to brew harvest ale, although a

Medal struck to commemorate the opening of the Llanidloes & Newtown Railway.

generous supply of this was commonly held to be essential to the bringing in of the sheaves.[11] His hatred of drink was surpassed only by his loathing of indolence: he would say he had more hope for a drunken man than a lazy man.[12]

The directors' sense of urgency was such that the ceremony of turning the first sod took place the very next day at Llanidloes. This was no mere formality but a noisy and colourful carnival, a kind of *mardi gras* in the rain. People streamed into the town from miles around, the toffs in their carriages, the farmers in their gambos, the farm bailiffs on horseback, the poor on foot. Cannon thundered, church bells clanged, and the children of Llanidloes National School looked forward to a rare treat − a tea party, complete with plum cake, provided by 'Mr Salter and other gentlemen connected with the town'. Nimble fingers had been busily stitching banners, which made a splendid sight when uplifted. The mayor and corporation, and shareholders of the railway company, marched proudly behind a banner bearing the motto, 'Success to Llanidloes and Newtown Railway', while dignitaries from other towns followed one wishing 'Success to the Town and Trade of Llanidloes and Newtown'. The procession, nearly a quarter of a mile long and headed by a brassy *brouhaha* of bands, made its way to the spot where the ceremony was to be performed: the site of what was to be the first railway station in Montgomeryshire. Naturally the rain teemed down, and the day did not quite go according to plan: the turf was to have been cut by the redoubtable Mrs Ann Warburton Owen of Glansevern, but since she did not consider herself to have been properly invited she stood on her dignity and stayed away. In her absence the ceremonial spade was wielded by the chairman of the Llanidloes & Newtown Railway, George

Hammond Whalley Esq, deputy lieutenant of Denbighshire and captain of Denbighshire Yeomanry, who regretted the absence of 'that exemplary lady' but did not allow it to ruin his enjoyment of the occasion. His elegant speech was loudly cheered by the 5,000 damp but enthusiastic onlookers, whereupon Whalley stripped off his coat, rolled up his sleeves and neatly turned the first turf into the mahogany wheelbarrow.[13] If it all seems a little excessive now, we must remember that entertainments were harder to come by then, and that for people who had never set eyes on a locomotive the prospect of railway travel was not merely a novelty but something of a miracle. There is, too, another consideration. This humble stretch of line, twelve miles in length, was seen at the time as part of a grand scenario: a line of railway stretching all the way from Manchester to Milford Haven, which would provide the mill owners of Lancashire with a new outlet and turn the Pembrokeshire port into another Liverpool, a gateway to the wealth of the New World across the Atlantic. Alas for dreams, it all came to nothing, but the enthusiasm of the day shines out from the columns of the *Shrewsbury Chronicle*:

> Of three schemes brought before Parliament in the session of 1853, the only one that was successful was the application for a bill to construct the line from Llanidloes to Newtown. That success was in a great measure due to the independent nature of the application to the legislature, as being totally unconnected with either of the great companies, and promoted by parties locally interested ... Conscious that any alliance with either the North Western or the Great Western would only fetter their course of action, they have nobly held themselves aloof from any proposals for alliance, and the result is that they now stand in the proud position of being the first company to introduce the iron band of civilization into the important county of Montgomery. Viewed even locally, the Llanidloes and Newtown Railway has the strong sympathies of all parties interested in the district; and it requires no great stretch of the imagination to look forward to the day when that line will form a link in the great chain of railway communication that must ultimately connect Manchester and the manufacturing districts of the north with the splendid harbour of Milford. Link after link in this important chain is being rapidly secured, and we hopefully look forward to a grand consummation of the whole at no very distant period.[14]

In time David Davies would himself become involved in the by then fading dream of the M&M (Manchester and Milford), but in the autumn of 1855 he was less concerned with romantic visions than immediate reality. He had a job of work to do, his most important yet, and nothing would stand in his way. He began recruiting the labour force he needed, and in the very early stages at least had a close ally in a neighbouring farmer, Edward Parry, who according to David Hamer of Newtown, a schoolboy at the time, was regarded at the outset as Davies's partner. Hamer, who remembered the line of the railway being surveyed across his father's farm and the cannon's roar at Llanidloes when the first sod was cut, wrote that Parry

> ... was a land surveyor, and people thought therefore that he was the best qualified to lead, but ... Davies was ... top sawyer ... The partnership only lasted two or three weeks, and then David Davies carried on alone. He commenced opposite Morfodwin near Llanidloes. The wise ones found great fault with this, as he had to keep several teams hauling material from Newtown, but David Davies knew what he was doing. He commenced on the higher ground so that he had the law of gravitation to assist him.[15]

There were no great engineering problems to overcome, as the steepest gradient was 1 in 132 (for a mile) and the next 1 in 220. There were, however, problems with the landowners, chiefly the vicar of Glanhafren, the Revd John Arthur Herbert, who declared that he would not let 'a bit of a sawyer' through his land and fastened his gates. The 'bit of a sawyer's' response was to say to his men 'Come on boys, we'll have a bit of fun with the old parson today. Bring them horses here.' The horses uprooted the gates, posts and all, without much difficulty − 'like Samson,' in the words of Matthew Humphreys, who in spite of that day of 'warming' on the river bed was now one of Davies's railway navvies. Humphreys noted how the old parson had stormed up and 'begun to cuss and swear', which amused David Davies no end. 'Thee art a funny old parson,' he taunted, and whether the reverend gentleman had a fit of apoplexy is unrecorded.[16]

In locking his gates in the vain hope that the despised sawyer would quickly admit defeat, the vicar was simply carrying to an extreme the opposition and resentment of many landowners towards the encroachment of railways on their territory. This was not a problem confined to mid Wales, for in the early days of railway travel there were widespread fears that the hissing iron monsters would poison the air, blight the crops and kill pheasant and other game. Mrs Ann Warburton Owen of Glansevern had been so fearful of the LNWR's proposals for the county earlier in the decade that she had frequently sought the advice of her lawyer, George Brace. He had pledged to do his best to 'resist the aggressiveness of the North Western' but had warned 'Trust none'.[17] When it appeared as if a railway might be taken from Welshpool to Newtown on the north side of the river through her grounds at Berriew, he advised her to have a painting made 'in lively colors' (*sic*) for submission to the committee which would make the final decision on the matter — 'a good picture conveys more to the Committee Men in five seconds than the addresses and explanations of Counsel for as many days', he shrewdly observed.[18] He was evidently perturbed by the conflicting advice she was being given, for within a week he gave another warning: 'The placing of confidence in the Railway Companies as suggested by Mr A. Johnes and Mr Howell I *can't at all understand* — it is quite beyond my comprehension . . . you should trust only your own efforts for the protection of your Estate', adding: 'the pleasure which your two neighbours take in the expected destruction of Glansevern is nothing less than despicable.'[19]

The wise Mrs Owen safeguarded her own interests by investing heavily in local railway companies, thus ensuring that the line was kept well away from her property.[20] Many other landowners, too, took shares in the undertakings or annual rents in lieu of purchase money. Had they insisted on their land being bought outright the companies would have been hard pressed to find the cash, as they simply did not possess it. Just before David Davies was awarded his first railway contract the directors of the L&N were able to tell shareholders that their approaches to landowners along the route had been so successful that half the value of the land required was being paid for in shares or rent.[21]

Early in the day, when the river mists still shrouded the Severn and the silken webs in the hedgerows gleamed in the first sunlight, David Davies made his way from Gwernerin across the iron bridge at Llandinam to superintend the work. In spite of being an employer he was still the old Davy, ready to roll up his sleeves and turn to with the lads. One morning he saw them struggling to roll heavy stones into trucks in a quarry and with a cry of 'Sweet boys, up with them!' helped them shoulder the stones into place. His effort was all the more impressive in that he was on his way to London on business and wearing a dark suit, which was so covered in dust that he had to go back home and change before making the journey.[22] In later life he was to say that this comradeship in labour had been one of the sources of his prosperity.[23]

Yet if he gave a lot, he also demanded much. Nearly a century after his death, the story persisted in Llandinam that if a workman did not thrust his shovel in the ground 'up to the maker's name' he would be 'down the road'.[24] He abhorred not only idleness but waste, and reprimanded an employee making a shoddy job of erecting a fence beside the permanent way with the classic remark: 'Dost know thou art wasting an eighth of every plank, and if we were all like thee I'd be losing £30,000 on this job?'[25]

Men were, however, crying out for this work, and some travelled far to obtain it. In the autumn of 1855, Frederic Kerr set out from Chester with his wife and young family in the hope of being taken on by Davies, but by the time they reached Welshpool they were desperately short of money. He turned for help to someone whose acts of charity were well known, none other than Mrs Ann Warburton Owen, and from Welch Pool (*sic*) he sent a letter asking if she could 'oblige' him with the 'temporary loan' of half a sovereign. 'I can undertake to repay the debt in the course of the present Month . . . The bearer is my little boy, and has undertaken to walk to Glansevern with this. He can answer any enquiries you may think proper to make.'[26] The outcome of this appeal is, regrettably, unknown to us.

There were up to six hundred navvies at work on the line,[27] accomplishing tasks with pick and shovel which are amazing to contemplate. 'Their powers of endurance were extraordinary,' Samuel Smiles – the apostle of self-help – wrote of the workmen who turned the speculators' dreams into reality. 'In times of emergency they would work for twelve or even sixteen hours, with only short intervals for meals. The quantity of flesh-meat which they consumed was something enormous, but it was to their bones and muscles what coke is to the locomotive – the means of keeping up the steam.' One of Davies's foremen was nicknamed 'The Preacher' and another 'The Sentry',[28] and although the workmen they superintended must have included many outsiders like Frederic Kerr, they bent their backs alongside local lads who spoke the broad Montgomeryshire of the gaffer. There were exhilarating moments such as the time the wages for a gang of sixty were left heaped in a barrow after a cry of 'Come on, lads!' from David Davies, who could resist drink and tobacco easily enough but not the allure of the hunt. Off they all went, following the pack of baying hounds which had streamed by in pursuit of their quarry. Jack y Saer, who was in the gang that day and went on to work in Davies's Rhondda collieries, swore that in the boss's absence not one gold sovereign disappeared from that barrow, nor even a silver crown or copper piece.[29]

In those early days the railway works made an extraordinary sight, for a stranger would have been hard put to find the logic in them. The stretch of line being laid down amid these quiet hills of mid Wales appeared to exist for itself alone, as there was no connection at either end with another length of track. Davies must have chafed at the delays resulting from the fact that his supplies had to be brought along the Shropshire Union Canal to Newtown before being hauled on wagons to Llanidloes. As the work progressed through the summer of 1856, however, he did not attempt to disguise his elation – for they were now drawing steadily nearer his home village of Llandinam. When the workmen took their meal break he sat with them, pointing out the timbered farmhouse on the hill to their right — his birthplace, Draintewion. And there on the valley floor, just across the river from the railway, was another place dear to his heart — Neuaddfach, where brother Joseph was now tilling the soil, sister Elizabeth was milking the cows and his mother was keeping house.[30] Yet by a supreme irony his new enterprise brought tragedy to Draintewion: on 19 August Richard Lloyd, thirteen-year-old son of Thomas Lloyd and his wife — the couple now living there — was killed on the railway near Neuaddlwyd.[31]

David Kinsey noted the tragedy without comment; with equal brevity he had observed, six months earlier, that 'Our Vicar first wore spectacles in Service time.'[32] In ways great and small, the village was changing. Even *The Times* was regularly arriving there, all the way from London — a single copy shared by three families.[33]

The trust which the L&N directors had placed in David Davies was being amply rewarded. 'It is satisfactory to be able to state,' reported engineer Hopkins in February 1857, 'that the entire cost of the works hitherto constructed has been within my original estimate.'[34] The company's balance sheet shows a payment of £1,343. 5s. to David Davies in the first half of 1856, and a further £2,113. 10s. by the end of the year.[35] Progress was being hindered, however, by the directors' deliberate decision to go slowly in the hope that their line might open at the same time as the next link in the chain to the border, the Oswestry & Newtown Railway:[36] a vain hope, as it turned out, and a bad miscalculation.

Whatever his private thoughts, David Davies was there to do their bidding, and the enthusiasm he brought to the task was enormous. Matthew Humphreys would remember to the end of his days how he 'would not stand by to view his men straining with some heavy work, but would always be first to run to assist and by doing so would put heart into his men . . . Often at night he would almost be too tired to walk home, but his loving wife would be there to receive him, to wait on him and to soothe him, and the maids would run to be first in opening the laces of his boots.'[37]

As he entered the second year of his contract, however, his thoughts were turning in a new direction: to the possibility of operating the line himself. With the oil lamps burning at Gwernerin he confided his ambitions to Margaret, and whatever her confidence in the man, she must surely have had her doubts. There was another mouth to feed now, their son Edward — the only child of the marriage — having been born on 16 June 1852. In the spring of 1857, however, Davies took the plunge and offered to lease the line on businesslike terms: a rent of £4 per cent upon all the outlay of the company when the line was open to

Penstrowed, £5 per cent when it reached Newtown, rising to £10 per cent when the Oswestry & Newtown line should be opened.

'The Directors, we believe, have agreed to these terms ... certainly there was never in Montgomeryshire a more gratifying or important event,' reported the *Shrewsbury Journal*. 'That 5 per cent and ultimately 10 per cent should be thus secured for this single link of the great route to Milford Haven, and that too by a man like Mr David Davies, who has never yet made a commercial mistake, and who may have as many partners in the enterprise as he chooses to accept, is the most extraordinary event in railway history.'[38]

There was fulsome praise for Davies at a special meeting of the directors in June, when chairman George Hammond Whalley went on record as saying that

> ... the success of the railway required an amount of energy, personal responsibility and devotion to the business which could be exercised by no better man than David Davies, as had been evidenced by his conduct in all matters of business with which he was connected. The public would have the benefit of that spirit of Liberality and those enlarged and comprehensive views which the board had found so valuable in their relations with him as contractor.[39]

Only a few years were to pass before Whalley would gladly have destroyed all copies of the newspaper carrying these words, so bitter an enemy did he become of contractor Davies.

4 *Well Now We've Got A Railway!*

'Aug 7. First Sod of Vale of Clwyd Railway Cut. D. Davies & Savin contractors.'[1]

With this economical entry in his diary for the year 1857, David Kinsey recorded not only the remarkable fact that while still struggling to carry the railway to Newtown, the sawyer-cum-contractor had taken on another heavy commitment, but the beginning of one of the most intriguing partnerships of the railway era in Wales: that between David Davies and Thomas Savin. It began in mystery, gave rise to a brief period of intense co-operative effort, and ended acrimoniously within the space of four years.

The mystery is why David Davies allowed the Oswestry draper to hitch his wagon to his star in the first place. Savin, eight years his junior at thirty-one, was clearly a young man on the make with a keen business sense. One suspects that it was his flair for publicity that lay behind those flamboyant display advertisements that reach half-way down the front page of the local paper, when he and Edward Morris prised open the purses of well-bred ladies with offers of superior Congou and Souchong teas, 'fine plantation' coffees and a host of exotic fruits, ranging from Egyptian dates to Portuguese bitter almonds. Savin obviously had energy and enterprise, but there was a streak of impetuosity in his nature graphically illustrated by the tale of his dashing into the ring on market day to buy a thousand sheep simply to complete the livestock sale so that he might begin to move the stock on his drapery stall.[2] It may have been apocryphal, but like many an apocryphal tale it had the zest of essential truth in it.

There must have been a dynamism about Savin that appealed to David Davies, but the instinct that so often allowed him to choose the right course signally failed him on this occasion. His celebrated prevision did not operate forcefully enough to enable him to see that this man would take him to the very edge of disaster.

There is no mention of Savin in the original contract for making this ten-mile line from Rhyl to Denbigh: it is simply between David Davies and the Vale of Clwyd Railway Company.[3] The company agreed to pay him £21,650 'in respect of all the works to be executed and materials to be supplied by him,' provided that he agreed to accept part payment of £2,000 in shares — an important stipulation at a time when promoters were often short of ready cash and liked contractors to invest something more than their labour. The contract stipulated that 'notices or orders' should be delivered to Davies's 'most usual place of abode or of transacting business in England'. (Typically of the time, England was taken to include Wales.)

In the pioneering days of railway making it was not uncommon for men to be paid at intervals of a month or more, advances being made on the notorious truck system, but there was to be none of this on the Vale of Clwyd. 'The workmen and labourers of every description engaged in the construction of the line shall be paid in cash, at least once a fortnight on Friday evening in an office or offices to be erected on the site of the works at the Contractors expense', Clause 13 stipulated. 'On Sunday no work will be allowed to be carried on excepting when the Engineer certifies in writing that it is necessary for the safety of the works.' One sees the hand of David Davies, the strict sabbatarian, here.

There was no easy escape for railway contractors whose works went awry. 'The Drawings are presumed to be correct,' ran Clause 14, 'but the Contractor must take all responsibility for their being so himself unless he points out before signing the Contract any errors that may exist, as no allowance will be made to him for any failure in the works on the allegation that the designs were insufficient or inaccurate.'

Under Clause 17, 'There shall be at all times employed on the works as many suitable men and horses and also experienced Foremen and Overlookers as shall be necessary for the efficient conduct of the works.' In the event of unsatisfactory performance, the engineer had the power to remove the contractor or to add to the number of men and horses on site, 'all the costs of such measures being borne by the contractor'. The type of fencing required, and the manner of its construction, were meticulously detailed. The railway was to be fenced on each side for its entire length,

> ... the posts to be of Oak or larch 7' 6" in length and 6 inches by 4 inches in section at the smallest part. They are to be neatly split from straight grained wood and the bottoms for a length of 3' 6" must be well charred, 3 feet of this will be under ground when fixed. All the posts on any continuous length of the Contract are to be of the same timber ... The posts where under ground to be charred, and all above ground to receive three coats of good Oil paint plain colour.

The line was to run from its junction with the Chester & Holyhead Railway 'in the parish of Henllan ... being ten miles or thereabouts in length.' There is something deliciously vague in that 'thereabouts'.

Thus did David Davies embark on an enterprise which was to absorb him for most of the following year of 1858, when a shortage of funds brought works on the Llanidloes & Newtown to a temporary halt. The

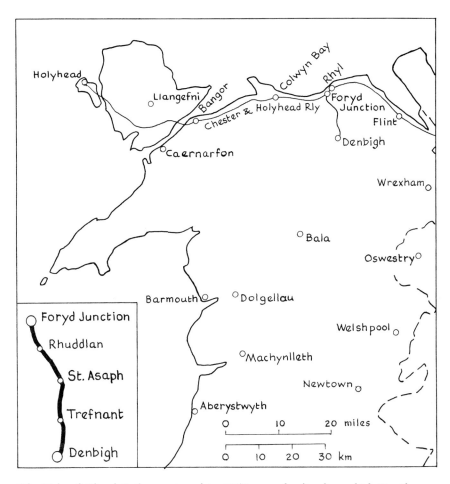

The Vale of Clwyd Railway, opened in 1858, was the first line which David Davies completed in partnership with Thomas Savin. It linked with the main Chester & Holyhead Railway, engineered by Robert Stephenson.

people of Denbigh, where the line was to begin, greeted the railway with the same enthusiasm as their counterparts in Llanidloes, and a printed notice dated 4 July 1857[4] informed everyone that the ceremony of cutting the first sod would be celebrated 'in such a manner as is consistent with its importance to the Towns of Denbigh, Rhuddlan and Rhyl, the City of St Asaph, and the whole of the Vale of Clwyd.' The 'Gentry, Clergy, Tradesmen, Farmers, Mechanics, and other classes in the adjoining Towns and Neighbourhood' were invited to join in the demonstration. This took place, as Kinsey noted, on 7 August, when the

Kinmel Troop of the Denbighshire Yeomanry Cavalry mounted their horses to head the procession.

Montgomeryshire had been celebrating as well. Three days before this, the first sod of the Oswestry & Newtown Railway had been cut in Welshpool by Lady Wynn, who wheeled the small ceremonial wheelbarrow over the specially-laid planks 'in a very graceful manner' before turning the turf with a silver spade.[5] She was unlikely to have soiled her hands.

In time this line would, like the L&N, form a link in the chain of railways running from the English border to Cardigan Bay, and this too would involve the firm of Davies & Savin.

There was something else to celebrate just before Christmas, when Kinsey noted in his diary: 'December 23. The Locomotive Engine arrived at Llandinam from Newport Being the 1st brought to the County.'

The 'Locomotive Engine' was the 2−2−2 tender locomotive *Dove*,[6] which Rice Hopkins the engineer had bought second-hand for the L&N for £400.[7] Its purchase was a great event, but it posed the considerable challenge of how to transport it nearly forty miles from the railway station in Oswestry to Llandinam. The *Dove* and its tender were carefully lifted on to carriages made of stout timber, and no fewer than fourteen horses hauled the engine along the turnpike road into Montgomeryshire; a further seven horses were hitched to the carriage carrying the tender.[8] As the strange procession made its way towards Welshpool through Llanymynech and Four Crosses, cottagers rushed to their doors, the women holding fiercely on to children whom they feared might dash below the carriage wheels in their excitement.

Newtown was reached on a Saturday evening, and there the engine remained in the town's ancient High Street throughout the whole of Sunday,[9] contractor Davies having given strict orders that even so important a task must not be allowed to interfere with the peace of a day he regarded as one sanctified for rest and worship.

It was more like spring than winter. As David Kinsey − now the village postmaster − went around Llandinam, he wonderingly noted that primroses and polyanthuses were in full bloom, and that birds were nesting.[10] For all that, Davies began the new year in a mood of frustration and impatience. The company's financial problems were such that he feared the work would be cut short before the few remaining miles to Newtown were completed, and some of the landowners, notably one General Proctor, were still proving obstructive.[11] He was also to find, in due course, that in paying £400 for the *Dove*, Rice Hopkins had bought a pup.[12] By then, however, Hopkins had placed himself beyond the scope of earthly wrath by going to an early grave. He died in London, just about the time the second-hand engine was arriving in Llandinam.[13]

For all his efforts on behalf of the Llanidloes & Newtown Railway, the most interesting thing people found to say about Rice Hopkins was that he was the son of the man who had laid the Penydarren Tramway which carried Trevithick's locomotive on its epoch-making journey from Dowlais to Abercynon in 1804. The second most interesting thing is that when the L&N plans were first placed before the Lords, they were rejected because at one point Hopkins had shown the line to be running eighteen feet below the level of the Severn.[14]

Hopkins had been in poor health for some time, as his death just before Christmas 1857 was said to have followed 'a protracted illness' which had 'occasioned some interruption and delay in prosecution of the works.'[15] Obviously, a successor had to be found as quickly as possible. The company minutes show that on 31 December four men 'presented themselves as eligible for the job of engineer' and were asked to state their terms.[16] They included a 'Mr Penson', and although it is tempting to think of the man who had given David Davies his first chance wishing to team up with him again he was unlikely, at the age of sixty-seven, to have been contemplating a new career. The name is so unusual, however, that the applicant was almost certainly a relation of his. Another applicant was Benjamin Piercy, who was eventually to get the job, but not before an interim period in which an Evan Hopkins took over. At their meeting on 3 February 1858, the directors noted Hopkins to be 'a Gentleman introduced to them by the Representatives of the late Engineer, and they have found great cause for confidence in him.' He certainly produced a lucid report for this meeting, stating briskly: 'The progress of the works must necessarily depend on the "ways and means" of the company. The contractor (Mr Davies) has bought sufficient timber for all the bridges and he could complete the whole line to Newtown in the course of the next six to eight months. According to a rough estimate I have made of the works done by him from Llanidloes to Penstrowed, including materials and his liabilities, they amount to £12,000 and upwards.'[17]

Evan Hopkins was appointed engineer a few days later,[18] but by the end of the month he was in sharp disagreement with the directors over money matters. These partly related to methods of raising the cash required to complete the line, but there was also the question of payments still owing to Rice Hopkins at the time of his death.[19] The upshot is that Evan Hopkins disappeared from the scene and by the end of May, Benjamin Piercy was being employed to 'set out the Line and complete the plans required to give notice to land owners.'[20] Piercy was appointed engineer on 27 August, with Joseph Cubitt as consulting engineer 'to give counsel and advice from time to time'.[21]

Benjamin Piercy was the kind of man with whom David Davies could feel quite at ease — not a 'self-made man' it is true, but one whose quickness of thought and lucidity of tongue enabled him to beat lawyers at their own game, and whose idea of relaxation was to go out and shoot something. Both were attributes which Davies rated highly. Once, while engaged on one of his railway contracts, Davies was rash enough to boast of shooting three hares before breakfast. 'Good heavens, that's nothing' countered Piercy, 'when I was in India I shot three tigers before breakfast!'[22]

Piercy, too, was a Montgomeryshire man. He was born nine years after Davies in the village of Trefeglwys, which lies in the Trannon Valley, four miles west of Llandinam across the hills from Gwernerin. His father was Robert Piercy, who as a local commissioner and surveyor became involved in one of the most unscrupulous acts of governmental banditry of its time, the enclosure of commons and waste lands. In 1852, at the age of twenty-five, Benjamin Piercy showed his mettle by refusing to be daunted when his plans for a railway in Shropshire were stolen from his hotel bedroom just before they were to be deposited before Parliament: he promptly applied himself to preparing a new set of plans.[23]

David Davies's fears that work on the L&N might be interrupted proved well founded, for no sooner had the line reached Penstrowed bridge, within three miles of Newtown, than the cash ran out.[24] In a sense this was fortunate, as it enabled Davies to concentrate all his energies on the Vale of Clwyd. For all his ambitions to make his mark as a railway contractor, it must have been a wrench leaving the familiar landcape of Llandinam, where he had spent all his thirty-nine years, for the unfamiliar pastures of Denbighshire. He took with him his newly-acquired partner Thomas Savin (who left behind a possibly disgruntled Edward Morris to run the shop on his own) and Benjamin Piercy, who had been appointed Vale of Clwyd engineer.[25]

Like the L&N, this was a predominantly rural railway, carrying butter and cheese from Denbigh to Rhyl as well as cattle, sheep, horses and pigs. Coal and other merchandise was taken inland, the junction with the Chester & Holyhead — the great Irish Mail line pioneered by Robert Stephenson — proving lucrative.[26] David Davies threw himself whole-heartedly into the job, working up to sixteen hours a day and sleeping curled up in the firebox of a disused engine — 'a locomotive with its stomach out' was his own graphic phrase for this.[27] His prejudice against strong drink was strengthened by his experience in the Foryd section near the coast, where the shifting sands and treacherous tides caused problems. When two men he had dispatched post-haste to put baulks in position to stem the river took an extended midday break in the local, an infuriated Davies did the job himself with the help of a labourer.[28]

Problems of this kind, however, were infinitely preferable to the tantrums of Montgomeryshire landowners and the soul-destroying task of squeezing money from penny-pinching L&N directors. By the end of August the job was practically finished, and arrangements were being made for the ceremonial opening of the line and a testimonial for the contractors. When word got around that the Bishop of St Asaph had been asked to address the 'masters' Davies and Savin on behalf of the workmen, however, the gangers held what today would be called a protest meeting at the White Horse Vaults in St Asaph. The Welsh language newspaper *Baner Cymru* carried an account of this meeting under the headline 'Ffordd Haiarn Dyffryn Clwyd' (Vale of Clwyd Iron Way), the writer — unidentified in spite of his use of the first person — informing his readers:

> I believe there will be strong objections to the Bishop having the office of addressing the masters, because the warmest wishes of the workers is to have David Evans to address Mr Davies and Richard Humphreys to address Mr Savin. [Evans was head ganger.] Honestly they are the most appropriate people to convey the feelings of the workers; and they can also carry the words of the workers to the ears of the masters in their own tongue, which is the pure Welsh. David Evans was the one to open the big cutting in the village, and most of the workers have been with him from the start of the line to today.[29]

The report added that Evans had been 'under the authority of Mr Davies for fifteen years', which suggests that he had been employed by Davies on his Llandinam farms; he could, indeed, have been the 'Davied Evans' listed as an agricultural worker at Gwernerin in 1851.

The report ruffled a few Clwydian feathers, a local bigwig rushing into print to declare that there was 'not the slightest shadow of truth in it . . . every arrangement effected by myself, in the name of the working men . . . was fully concurred on.' He spoke of the 'enthusiastic applause' which had greeted the announcement that 'the Lord Bishop of St Asaph had condescended . . . to become the mouthpiece of the labouring men.'[30] All the same, when the time came for the presentation of two sets of tea services to the contractors the words of the condescending bishop were followed by an 'Address to Messrs Davies and Savin' read by 'Mr Roberts, one of the foremen', so perhaps the point had been effectively made.[31]

The official opening of the line took place in October 1858, when the *Chester Courant* hailed railways as 'the harbingers of prosperity' and the Revd Hugh Morgan said that since the arrival of the Chester & Holyhead Railway, Rhyl had changed from 'a straggling village of lodging-houses' to 'a town dignified with its parade and terraces'. In his long-awaited address the bishop said the 'upper orders' had 'a sincere wish to do good to the lower orders.' He also preached the virtues of temperance and self-denial to the workmen, and offered some gratuitous advice to their wives by informing them that 'many an untidy slatternly wife has driven her husband to the alehouse.'[32]

Mr Roberts the foreman had no uplifting message for bishops' wives but his words tell us far more about the conditions of the time. In welcoming the completion of the task 'with so small a sacrifice of human life' he implied that some lives had been lost in making this ten-mile stretch, and after a conventional observation about the need for 'masters and men to work together in unity' he complimented Davies and Savin on the way they had paid wages weekly in coins of the realm without resort to the truck shop, 'thereby increasing our domestic comforts, and rendering our firesides cheerful and happy.' He ended on a high note, expressing the hope that the contractors, having done their duty 'faithfully and honourably' to their fellow men, may one day 'relinquish the cares of this world without regret, and enter upon eternal life with unfading joy.'[33] Even the bishop could not have done better.

It is significant that although he was the senior partner, David Davies asked Savin to make the formal reply on their behalf; at this stage of his life he was still nervous of public speaking. He did bring himself to say a few words, however, after listening to Savin's well-turned little speech praising the workmen for 'refraining from an over-indulgence in spirituous liquors.' He spoke with characteristic directness, saying how much he appreciated the workmen's gift, 'particularly as it has come from that class of men that I so much respect and love, being honest, sober and industrious men.' He went on:

> To you, as a class of men, Great Britain owes a great portion of her honour. If you take a view around Great Britain, and look at the mighty works of man in railways and other important undertakings, you will find that this, in a great measure, has been done by the lower classes of industrious and sober men, both masters and workmen.[34]

It is interesting to see David Davies place himself firmly in the 'lower classes', no higher socially than the workmen he employed.

The job completed, Davies and Savin resumed operations in Montgomeryshire. The works on the Llanidloes & Newtown line were still idle, but they had other matters to engage them: they had obtained the contract for making the Newtown & Machynlleth Railway, another link in the chain between the English border and Cardigan Bay. The inevitable turning-the-first-sod ceremony took place towards the end of

November in Machynlleth. There was the usual clamour of church bells, the thunder of cannons and the blare of brass bands, but a distinctly Welsh note was struck with bilingual banners saying 'Commercial and Agricultural Prosperity' on one side and 'Llwyddiant i Reilfordd Machynlleth a'r Drenewydd' on the other. The chairman of the company, Earl Vane, recalled how pessimists had predicted failure for the enterprise, saying 'You may have your mail coach and four horses, gentlemen, but never a railway!' We are told that he then 'created a perfect furore' by wielding a pick-axe 'in right good earnest' after taking off his coat and rolling up his sleeves, all this exertion putting him in the right mood for the cold collation at Machynlleth Town Hall.[35]

For some reason Savin was not present, and David Davies drew the laughter he was expecting when he made the wry remark that he was sorry about this as 'it was part of Mr Savin's business to give thanks'. Having eased himself into the unfamiliar task of speech-making, he made the important point that this line had brighter prospects than the others with which he had so far been associated, as 'there was more money subscribed in proportion to the capital required.' His next words not only give us an insight into his thoughts on the Welsh character, but show that even then he was having to restrain his partner. *Eddowes' Shrewsbury Journal* reported him as saying:

> It was not owing to any want of money in the country that they could not get on, but from a want of confidence. There was sufficient money amongst the Welsh people, and they need not go to England for it; the people lacked confidence, and if they could see the line would pay 5 or 6 per cent they would soon come forward. They all knew the Welsh were not such great speculators as the English, and that they would either be noblemen or beggars. Some of the English, through their speculations, had become noblemen, and others had become poor. It was not so with the Welsh, for they would not risk without they could see the road clear; they were quite right, and he was one of them himself. (Laughter and cheers.) His partner was, he might say, half an Englishman and half a Welshman, and a greater speculator than himself; and, to tell the truth, he was obliged to apply the brake to keep him from going too fast. (Great laughter.) There was a word very common to his partner, 'Go on, it's all right.' He liked to see that it *was* all right.[36]

What Savin thought of all this when it came to his ears one can only imagine. The one thing he knew for certain is that, with David Davies, it could not have been a case of *in vino veritas*.

In its report of this day of days for Machynlleth, the paper noted that the railway would link with Oswestry and Shrewsbury and 'bring the iron road within 18 miles of Aberystwyth, the Brighton of Wales'. Davies and Savin had agreed to make the railway for £130,000, and £23,000 of this would be paid to them in the form of shares. The line would be twenty-three miles long, 'beginning with a junction with the Llanidloes and Newtown at Caersws, and passing by Carno, Talerddig, Llanbrynmair, Comminscoch and Gwastadcoed, to terminate near the National Schools at Machynlleth.' The 'celebrated lead mines of the neighbourhood' would receive a fresh impetus, and the 'railroad' (what was to become an Americanism was then in common use) was welcomed as 'the natural road from the heart of Wales to the heart of England'.[37]

In Llandinam there was a new squire, John Offley Crewe-Read having died at another of his country seats, The Wern in Flintshire, at the age of sixty-eight.[38] His brother Bagot took over at Llandinam Hall, and in the village itself David Kinsey made a solemn vow not to drink more than four glasses of any intoxicating drink in the course of a day.[39] Young David Hamer, who a few years before had been so excited at the sound of cannons firing at Llanidloes, noticed work resume at long last on the L&N in the first days of 1859 with the construction of the Scafell cutting, and the tank engine *Enterprise* — which became known as the *Black Donkey* — arrived.[40] On 1 February thirty tons of coal for the poor were run up the line from Llandinam to Llanidloes, an act of charity by company chairman G.H. Whalley.[41] On 5 April Kinsey noted: 'Davies & Savin started with their Waggons to Oswestry to bring home the New Engine "Milford" to Llandinam'.[42] By the following month the first engine brought to Llandinam in this way, the *Dove*, appears to have been regularly employed in carrying coal and other goods to Llanidloes,[43] and Kinsey had made an even more stringent pledge: to drink only two glasses a day, not four. 'Tippling the greatest evil of our land', he had sternly observed. In an attempt to disguise his intentions, he sometimes wrote the words in his diary back to front.[44]

Now all the difficulties appear to have been overcome and it was only a matter of weeks before the whole length of line between Llanidloes and Newtown was opened for goods and passenger traffic. The company's minute books record the satisfaction of the directors with the partners who were at last bringing their hopes to fruition. 'Your railway is being constructed at a cost below that of any railway yet brought into operation,' engineer Benjamin Piercy informed them,[45] and when Davies and Savin declared themselves 'unable to go on with the works unless £3,000 be forthwith provided', they immediately arranged a loan from the North and South Wales Bank in Liverpool, where the general manager was George Rae.[46] The contractors had been issued with £20,000 worth of shares in January 1859,[47] another £4,000 worth of paid-up shares following in May,[48] and the balance sheet on 30 June showed that since the beginning of Davies's contract in 1855, a total of £26,380 had been spent on the works, the company having a bank balance of £531 after an overall expenditure of £52,549.[49]

Sadly, the man who had set David Davies's footsteps firmly on the path to the iron road by giving him his first job as a contractor, Thomas Penson, did not live to see the line completed. On 20 May 1859 he died at his home, Gwersyllt Hill, near Wrexham, aged sixty-nine, having achieved in his latter years the dignity of being Deputy Lieutenant of Denbighshire.[50]

Although the line was still to be inspected and given official approval — that was not to happen until early in August — Davies and Savin laid on free trips for the locals in the middle of June. Eight hundred people clambered excitedly into the 'new and splendid carriages' which carried them from Llanidloes to Newtown, and no fewer than 2,000 made the journey in the other direction. The mill owners of Newtown entered into the spirit of the day by closing all the factories, and the shopkeepers put up their shutters as well. At half-past six, the time the train was due to leave, only two people were to be seen in the main streets of the town, 'so universal was the rush to the terminus'. Two engines busily got up steam to draw the thirty carriages crammed with people who, in the words of the *Oswestry Advertiser*, 'had somehow stowed themselves away'.

> The old beadle of Newtown in his full uniform, wand in hand, was very conspicuous, the Newtown Band also gave their aid ... The only drawback to the pleasure of the excursionists was on the return from Llanidloes, when some young vagabonds stoned the people in the carriages; but as one or two of them received their deserts on the spot, and as the police will look closely after them on any future occasion, it is hoped that no further mischief of the kind will take place.[51]

The reporter who observed this summary justice being handed out noted also that thanks to the coming of the railway, the price of coal had been cut by one-third, from 30s. a ton to £1. To David Davies, however, progress did not involve any slackening of his strict moral code, and in mid-August it was made known that although there would be three trains a day on weekdays, none would run on Sundays. The *Oswestry Advertiser* confessed itself 'at a loss' to know why this should be so, 'as we can hardly suppose that the directors of this company intend to follow the same dubious policy as the managers of the Vale of Clwyd'. The first train was timed to leave Llanidloes at half-past seven in the morning, to arrive in Newtown thirty-five minutes later, with intermediate stops at Dolwen

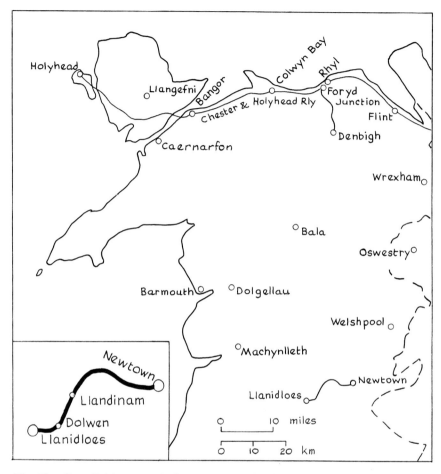

The Llanidloes & Newtown Railway was completed in 1859, within a year of the Vale of Clwyd Railway.

and Llandinam. The fares were advertised as 2s. 6d. first-class, 1s. 6d. second and 1s. third, return tickets being issued (for first and second-class travel only) at 3s. 9d. and 2s. 6d.[52]

Such was the enthusiasm on the railway's official opening day that even the unfinished gasworks in Llanidloes was spruced up with banners and flags. The staff at the Lion Hotel had been kept busy decorating the lion motif with evergreens and above it was a banner saying 'Welcome, Whalley, Champion of our Rights'. The prize for the longest slogan would certainly have gone to the Britannia Inn for its 'Success to the Llanidloes and Newtown Railway, with a Continuation into Wales'. At the railway station 'gay archways were thrown across the line and mounted with colours and all manner of beautiful devices.'

The inevitable parade to the station was headed by the Plas Madoc Silver Band, who oompahed away to their heart's content while, at a respectful distance — far enough away, at any rate, to allow themselves to be heard — a group of juvenile performers on the tin whistle 'created much amusement by their novel kind of music, playing the most lively airs.' The mayor and corporation naturally led the procession, which included Mrs Ann Warburton Owen of Glansevern riding in state in a carriage and forty navvies wearing specially-struck medals. Later 3,000 people crammed into a 'monster train' of forty-eight trucks and carriages drawn by two locomotives, the *Milford* and the *Llewellyn*. 'More than 2,000 of the passengers were in open trucks ... the train, as it wound its way through the valley, presented a scene not easily to be erased from the memory'.[53]

Mrs Owen of Glansevern excelled herself that day, with a speech of hyperbolic splendour:

> Different epochs of the world have been celebrated for discoveries conferring signal blessings ... the discovery of the telescope and microscope, gravitation by Newton, and the blood circulation by Harvey, but in my mind there floats an idea that the present age, by the application of steam, has done more than all former times to bring comforts to the hearths of millions, and that the iron road is destined to act beneficently in the humanising of nations next only to Christianity itself. With such an idea, perhaps I should say with such a conviction, may we not all rejoice at the opening of the first railway in Mid-Wales at Llanidloes.[54]

Llandinam had its own celebration next day, when the 600 workmen who had laid the iron road were given a feast by the contractors. They sat at long tables in a marquee on benches made of railway sleepers, and gorged themselves on gigantic rounds of beef and huge pies. The bells of St Llonio's pealed and cannon blasted on the surrounding hills. The people of the area served by the railway collected enough cash to present David Davies and Thomas Savin with handsome silver salvers and cake baskets, while the workmen were alone responsible for presenting gold watches, each worth twenty-two guineas, to the contractors' sons, five-year-old Edward Davies and six-year-old Tom Savin.

David Davies rose to the occasion on his home ground, delivering a vigorous little speech in which he reminded the company that he had been born 'in a little thatched cottage close by on the mountain'. After observing that often in the past he had worked side by side with many of the people now in his employment, he made a semi-jocular remark to the effect that he liked to see workmen save their money because, 'if they had not been in the habit of doing so, they wouldn't have been able to buy a watch for my son!'[55]

There was a poet among the workmen — or, at least, a McGonagall — who was bold enough to step forward and sing the verses he had composed especially for the occasion:

> Well now we've got a railway,
> The truth to you I'll tell,
> To be opened in August,
> The people like it well
> We've heard a deal of rumour
> O'er all the country wide,
> We'll never get a railway,
> The people can't provide.
>
> Well now we have the carriages,
> For pleasure trips to ride;
> The Milford it shall run us,
> And Henry lad shall drive;
> There's also Jack the stoker,
> So handy and so free,
> He lives now at Llandinam,
> A buxom lad is he.
>
> We have a first rate gentleman
> Who does very nigh us dwell,
> And he has got a partner,
> The people like him well;
> Look at the trucks my boys,
> Their names you'll plainly see;
> They've took another Railway,
> There's plenty of work for we.
>
> Well now our gen'rous masters
> Do handsomely provide
> A store of meat and drink my boys,
> Come out and take a ride;
> For we are in our ribbons,
> And dress'd so neat and trim;
> Drink up my charming Sally,
> We'll fill it to the brim.
>
> When these few days are over,
> The navvies they will part,
> And go back to their gangers

With blithe and cheerful heart;
And Jack he will be hooting,
And getting drunk full soon;
I wish there was a railway
To be opened every moon.

And now I have to finish,
And shall conclude my song;
I hope and trust my good friends,
I've stated nothing wrong;
All you young men and maidens,
That are so full of play,
I hope you'll all take tickets
On that most glorious day.

This performance was greeted by 'roars of laughter and tremendous cheering', and when it was finished Colonel Wynn purchased the first copy, 'for which the fortunate bard received a shilling.' *Noblesse oblige.*[56]

David Kinsey had been busy too, composing 'An Acrostic to commemorate The Opening (at Llandinam) of the Llanidloes and Newtown Railway'. There is no mention of his reciting it at the feast, but he may well have entertained his drinking partners at The Mermaid in Llandinam with a composition which, for all its limitations, at least had lines with initial letters spelling out the words 'Messieurs Davies and Savin':

Montgomeryshire your praise will sing upon this festal day,
Encircled round from every town and hamlet far away,
Sabrina's vale doth echo, hark! the whistle soundeth shrill,
See the 'Milford' and the 'Enterprise' are crossing now the rill;
I see them, now I've lost the sight, they fly along the line
Engaged in haste for Newtown, to bring the friends to dine.
Unto Llanidloes now they go, how swiftly on they ride:
Returned again! see! both the towns *united side by side.*
Some Token of esteem this day, the contractors we present,
'Donation's purchase,' by the friends surrounding now this tent.
Another Testimonial too, given by those 'sons of toil,'
Very genuine fruits of industry, while turning up the soil.
In Denbighshire you graved your names upon the 'Clwyd Vale'
                                    line,
Echo'd forth your names shall be, safe handed down by time,
Sabrina's sons the chorus swell, loud join now the great guns!
And hand these testimonials to Messrs Davies, Savin and their
                                    sons.

Newtown now to Llanidloes joined by both contractors' skill,
Drink each this toast, long may they live! to cross the Radnor
hills,
So that their sons as years roll on, and these heir-looms handed
down,
Affirm and say, 'our fathers made a road to MILFORD TOWN!'
Viewing these presents with delight, the inscriptions tracing o'er
In memory of their fathers' deeds till time shall be no more.
Now to conclude, God guide their steps to gain that 'perpetual
shore.'[57]

5 The Little Urchin

The celebrations in Llandinam were made all the happier for David Davies by a decision reached at Liverpool Police Court eight days before, on 24 August 1859. The magistrate, Mr Jeffery, had found the steamer *Sea King* to blame for a collision with the SS *Lion* in Liverpool Bay on 29 July.[1] Both vessels were on the Liverpool–Rhyl run when the *Lion* was struck on her starboard quarter by the *Sea King*; the dispute was whether the *Sea King* had been recklessly overtaking the *Lion*, or had fallen victim to some crass seamanship by the man at the *Lion's* helm.

The passengers aboard the *Sea King* were quite convinced that they had the answer: they wrote to the editor of the *Northern Daily Times* complaining of the 'shameful conduct of those in charge of the steamer *Lion*, in attempting to cross our bows in a narrow part of the channel.' The skipper of the *Lion* was equally convinced that the *Sea King* had been at fault.[2]

David Davies's interest in this is that he was part owner of the *Lion* with Thomas Savin — an aspect of their business relationship which has so far escaped notice. They had joined forces with James Napier to form the firm of Napier, Savin, Davies & Co, an association almost certainly arising out of the Vale of Clwyd railway contract. In finding in their favour, Mr Jeffery made some stern remarks about the racing that occurred between steamers in that waterway. The 'spirit of opposition' which existed was 'dangerous to both life and property', and on this occasion there had been 'a very narrow escape indeed.'[3] In December 1859, it was reported that the plaintiff James Napier had been awarded damages of £45 11s. 5d. at South Lancashire Assizes against the owners of the *Sea King*.

This incident apart, ownership of a steamer must have been a welcome diversion for David Davies from his two basic concerns of farming and railways. It was certainly more fun than having to sit through the diatribe that assailed him when the first turf of the Mid Wales Railway was turned at Rhaeadr on 2 September 1859, the very day following the feast at Llandinam. It came from the lips of George Hammond Whalley, the temperamental chairman of the L&N, who only two years before had been so lavish in his praise of the contractor's energy and devotion to the business. He now had no good words to say for either Davies or Savin, who together had been awarded the contract for making a line from Llanidloes to Llandovery which was seen as a stepping stone towards that 'grand consummation', the Manchester to Milford.

Whalley was a complex man with a great regard for pedigree, especially his own. The eldest son of James Whalley, a merchant and banker of Gloucester, he claimed descent from a first cousin of Oliver Cromwell. He had launched himself on what appeared to be a career of intellectual distinction by gaining first prizes for rhetoric and metaphysics at University College, London, and being called to the bar at Gray's Inn in 1835 at the age of twenty-two.[4] Nature, however, can be capricious in her ways, and having endowed him liberally with brains she withheld from him the ability to use them properly. He saw jesuitical conspiracy everywhere he looked, and became an object of gentle derision in Parliament − a character who, in literary terms, degenerated from Don Quixote to Mr Dick.[5]

The seeds of this decline were to be seen in his behaviour on that wet September day in Rhaeadr, when he stood before the gathering as a man of substance: Liberal MP for Peterborough − elected barely four months earlier − deputy lieutenant of Denbighshire and captain of the Denbigh Yeomanry, with a seat in Rhiwabon.[6] He was also a man seething with ill-disguised fury: the contractors, whom he was willing to indulge and patronize when they kept their place, had got more than a little above themselves. With the support of Benjamin Piercy, who was engineering the line, they had dared to disagree with him on the route the line should take: he wished it to by-pass Rhaeadr, but had found himself overruled. What is more, he had failed to win the chairmanship of the board of the Mid Wales company, a defeat directly due to the way David Davies had used proxy votes entrusted to him. The fact is that Davies and Savin were themselves important figures in the affairs of the Mid Wales because they possessed what the company signally lacked: money. Eight months earlier, in January, they had stumped up the whole of the required Parliamentary deposit of £36,300,[7] a gesture as grand as the name then boasted by the company: it called itself The Manchester, Liverpool, Swansea & Milford Haven Junction Railway.

While Davies and Savin may well have had some idea what might happen, it is doubtful if many of the guests who sat down to luncheon in the marquee (or, to use the terminology of those Crimean times, 'Balaclava tent') were prepared for the uproar that engulfed this genteel gathering. Whalley, who in spite of his defeat had been allowed to preside as 'chairman for the day', shattered the party mood by accusing the contractors of putting their own interests first by devising a route to suit themselves. (He conveniently overlooked the fact that much of the money subscribed had come from Rhaeadr, a town excluded from his own preferred route.)

'The railway from Milford Haven,' he thundered, 'must be free for traffic, and no pettifogging interests of traders and monopolisers should interfere with the success of the line. I cannot conceive that the line ought to be made to enable railway contractors to carry their lime and coal cheap. I earnestly hope the contractors will keep themselves to the business of contracting, and the board keep their position as directors'.

He threw a crumb of courtesy in the contractors' direction by acknowledging them to be 'honourable men, most efficient and most able men', but thought that in this particular case 'they ought not to attempt the higher department of the railway system, that of jobbing, which was a very different branch.'

These highly charged remarks were greeted with a burst of laughter and some cheers, such acrimony being an unusual departure from the round of self-congratulation that usually distinguished these occasions. Mr Johns, a London director of the company, sprang to his feet to protest on behalf of Davies and Savin, who were 'heroes in their own district'. Whalley, unabashed, observed that 'Mr Davies is the working contractor, and Mr Savin the scientific one', and said the secret of success was to keep the line clearly drawn between servants and masters. 'Contractors and engineers are like fire and water − they are very good servants but shocking bad masters,' he added, which in the words of *Eddowes' Shrewsbury Journal* incited 'great uproar'.

The company secretary, R.S. France, sprang on to one of the long tables at which luncheon had been served to make an appeal for order, whereupon the ladies, deciding enough was enough, all tripped out of the Balaclava tent, where only the whiff of gunshot was needed to make it resemble Balaclava itself. The band, the *Journal* excitedly reported, 'began to blow, scrape, squeak and drum with a 40 band power.' Mr France remained on the table in spite of efforts to pull him down and, shouting above the cacophony, reminded those still disposed to listen that for fully twelve months the Llanidloes and Newtown Railway had been a deserted undertaking facetiously likened to 'an isolated Indian fortress with no-one to go to its rescue'. It had taken Davies and Savin to deliver it from this parlous condition, and he called for three cheers for them.

Savin then rose to say that he was no stump orator but he and his partner would perform all they were engaged to do, 'which was a thing he did not remember Mr Whalley to make a common practice of'. This jibe goaded Whalley into saying that he declined to be an equal of 'such persons as Mr France and the contractors.' In fact, he would 'rather be anything whatever than be considered their equal' for he was 'a gentleman, a magistrate, and a Member of Parliament', and 'utterly incapable of doing anything dishonourable or unbecoming his position.' This brought gales of laughter from the assembly, and the company vice-chairman, Henry Thomas − who as chairman of Glamorgan Quarter

Sessions was accustomed to dealing with the recalcitrant — chastised Whalley by reminding him that 'the distinctions which existed in feudal times were rapidly passing away.'

David Davies then brusquely observed that the whole dispute might be settled in a few words. Everyone knew that he and Savin had put up the deposit money, and they were 'ready to come out of the concern this moment if the expenses were paid and they were relieved of the responsibility.' They wished to be straightforward and independent, and 'the moment the company found them not to be so they ought to kick them out'.[8]

Three days later a vengeful Whalley chaired a meeting of shareholders at the Queen's Head in Llanidloes which 'resolved that Messrs Davies and Savin should be forthwith called upon to return to this company the £20,000 worth of shares which . . . was a loan to them to aid in obtaining the deposit for the Mid-Wales line.' Until the shares were returned, the resolution added, 'no steps be taken for granting a Lease' (to work the line).[9] This appeared to be a fringe event, for the following day a more representative meeting registered satisfaction with the decision by Davies and Savin to vest their voting rights in four members of the board of directors 'for the benefit of the company at large'. The meeting also confirmed the decision to grant the contractors a lease of the line, only Whalley and a shareholder named S. Meddins voting against.[10]

All this was, in the end, much ado about nothing. The mêlée in the marquee turned out to be the most energetic happening for many moons, and by the time work on the line actually began Davies and Savin had parted company and another contractor had been appointed.[11] Whalley's outburst, however, had at least the merit of honesty, giving us an insight into social attitudes which were seldom expressed with such robustness. It is interesting that in its next issue the *Oswestry Advertizer* felt obliged to pass comment on Whalley, 'this paradoxical gentleman'. Taking up his boast of being a gentleman, a magistrate, and an MP, it addressed him directly:

> What constitutes a gentleman? Members of Parliament are sometimes traders, and so are magistrates. Traders may be gentlemen and not members of Parliament. Do you claim to be a gentleman from your long descent and gentle blood, or because you are a member of Parliament and a magistrate? We presume not from the former, for we have been told you never attempt to disguise the fact that you are the son of a shopkeeper. If from the latter, then you must know that money can generally procure a seat in Parliament, and a place on the bench. If your qualification is a money one, then surely may the contractors, who deposit

£33,000 on the Mid Wales Railway, take their place even by the side of Mr Whalley, Member of Parliament for Peterborough and magistrate for Ruabon [Rhiwabon]. And if your claim to be a gentleman is founded on your general good conduct, then the public must be their own judges.[12]

Such virility of expression was not unusual in the local press in those days, and editors more favourably disposed to Whalley were equally vehement. One of them made dismissive references to 'Contractor Davies' and 'Sawyer Davies' in a leading article in which he

> ... beheld with sorrow the *scandalous* way in which the founder of our local railways was treated by men, who, but for that gentleman's unremitting labours, would have been to this day sawyers of wood, and dealers in haberdashery. The time will come when 'the little urchin of no account', mentioned in a *characteristic* speech by Contractor Davies, at Welshpool, will have due honour paid to his name and memory. The man who planned railways to connect the isolated valleys of North and South Wales, and who fought hard, hoping to secure their independence, can never be forgotten by the patriot-loving sons of Cambria. Moneymongers and sharebroker's puppets may dim the verdure of his laurels, but time will make them bright as ever. The little terrier who keeps guard at Savin's town may bark and snarl, and Sawyer Davies's 'Blood may boil'; *but honour will in the end find its way to whom it is due.*[13]

The *Eatanswill Gazette* could have done no better.

6 Large Sceams With Great Risk

With the dawn of a new decade on 1 January 1860, David Davies had every reason to feel pleased with himself — and no doubt he did, since a proper regard for his own achievements (or just plain self-satisfaction) played a fundamental part in his make-up. He would not have been able to indulge the feeling for long, however, as there simply was not the time. His railway interests were ever expanding, and when he returned home to Gwernerin after a long day he moved, as it were, from one business to another. The oil lamps burned late into the night as he wearily scanned auctioneers' bills and caught up with a multitude of correspondence relating to the farm. Much had been done in his absence, for in Margaret he had a wife who was in effect his farm manager, a job she performed so capably that the books were showing a healthy profit.[1] There were good workers about the farm — a bailiff, three carters, a groom and two maids,[2] but the railways absorbed so much energy and time that she feared her husband might be over-taxing his strength. Someone was needed to take the burden of paperwork off their shoulders — someone trustworthy and discreet, honest enough to be entrusted with large sums of money and a multiplicity of business secrets.

The man chosen was to be termed not a private secretary, still less a personal assistant or administrator, but a 'confidential clerk', a suitably shadowy title for someone who was expected to shun the limelight. David Davies went about the business of selecting him with characteristic thoroughness. It was not a wholly attractive procedure, involving a detailed examination of the man's personal life: Davies even went to the length of tailing him to the railway station after a meeting to make sure he didn't slip into a pub on the way.[3] The man who passed these stringent and somewhat ludicrous tests was Thomas Webb, a newspaper reporter of unusually abstemious habits. When Davies was at last convinced of his rectitude he followed him out of a meeting and asked him how much he was being paid by his employers. 'A guinea a week plus travelling expenses' was the reply, whereupon Davies offered him more cash on condition that he moved to Llandinam.[4] The boyhood capacity for poaching which David Davies had shown in the fields around his native village was thus turned to other uses in his maturity.

About this time, Davies also took on a younger man to help deal with the clerical work required by his railway contracts. He was David Evans, who came to take his place at Gwernerin in a predominantly youthful household. The eldest, apart from David and Margaret themselves — who were just turned forty — was the farm bailiff, John Reese, who at the time of the 1861 census was twenty-six. The youngest employee was fourteen-year-old John Edwards, one of the three carters employed on the farm. There was a sixteen-year-old housemaid, Elizabeth Gravener, a seventeen-year-old carter, John Davies, and a nineteen-year-old dairymaid, Elizabeth Jones, who unlike the others had not been born locally — she hailed from the Cardiganshire country town of Llandysul.

By now the farm was sixty acres larger, and none of Margaret's sisters-in-law was living there any longer — Sarah, Elizabeth and Jane had all left, Elizabeth to serve as her mother's dairymaid in Neuaddfach. David Davies went down on the official return as 'Farmer 300 acres and Railway contractor employing 700 men' and his son as 'Edward Davies, age 8, Scholar.'[5]

In describing David Davies and Thomas Savin as 'heroes in their own district'[6] Mr Johns of London had not been guilty of hyperbole. After so many false hopes had been raised by empty talk and futile speculation, they had actually delivered the goods: trains were running in Montgomeryshire, prices were falling, horizons were broadening and everything they touched seemed to flourish. Having rescued the L&N from stagnation and won the Newtown to Machynlleth contract, they now came to the rescue of another company involved in this piecemeal development: the Oswestry & Newtown Railway. The contractors, Davidson & Oughterson, had plunged into bankruptcy with only eleven of the thirty miles of railway begun,[7] and the news that Davies and Savin had taken over the contract was jubilantly received. 'The line from hence (Newtown) to Oswestry was begun on Monday last, and there is no doubt that the works will be prosecuted with the utmost energy, as Messrs Davies and Savin are not the men to sleep when there is work to be done' a local paper reported in the autumn of 1859. 'The Newtown people are heartily glad that the contract is given to the gentlemen, who have shewn that they well deserve it.'[8]

A few months earlier, official returns had offered a good indication of the number of jobs provided by all this activity. There had been 215 labourers at work on the still uncompleted Llanidloes & Newtown Railway, 284 on the Newtown & Machynlleth, and 182 on the Oswestry & Newtown, in addition to superintendents, accountants, time-keepers, foremen and clerks. In England and Wales as a whole, 94,812 people were employed by the railway companies, from managers and secretaries to platelayers and labourers. Over 7,000 miles of track had been laid and there were 2,710 stations.[9]

Although their confidence at this time seems to have been unbounded, even Davies and Savin must have hesitated before involving themselves

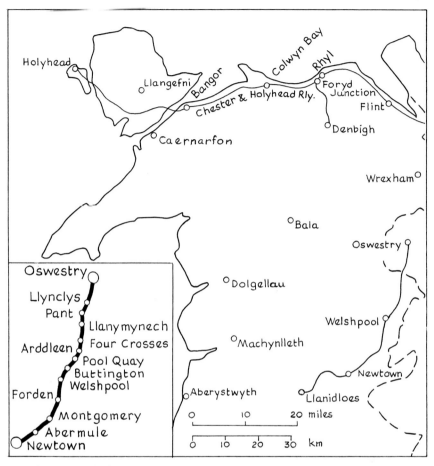

David Davies's third line, the Oswestry & Newtown, completed in 1861, was another vital stage in the formation of a railway from the English border to the Welsh coast.

with the Oswestry & Newtown. The company was heavily in debt and saddled with gigantic lawsuits: the chairman, Sir Watkin Williams-Wynne, was being sued for the staggering sum of £75,000.[10] The directors were quarrelling among themselves over the best means of overcoming their difficulties and the most influential man in the district, the Earl of Powis, finally lost patience and resigned from the board. 'I think you should for your own sake watch somewhat jealously the proceedings with regard to the contract' he loftily advised Sir Watkin, who in his reply expressed 'grief and astonishment' at his lordship's decision.[11]

The company's desperate financial problems meant that Davies and

Savin had no hope whatever of being paid in cash. Their solution was to accept payment in shares and debentures,[12] a system much criticized at the time but which David Davies was to defend as one which had provided Wales with 'something like 700 miles of railway which would not have been made for at least another century if we had waited for the localities to subscribe the necessary funds'.[13] To speak of 'another century' was obviously absurd, but his point was a valid one. Even more significant than this method of payment in kind is the fact that between them Davies and Savin managed to raise £45,000 to settle outstanding debts so that work on the line could resume at the end of October 1859.[14] The navvies continued to make progress through the winter in spite of appalling weather and by 1 May 1860 traffic was open from Oswestry to Pool Quay, a few miles short of Welshpool, and 'cheap trains' were advertised taking excursionists to the 'far-famed and commanding heights of Llanymynech Hills'. Later that month there was a joy-ride for the venturesome, who clambered into open trucks laid with rough seats for the occasion at Pool Quay. More trucks were attached at Cefn Junction (Buttington) and when Welshpool was reached 'the shrill whistle of the engine – for the first time heard in that beautiful locality – was all but overpowered by the cheers of the assembled people ... Congratulations were passed, and crowds of the very old, and the very young, to whom an Engine had heretofore been a figment of imagination, gazed with wonder at *The Montgomery*,[15] while their more travelled neighbours adjourned to the Bowling Green, where Mr R. Owen made a short pithy speech.'[16] This was followed by one from Thomas Webb, who at this time was working for both Davies and Savin: an arrangement which would prove contentious when the contractors spectacularly quarrelled. Webb had no sooner finished speaking than a warning whistle was heard: the engine driver was keen to make the return journey before nightfall. This was scarcely surprising as the track had still to be ballasted.

The Oswestry–Welshpool line was officially opened in August 1860, and in spite of Davies's strict sabbatarianism there were two trains every Sunday and six trains each way on a weekday. The opening of the line was an excuse for more junketing, punch and wine 'of the choicest and best descriptions' being supplied in abundance by the management of the Queen's Head in Oswestry. Perhaps it was this abundance that accounted for the fact that when the special train returned to Welshpool for still more celebrations, the bands of the Montgomeryshire Yeomanry and Montgomeryshire Militia were left behind, leaving the Oswestry Rifle Corps Band to do all the work. Revelling in their unexpected eminence, they performed 'with triple vigour'.[17]

The company's records show the directors to have been appreciative of the contractors' efforts. 'Messrs Davies and Savin have, notwithstand-ing the unusually wet weather, proceeded with the works, and provided materials and rolling stock to the amount of many Thousands of Pounds beyond the payments which the company have made, or had until now the means of making to them,' they noted on 2 August 1860.[18] Completing the link with Newtown should have been a simple affair, as the Severn Valley provided an obvious route through what railway engineers would have called 'easy country'. Nature is, however, often less obdurate than humanity, and another ten months were to pass before the fourteen and a half miles of single line between Welshpool and Newtown were inspected and approved.[19] This was chiefly due to the deter-mination of Mrs Ann Warburton Owen to protect her Glansevern estate from the intrusion of the railway. Seven years after her envious neighbours had gloated over its 'expected destruction', she was now confident of success. Her heavy investment in the company, to which she subscribed £10,000,[20] meant that she was no mere voice crying in the wilderness, but someone of influence: the combination of money and a forceful personality is a powerful one. The result was that the railway was taken well clear of Glansevern, but at considerable expense: a five-span iron skew viaduct was required over the river at Cil-Cewydd as well as several timber viaducts, and the new route also entailed a climb to Forden.[21]

It is doubtful if Mrs Owen lost a moment's sleep over the trouble she was causing; she would have considered herself a woman of breeding, to whom railway servants should naturally defer. The daughter of Thomas Sloughter, a captain in the Light Dragoons, she had married first a clergyman and then a barrister, surviving both gentlemen and living to a ripe old age. Widowed for a second time at the age of fifty-five, she did not obviously feel the want of a male shoulder to cry on, and indeed was more likely to weep in anger than sorrow. When she first sprang to the defence of her beloved Glansevern in 1853 she was over seventy, a Boadicea who did not shrink from any challenge. 'Mrs Owen was a lady of considerable shrewdness and ability, and of rather uncommon business capacity', Richard Williams was to write of her in a collection of brief biographies he respectfully entitled *Montgomeryshire Worthies*. She tended to the 'social and moral improvement of her poorer and less fortunate neighbours,' was a 'staunch advocate of political reforms,' took the 'liveliest interest in the promotion and passage of Liberal measures' and, not least, 'paid great attention to the welfare of her numerous tenantry in Berriew and Llangurig, and in Lancashire.'[22]

It was on behalf of this tenantry that she wrote to David Davies in the autumn of 1860. The lady of Glansevern and the contractor of Llandinam appear to have been on good terms, and she is unlikely to have been troubled by the fact that his reply contained spelling errors, a minimum of punctuation and was plainly that of an untutored man: it was the trickeries of the educated that infuriated her, not the infelicities of self-made men. His letter, written at Gwernerin on 27 November 1860, gives us an insight into his mind at a critical time. The construction of the line from Newtown to Machynlleth was posing awesome problems, as the great barrier of the Cambrian Mountains stood in the way, but something else was bothering him: the behaviour of his partner, Thomas Savin.

These were the words Ann Warburton Owen read, penned in the sprawling, untidy hand of David Davies.[23]

Madam,
 I do not know whether you saw my Partner at Pool on Saturday or not I was Oblige to go to Carno with Sir Watkin or I should have Called to see you about the Wharfs If your Tennants would meet me Some Morning at the Place about 9 O'Clock I Pass there about that time I should be Most happy to do all I can to accomodate them as you are Highly Entitled to a Wharf where you like on the line for your good Support to the Railways. Please Excuse Me Being so long Writing It is the first time for me to Put a Pen to Paper since I Received your note I am working Day and Night to get the line finished & do not have time to write a line more than once a week you may have heard that there is a chance of me having nothing to do with the Railway after a Short time as my Partner and Self has Differed he will Insist on going into Several large Sceams [schemes] with great Risk I will not follow So we differ I want to Stick to the Montgomeryshire Railways and not go Into Strange things at great Risk ...
Your Most Humble
Servant
D. Davies

The 'strange things' were to lead to an irrevocable and tragic break between the two men: tragic in that it deprived Wales of a dynamic business partnership which had scarcely begun to fulfil its potential. It foundered on Thomas Savin's dream of a railway going all the way up the coast from Aberystwyth to Porthdinllaen, on the north coast of the Llŷn Peninsula, with a string of resorts along the way and large hotels at Aberystwyth, Borth and Aberdyfi. The idea was to offer travellers rail tickets combined with hotel accommodation: in other words, package holidays. There seems nothing odd about this in the twentieth century, but at the time such defiance of financial rectitude had almost the whiff of brimstone about it. It certainly frightened David Davies, who is a Chance of me having nothing to do with the Railway after a short time as my Partner and self has differed he will Insist on going Into Serial large Schemes with great Risk I will not follow so we differ I want to Stick to the Montgomerie Railways & not go Into Strange things at great Risk I should be happy to do what I can for your Tennants Before I leave as I

An example of Davies's untutored hand: an extract from a letter to Ann Warburton Owen, 27 November 1860.

inevitably took risks as a contractor but was never tempted by adventurism of this kind. He was to say bitterly of Savin that he 'wanted to carry out great ideas just because they were great ideas, and not because he thought they would pay.'[24] In this lay the fundamental difference between the men: Davies often took a path which others feared to tread, but he had to see where he was going – he never relied on blind faith alone. He was guided by an odd mixture of realism and intuitive insight.[25] He would 'often speak as one seeing the invisible',[26] but the important thing is that he saw it to his own satisfaction.

For David Davies, Savin's scheme was sheer madness. He was anxious to reach Aberystwyth, thus providing the people of 'quality' who spent the summer months in this fashionable resort with the means of getting there without recourse to the tedium and discomforts of the stage coach. A railway up the coast, however, was a different matter altogether, and the idea of tempting the rich with the prospect of feather beds and port-and-lemon in luxury hotels did not appeal to him in the slightest. The two men argued fiercely, Savin accusing Davies of excessive caution and a woeful want of faith, and Davies striving with increasing desperation to hold Savin back from what he regarded as wild-goose schemes. 'Come on!' Savin would say time and again, as he urged his partner to share his vision, but Davies resolutely refused to come, and this marriage of conflicting temperaments began to look increasingly fragile as the spring of 1860 gave way to summer.[27]

Although Savin's bankruptcy six years later proves demonstrably that Davies was justified by events, we must remember that things did not seem so clear-cut at the time. Savin was by no means a lone dreamer but had the strong support of both the Oswestry & Newtown and the Llanidloes & Newtown railways, which between them offered to put up £100,000.[28] A line up the coast was bound to come some time; the question was, who should build it, and when.

Davies's powers of prevision did not enable him to see, at this moment, the time when there would be a railway snaking along the coast all the way to Pwllheli, if not to Porthdinllaen, and that as a director of the Cambrian Railways he would be helping to run it. He was obsessed by another vision: that of financial ruin, brought on by the recklessness of his partner. There must have been times when he looked back with longing to the simplicity of his days in the saw-pit, and thrust from his thoughts Biblical texts warning of the snares that lie in wait for the ambitious. There were problems enough in constructing the railway to Machynlleth, without being enmeshed in money worries, and the most fearsome problem of all was summed up in the one word 'Talerddig'.

It is hard for us today to appreciate what overtones it had for our ancestors. The British Rail diesels trundle through the Talerddig cutting on the Shrewsbury–Aberystwyth line as a matter of course, and the passengers carry on with their crossword puzzles regardless. But a century ago, this was one of the wonders of Wales. It was the deepest rock cutting in the world when completed, 115 feet from top to bottom, and in successfully accomplishing the task David Davies had achieved what many believed to be the impossible.

The merest glance at the map shows us the scale of the challenge: there between the border and the coast stands the mass of the Cambrian Mountains. It was hard enough to carve roads across them, but even harder to find paths for railways, the gradients of which have to be so much easier. The only practical route was by way of the narrow valley cut by the river Carno beyond Caersws, squeezing through the cleft in the hills between Llanbrynmair and Comins-coch to emerge at last into the Dyfi Valley four miles from Machynlleth. For several miles the way was comparatively clear until Talerddig was reached, and there the steep slopes of Newydd Fynyddog and Moel Caetwpa presented a solid wall in the path of progress. The only answer was a tunnel or a cutting, and the man engineering the line, Benjamin Piercy, favoured a cutting.[29]

David Davies supported him, and for the shrewdest of reasons: a cutting would serve a double purpose, slicing a way through the mountains and providing him with a ready-made quarry for the stones he needed to build railway stations further west. Yet the task remained a daunting one, for early in the 1860s the making of a railway was still primarily a pick-and-shovel job. Gunpowder was used to blast the rock when a tunnel or cutting was being constructed, but there were still no steam shovels to lighten the burden of labour. This was not because the technology was lacking; Terry Coleman points out in *The Railway Navvies* that steam-driven mechanical diggers were in common use in the United States and Canada, where labour was scarce and expensive, but in Britain the contractors preferred to hire the skilled workmen who were available in large numbers.[30]

When David Davies and Thomas Savin started to quarrel in earnest, the work had already been proceeding for some time. In August 1859 the *Oswestry Advertiser* reported that Piercy had found it 'necessary for the more complete drainage of the works to open a new course for the river Carno out of the Talerddig Bog, which work is nearly completed. The great cutting at Talerddig is being excavated, and the works are being pushed forward with vigour.'[31]

The muscle power was provided by more than 200 hand-picked navvies, the cream of David Davies's work-force. Many of them were Llandinam lads he had known for years; they followed him around from job to job, and some were to end up in his coal mines in south Wales. The workman in overall charge was David Evans,[32] almost certainly the

The Talerddig cutting: David Davies on the gantry in his silk topper, directing operations.

man of that name who had been head ganger during the construction of the Vale of Clwyd Railway. They must have felt, at first, that they had come to the end of the world, for they were surrounded by a wilderness of marsh and rock, miles from anywhere. Around them loomed the mountains, and the desolate cry of the curlew seemed to mock the vanity of their ambitions. There were times when it needed all the jauntiness of the gaffer to keep up their spirits: there is a famous photograph of him standing perilously on a gantry, directing operations. Davies appears to be wearing a frock coat, and is no more protected from falling rock by his silk topper than are the workmen by their soft felt hats. The excitement aroused by the boldness of this challenge lives for us still in the words of the reporter sent there by the *Shrewsbury Chronicle* in September 1861, when the work was in its final stages.[33]

> We intend simply to describe a very pleasant day which we spent on Saturday last by courtesy of the contractor, Mr David Davies, in visiting the works of the Newtown and Machynlleth Railway. An engine and a carriage was waiting at Caersws, where preparations for erecting a permanent station and warehouses were in progress. The engine bore us rapidly across a rich open plain formed by the junction of the Llandinam, Trefeglwys and Llanwnog valleys ... The Carno was again and again crossed, each time the little babbling brooklet getting smaller and smaller. Pontddolgoch and Carno villages, at each of which there is to be a station, appear ... and the speed visibly slackens as we pass groups of busy workmen erecting bridges, ballasting rails, sawing timber, or building stations. At length ... we arrive upon a bleak and desert moor, where we alight from the train, the better to see the great cutting of Talerddig, which is destined to become − is, in fact, already − another of the many wonders of Wales.
>
> Surrounded with an almost impassable bog, the towering rocks of Talerddig, with the deep ravine on either side, seemed determined to dispute the way against all comers. This cutting was a bold idea on the part of Mr Benjamin Piercy, and the bog through which it is approached proved nearly a Slough of Despond to the surveyor who took the levels. No wonder the railway contractors, accustomed to ordinary difficulties, fled when they saw this monster mountain in the path. Mr David Davies, however, had never allowed the word 'cannot' to enter his vocabulary, and he undertook to ... go through Talerddig and bridge over the yawning chasm beyond ...
>
> Two years of hard labour, continued through all seasons, and for the most part night and day, have succeeded in cutting through the hill of Talerddig, a distance of nearly 400 yards, so that in a week or two of favourable weather the steam engine will be enabled to pass through the midst of this solid mass of stone having on either side walls 115 feet high; and we are very much mistaken if such a sight will be seen in any other part of the world.

Remarkably, at a time when mishaps to workmen were commonplace, not a single life had been lost.[34] Some months earlier, the reporter noted, 'a slip occurred near the bridge which crosses the road at Talerddig Village, by which some trucks were smashed and the roadway blocked up, but nothing worse happened.'[35]

It was during the construction of the Talerddig cutting that David Davies had his famous dream of water rushing in to threaten the entire works. He was in London at the time, but was so troubled in spirit that he hurried back the next morning. Sure enough, he found floodwater swirling into the cutting and was just in time to prevent serious damage.[36] As the story spread, it confirmed his reputation as a man with second sight and there were those who saw it as divine intervention. After this, the civil action in which he was involved over the 'quantity of earthwork' at Talerddig seems trivial, although the statistics are impressive, the referee finding 'that the number of yards in the Talerddig Cutting, after allowing for sinkage, is nine thousand, seven hundred and twenty-five of Bog, and two thousand one hundred and sixty eight of Clay.'[37]

By the time David Davies laid on that visit for the man from the *Shrewsbury Chronicle*, an arrangement that suggests a flair for public relations in advance of its time, the break with Savin was complete.[38] It enabled Davies to protect his fortune, but at some cost both to his pocket and to his reputation. The unravelling of the knot that tied him to his business partner entailed countless trips to London, and he had to suffer public accusations of double dealing. His fiercest critic was his old adversary George Hammond Whalley, who lambasted him at the half-yearly meeting of shareholders of the Oswestry & Newtown Railway in August 1861. The wrangle that resulted was one of the reasons the meeting lasted nearly eight hours. It began when a shareholder, identified in the press only as 'Mr Jones', rose to ask if any of the company's outstanding debts were not contained in the balance sheet. Whalley, who was chairing the meeting, immediately accused David Davies – who was sitting next to Jones – of prompting the question. Jones denied this, but the chance of pursuing his vendetta against Davies was too good for Whalley to miss. While professing 'great reluctance to refer to him personally', he tore into Davies for the way he had dissolved his partnership with Savin. He contended that he had been forced to have words with him in private which, regrettably, he now had to repeat in public. His most damaging accusation was that Davies had tried to backtrack after proposing an end to the partnership. When Savin took him up on the idea, Davies had replied, 'Oh, I never intended it, it was only a dodge.' Savin had, however, insisted on its taking effect.[39]

This outburst by Whalley brought back unpleasant memories of his performance in the Rhaeadr marquee two years previously, and curiously the man who now tried to pour oil on troubled waters was the very same Mr France who had leapt on to the table then in an attempt to quell the disorder. Rising bravely to his feet, he said they were there to decide financial arrangements, 'not to listen to the squabbles of Messrs Davies and Savin' — a protest greeted with cries of 'Hear hear' from the discomfited shareholders. Whalley retorted that he must be allowed to conduct business in his own way, and alleged that when they had been struggling to complete the line Davies had spent his time 'making frequent journeys to Manchester and London', telling people that 'in his perfect knowledge Mr Savin was insolvent and would be bankrupt in a fortnight.'

Whalley then noted that Davies had persuaded Savin's confidential clerk to join him — a man party to all the company's secrets. This was Thomas Webb, who after working for both partners had apparently been serving Savin alone just before the split.[40]

David Davies, who had been barely able to restrain himself, said afterwards that he had been prevented from making a proper reply to these accusations at the meeting. According to the report in the *Railway Times*, however, he did manage to say that 'if any other person had abused him as their chairman had done, he should have been at him, and if he had had strength enough, he would have given him a thrashing.' He was 'as hard as steel', and Whalley's words 'did not cut through his skin.'[41] They hurt enough, however, for Davies to send a long reply through the columns of the local press. The letter published by the *Shrewsbury Chronicle* was dated 'Llandinam, September 7'.[42] It was signed by David Davies, but the phraseology suggests that Webb played an important part in its composition: the confidential clerk was already earning his keep. After noting that Whalley's observations had reflected 'on my personal honour', Davies contended that 'the object was to throw dust in the eyes of the shareholders, as much as to abuse me personally,' and the letter continued:

> Mr Whalley, on this occasion, seemed to feel the necessity of being even more unscrupulous in his statements than he ordinarily is. To such of your readers as we are respectively known, it is hardly necessary for me to do it, but for the benefit of others I take leave to give the most unqualified contradiction which language can supply to each and everything he said in regard to myself. Many of his assertions carry absurdity and contradiction on their very face. For instance, he says that I made 'frequent journeys' to Manchester and London for the purpose of circulating reports injurious to Mr Savin. Why, sir, at the very time he speaks

of I, of all men living, had a direct interest to do all I could to
sustain and preserve Mr Savin's credit. Bound to, although
struggling to be freed from him, my fortune for the time being
hung upon our mutual credit, and it would have been insane in me
to have adopted any such course, for the obvious reason that we
must have gone down together, if at all. . . Then there is the
'private remonstrance' to me from Mr Whalley!! He pretends to
forget that 'the boot was on the other leg' and that *I* had a private
remonstrance with *him.* I had to tell him that a chairman of a
company was honourably no less than legally bound to protect the
property and interests of the shareholders. That, in utter disregard
of so plain an obligation, Lloyd's Bond and preference shares to a
large amount were being issued, for which I at least knew, and he
ought to know, there was no consideration whatever, and that
these and similar proccedings had been adopted in furtherance of
the interests, not of the company, but of the speculations of Mr
Savin and his colleagues. I had to remonstrate on other grounds
quite as strongly. For this expression of my opinion Mr Whalley
promised me an action of libel, of which, however, like other of
his promises, I have heard nothing since, and suppose never shall.

Having fired these broadsides, Davies went on to deal with the
dissolution of the partnership.

Does he [Whalley] really not know how I suffered in health and
pocket during the short period I was reluctantly compelled to
continue bound to the party of which he has become the leader! I
can well appreciate his soreness at my escape, and the vexation of
others at losing the opportunity of still further using my hard-
earned savings for their own purposes, but to my loss. Can he be
ignorant of the numerous useless journeys I took to London and
elsewhere, when I could ill afford the time, in order to compel a
dissolution and secure what I could of my admitted share of the
partnership property which was being rapidly absorbed in
speculative extensions and wild-goose schemes!

Davies spoke of a ruse attempted on him when he was about to sign
the deeds relinquishing his rights and property for a certain sum. When
he asked to see the securities he was to have in exchange, they were not
forthcoming. Moreover, before matters were finally settled he had to
sacrifice several thousand pounds, 'Mr Savin not being prepared to carry
out the "certain stated terms" Mr Whalley alluded to.'

So alarmed, indeed, had I become, lest all that I had in this world
should be swallowed up in the gulf represented by schemes of last
session, four hundred miles long, that I employed the most able

counsel I could procure, and had to resort to the most energetic
and determined means before I could get anything . . . not
withstanding, I had protested at every step against the course of
proceedings in which my money had been so thrown away.

Whalley's warning on Webb's knowledge of secret negotiations
between the Oswestry & Newtown and other companies drew from
Davies — or, perhaps, his amanuensis — the acid comment that 'if the
object be to outwit others, profound mystery is essential, but where
people are straightforward and above board I ask what secrecy is
necessary?'

> Surely Mr Webb is entitled to judge for himself as to the
> employments of his own talents and character, and if he considered
> that the time had come when he ought to sever his connection
> with Mr Savin, I do not see that Mr Whalley, or Mr Savin, or any
> other person had a right to remark upon it. On the other hand,
> when Mr Webb intimated a wish to join me, I considered myself
> justified in accepting his services if I chose.

Davies then made the remarkable allegation, which he was to repeat
on other occasions, that he had received no payment for his work in
constructing the line.

> It is true that I did not originally subscribe to the Oswestry &
> Newtown as much money as others . . . but it is well known that I
> contributed eighteen months of very hard and very anxious labour,
> continued by night and by day, for which I never received one
> shilling; now, indeed, in the bitterness of spite, I am deprived of
> even a pass. When we at first took up the Oswestry & Newtown
> the risk was very great, and for this, as well as for the labour and
> time bestowed upon it, I was entitled to receive a liberal profit
> when the contract turned out, as it did, so good an one. The
> money I so hardly earned, and which I ought to have received,
> was, however, squandered in 'sumptuous living', and the
> manufacture of through lines and extensions; and because I (the
> only one, by the bye, who had anything to lose) would not consent
> to be fooled to the extent which was wished, I now come in for so
> large a part of Mr Whalley's abuse.

He concluded by saying that, 'when the shadow of a London & North
Western rebate shall have faded before the eyes of the deluded
shareholders and they find only the unpleasant reality of enormous
subscription debts, they will be convinced who are their friends and who
their enemies.'

Thomas Webb was not content simply to pen these sonorous phrases for his master; he wrote a letter entirely on his own behalf which appeared in the same issue of the *Shrewsbury Chronicle*.[43] 'Under ordinary circumstances any statement coming from George Whalley receives about as much attention from me as is usually accorded to the observations which he throws away upon a well known assembly of *gentlemen*,'[44] he loftily began, in an oblique reference to the House of Commons. The change in his own 'humble personal arrangements' — the move from Savin to Davies — was, in his view, 'scarcely of interest to the public,' but it was one he had been perfectly entitled to make after concluding that 'so far from Mr Whalley and his allies being actuated by patriotism and disinterested public service . . . their objects were far more sordid and vulgar.'

> . . . the charge against Mr Davies of having *enticed me away* from Mr Savin is really too absurd to reply to. In point of fact I made up my mind to leave the position I lately occupied long before I knew Mr Davies would have me . . . When I obtained my present appointment I was quite prepared for the observations of people cast in the same mould as Mr Whalley, and possessing sufficient impudence to attribute their own principles to others.

The letter was signed 'T. Webb, Railway Offices, Llandinam,' and dated 7 September.

The agitation felt by David Davies over the entire business is evident from the letter he sent to the mistress of Glansevern on 26 August, just before that half-yearly meeting of shareholders at the Town Hall, Welshpool. It was notable on two counts: this was the first time he had felt bold enough to write to Mrs Ann Warburton Owen on his own initiative, rather than in reply to a letter from her, and its rough-and-ready style contrasts vividly with Webb's polished phrases in the 'ghosted' letter to the newspaper. It is headed 'Newtown, August 26th 1861' and reads:[45]

> Madam
>   I take the liberty I think for the first time to write to you on Railway Matters as this is a most Important time in the affairs of the company you have so large an Intrest [*sic*] in the Ordinary shares, I was Oblige to leave the Contract in an unfinished State Because my late Partner and some of the Directors would Promote Railways in all Directions without the means to carry them out   I did work hard at the Oswestry & Newtown for 18 months & did not get one Shilling for my Risk Anxiety & Labour   at the next meeting the Shareholders are asked to subscribe for the Welsh Coast Railway in Preference Shares 75000 Oswestry & Whitchurch 30000 Mid Wales 70000 Total 175000 If

you support this in my Opinion your shares are worth nothing
I did oppose these Extensive Sceams [sic] before one Shilling was
Spent in them & left because they were taken up by my late
Partner   I would thoroughly Recomend [sic] you to leave your
Proxy in the Hands of Mr Naylor as his Intrest [sic] is Identical
with your own & he will not deceive you   Our Own Directors
are the Promoters of the new lines and your Proxy is not Safe in
their hands   you will See from the Pamphlet the Capital
Acount [sic] I foretold all these troubles last year before I left so
now they are become facts.
I Remain
your humble servant
David Davies
Contractor

So Davies and Savin went their separate ways − Davies to prosperity,
Savin to ruin. There was a poignant moment when David Davies called
his workmen together near Machynlleth and stood on a wheelbarrow to
offer them a choice − either to stay with him and complete the line to
Newtown, or to join Savin in taking a line to Aberystwyth: 'Those who
prefer the Aberystwyth line, stand to the right, and those for the
Newtown line to the left.'[46] Davies is said to have confided in his
workmen, explaining how the split with Savin had come about,[47] but it
was not only Whalley who disapproved of Davies's behaviour at this
time. One of the Oswestry & Newtown Railway shareholders, writing to
the *Railway Times* about the company's 'misfortunes', declined to give
Davies any further consideration because it was 'notorious that he has
dissolved his connection with, and given up the concern to, Mr
Savin.'[48]

Savin did not stay in Whalley's good books for long. Two years later,
as he juggled the finances of the Aberystwyth & Welsh Coast Railway
in a desperate bid to stay solvent, he faced the bitter enmity of the man
who had once so eagerly sprung to his defence.[49] The truth is that
Whalley's attachment to Savin was useful only insofar as it fed his hatred
of the sometime sawyer.

7 Comradeship in Labour

In spite of being paid 'not one Shilling' for his work on the Oswestry & Newtown Railway, David Davies was by now a wealthy man. No longer was he laying up treasure in Heaven simply by outbidding his neighbours in gifts to the chapel; he had joined the ranks of those who dished out largesse to the needy. At the beginning of that year of 1861 he had given fifteen tons of coal to the 'aged poor' of Llandinam, 'these being 42 Recipients above 70 Years of Age,' as David Kinsey noted in his diary.[1] It was the first of many such gifts he was to make over the next twenty-nine years.

Although Llandinam was still small, with only 131 people in the village itself,[2] there was a growing sense of being part of a wider world. The railway had given people more scope and variety; business opportunities were expanding. Merchants in Llanidloes were now able to obtain coal and lime direct from Llanymynech,[3] and Llandinam was on the route. The ever enterprising David Kinsey had set up a coal yard in the station the previous November,[4] just in time to do a brisk trade as the temperature plunged to give London what he believed to be its coldest Christmas Day on record.[5] The sense of progress was such that an old man living in Llanidloes — another David Davies, in fact — was persuaded to list the changes that had taken place in the town since his youth. One of the most obvious was that forty or fifty years previously, it had been customary for poor people to have large 'middens' — smelly and unsightly heaps of rubbish or dung — outside their front doors, and sometimes deep pools nearby in which to soak the straw, bracken and oak leaves they had gathered for the making of manure. It had been dangerous then for people to step out of doors at night into the unlit streets, for they might easily end up sprawling into the midden or falling into the pool. 'Our town is healthier now,' wrote Davies cheerfully, 'and its streets are free of filthy pools and middens.'[6]

In matters of belief and custom, however, the old world took a long time a-dying in the Welsh countryside. There is something medieval in a happening recorded in Kinsey's diary on 30 December 1860, when Elizabeth Hamer had to pay for 5s. worth of bread to be shared among the poor at Llandinam Church after she had been found guilty of spreading scandal.[7] A few months later a happier event occurred: an eisteddfod was held in May at Llanidloes, the first ever according to Kinsey.[8] This came two days after another 'first' — the first Sunday train between Newtown and Llanidloes, manned by a volunteer crew who had no moral objection to breaking what chapelgoers thought of as 'the Sabbath'.[9] Anne Watkins was 'buried from the workhouse' on 15 May,[10] in the plainest of coffins, but all was jollity just under a month later with the opening of the Oswestry & Newtown Railway. Nothing could prevent Mrs Owen of Glansevern playing a leading role on occasions of this kind, and this time she presented a silver bugle to Captain Johns and his men of the Railway Volunteers. The instrument was evidently a handsome affair, showing the locomotive Glansevern on one side and a train passing over a railway viaduct on the other.[11] There was a curious link at this time in Montgomeryshire between railway making and spare-time soldiering, George Owen and Benjamin Piercy being among those who joined the Volunteers and paraded when they could in the uniforms of the Queen. In *The Story of The Cambrian* C.P Gasquoine tells how in after years 'it was the habit of their children to ask these gallant men whether they had "ever really killed anyone" with their formidable swords, and some of them were wont to answer that, perhaps not, but they had taken part in the "battle of Aberystwyth", a somewhat mysterious affair among the plum stalls in the market-place...'[12]

David Davies now had no more to do either with the Llanidloes & Newtown or the Oswestry & Newtown Railways, as the arrangements he had made for working the lines were made void by the break with Savin. 'My offer to lease the Llanidloes & Newtown Railway was made when the company confined itself to its own business,' he explained. 'This small company, in connection with the Oswestry & Newtown, has since been used as a basis upon which to project visionary and expensive railways in all directions.' All this, in his view, was bad news for the shareholders. The 'enormous' increase in the required capital meant that 'the sum which would have been sufficient to pay ordinary shareholders 6% will now scarcely do more than pay its preferential dividends.'[13]

The *Railway Times* took a haughty metropolitan view of things. 'The jobbers and speculators which infest this undertaking are excessively wroth with the *Railway Times*,' it observed in a leading article on the Oswestry & Newtown, going on to describe them as an 'unprincipled gang of adventurers driven desperate by the failure of their hopes and the exposure of their nefarious doings.' The editor had a deep contempt for Whalley, whose 'language and conduct' were such that any attempts to convert him into 'a useful, respectable, trustworthy and independently-minded gentlemen' were no less than 'a social error'.[14]

With the burden of worry over Savin off his shoulders, David Davies applied himself vigorously to the task of making the Newtown & Machynlleth line. Although the engineering problems were acute, the enterprise was thankfully free of litigation, which meant − as the

Shrewsbury Chronicle noted approvingly — that 'the money raised upon the shares has gone to make the works and not to be expended in law.' So unusual a circumstance was this that the paper called it 'one of the peculiar features of this Welsh line'.[15]

Davies guaranteed to complete the line for only £9,000 a mile, a sum which included the erection of permanent stations. In the autumn of 1861 he had 1,100 men at work on it, some at Talerddig and others further west between Llanbrynmair and Machynlleth.[16] He drove them hard, having no time for slackers but shrewdly offering cash incentives on top of basic pay: he awarded £50 merit money to an engine driver and promised to share a prize of 100 guineas among his most assiduous gangers.[17] The men never knew where he might turn up, giving a rebuke here and a pat on the back there, talking to them in their own language. His name had spread far as a boss with a difference, one who had not come into the business after years of soft living but a man who knew what it was like to have an aching back and blistered hands. Like them, he was up and about when the gentry were still lying abed. He would leave the Gwernerin farmstead at 5 a.m. to catch the workmen's train up the line to Talerddig,[18] and a century after his death the story persisted that in order to be at a remote point on the line first thing in the morning he would put up overnight at the home of one of his workmen.[19] He would treat the men not as mere hired hands but as his comrades, telling them of his hopes and his fears and infusing them with enthusiasm. If one of his visits of inspection coincided with a meal break he would sit down with them, accepting bread from one, cheese from another and butter from a third.[20] When he became a colliery owner physically remote from his employees and conducting his business affairs through intermediaries, he must have longed for the simplicity and delight of those years of good fellowship. He would speak warmly of this 'comradeship in labour' and regarded it as one of the cornerstones of his success.[21] It was, of course, a comradeship of unequal returns: he made a million, while the men who sold him their labour continued to struggle on from one pay-day to the next. Unlike the factory owner Robert Owen — another Montgomeryshire man, born in Newtown in 1771 — he had no vision of the country being run as a vast co-operative enterprise. There were masters and men and his implicit belief was that while the men should always be treated fairly, the masters — as the initiators and financial risk-takers — were entitled to handsome rewards.

It is likely that, all his life, David Davies spoke English in the dialect of Montgomeryshire.[22] The Journal of the Powysland Club for 1890 provides us with an example of this dialect:

'Well, John, how bin-ee today? What sort of a fair han-ee had?'
'Middlin'; I munna complain. I sold all my ship, an' got two poun'
ten for the yews.'
'Well done. I wish I could ha' sold my pigs so well, but I'm afeard
I shall have to take 'em home today agen. This 'Merican bacon, I
do think, does spoil the market.'
'Times has been very bad, that's serten, but they'm a little better
now, binna they?'
'I dunno no, indeed. Besides rent, there's tithes and rates and
taxes, so many on 'em all, and servants is so hockard. I sometimes
feel jest ready to jack it up.'
'Wait a bit; dunna break your heart, man. This County Councell
does talk a dell about bringin' down the rates.'
'Ay, talk, and talk they 'ool; but I hanna seen much sign on it
yet. It inna them as talks most as does most. Small-neck'd bottles
always keeps the most noise.'
'You are quite right, Tummas, an' very often it's them as canna
look after their own business as thinks they can mind other
people's, and 'ool spend a lot o'time and money about it, too.'
'Bother take their lecsions, I say. There's summat or other all the
time − Parliament, Local Board, County Councell, Guardians or
School Board, there's no pace to be had. It dinna use to be so.'[23]

Those bothersome 'lecsions' were to bring David Davies both
jubilation and heartbreak, but they did not concern him just yet. All his
efforts were going into the brave, perhaps rash, promise he had made, to
have the rails laid all the way to Machynlleth − though not the line
ready for passengers − by May Day 1862.[24] 'Mr Davies is undoubtedly
entitled to our thanks, for he evidently leaves no stone unturned to
complete the line in the time specified' the shareholders were assured at
their meeting on 26 February that year by the chairman, Captain Robert
Davies Pryce. 'From what I saw this morning, in his anxiety to prosecute
the works the men are actually treading upon each other's heels.' At one
place, over one hundred masons were at work − and there was plenty
of scope for skilled craftsmen like these. 'The earthworks remaining to
be done are being pushed on as rapidly as possible,' reported the
engineers, Benjamin Piercy and his brother Robert, 'and the great rock
cutting at Talerddig will soon be taken out to its full width.'
Three heavy bridges still had to be built near Comins-coch over the
Afon Twymyn, 'but as your contractor is now able to take the stone and
other building material to the spot by rail, there is every prospect of these
being finished by early in the summer.'[25]
On its eastern side, the railway linked with Davies's first line, the
Llanidloes & Newtown, at Caersws Junction − otherwise known as

Moat Lane — half a mile from Caersws. Even midway through the twentieth century the prospect of a long wait at Moat Lane was dreaded, as this dreary junction in the middle of nowhere embodied all that was dispiriting in rail travel. A century earlier, it was infinitely more gloomy. On 21 March 1862, the *Shrewsbury Chronicle* carried a graphic account of a journey headed 'From Oswestry to Moat-Lane (34½ miles) in four hours and a half.'

Sir, — On Monday the 24th ult, I had occasion to go by the train leaving Oswestry at 7 o'clock a.m. to Moat-Lane, on the Newtown & Llanidloes line. The first misery was to wait in the worst hut of a booking office amongst navvies, or starve outside for a quarter of an hour, the train not starting in time. When it appeared I found the carriages linked to a huge goods train, which was too cumbersome to shunt to the side of the platform. Having overcome our first trouble we made a very fair start, leaving disappointed third-class passengers behind. We got to Pool at 8 o'clock, but our punctuality only increased our misery, for we had to wait *one hour and twelve minutes*. I got out some distance from the station, where our carriages and part of the passengers were doomed to do penance. Those who got out, had just an occasional glimpse at the fire in one of the celebrated huts, as at Oswestry. We very slowly proceeded towards Newtown, and, contrary to the rule, instead of passing, we stopped at every station from Pool to Moat-lane, and at a great many places where there are no stations. We were ultimately put down at or rather near Moat-lane station at 11 o'clock. A gentleman going by the same train informed me that it was the intention of the company to improve their arrangements on the first of this month, but I find the time-bills are exactly the same...

A TRAVELLER

Little wonder that David Davies's brother Joseph — who fancied himself as a long-distance runner as a young man — was able to boast of racing a train from Moat Lane to Newtown when the railway was still new.[26] But although trains were often dead slow, some were much too fast. Some reckless driving near Newtown in November 1861 culminated in a fatal accident at Abermule, scene of a far worse crash sixty years later. A goods train running to Newtown and Montgomery ran off the line and down an embankment, and with a relish for gory detail the *Railway Times* informed its readers that the driver, Henry Baker, had been 'thrown a considerable distance and dashed to pieces' and that the 'stoker', Herington Kerr, had been 'crushed under the engine'. Another man who, mysteriously — and almost certainly illictly — had been on the footplate, was lucky enough to escape with bruises, while the guard saved himself by jumping out of his van. 'It is to be feared,' the report severely continued, 'that Baker was driving at a furious pace; he had on more than one occasion been warned...'[27] Kinsey's diary records other accidents that year:

Aug 29:   First Cheap excursion trip from Llanidloes to Liverpool. Accident at Caersws Junction   Engine & Carriages thrown off.

Oct 29:   William Morris Pontddolgoch killed on Railway by Waterloo Bridge, Returning from Newtown Fair (miss'd his coach)

Dec 25:   Edward Richards Llanidloes killed by Talerthig [sic] cutting

There was a tendency to take such things for granted, to view them as 'acts of God' rather than the result of human folly. It seems incredible that no blame appears to have attached to David Davies for the collapse of one of his bridges on the Newtown & Machynlleth line, not once but twice. The first time this happened was on 25 April 1862, and at that stage the bridge was still regarded as a temporary structure. It had been flung across a chasm at Comins-coch, on the stretch of line being put down between Machynlleth and Llanbrynmair. One of Davies's engine drivers, Henry Clough (perhaps the 'Henry lad' named in the ballad sung at the opening of the Llanidloes & Newtown) was taking a locomotive across the bridge when it gave way, plunging engine and driver into the river.[28] Davies is said to have wept at the news and to have made 'ample provision' for Clough's widow and three young children.[29] The engine was the *Llandinam*, the 0−6−0 saddle tank purchased from Manning Wardle for the Llanidloes & Newtown, and at first the task of retrieving it from the River Twymyn appeared insuperable. Next day, however, ropes were attached to it and 200 muscular workmen hauled it out of the ravine along a specially-laid length of track.[30]

Within four months of this tragedy, the *Oswestry Advertiser* was reporting the collapse of 'what was intended to be the permanent structure' at this very same point. The brick arch had given way under the weight of soil deposited on the bridge, and once again the contractor managed to escape prosecution. Far from expressing any horror at what appears to be a second case of criminal negligence, the newspaper noted that 'the loss to the contractor is estimated at £500,' and that the 'vast amount of lime used in the structure killed thousands of fish including salmon, sewin and trout ... such a wholesale destruction of fish was

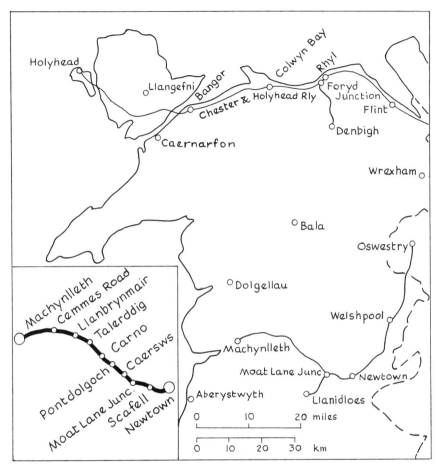

In spite of the difficulties of the works, David Davies kept his promise to complete the laying of the Newtown & Machynlleth track by May Day 1862.

scarcely ever seen.'[31] The fact that there was no loss of human life on this occasion passed without comment.

Henry Clough had died on the very brink of success: only a week after the first fall of the Glyn Bridge at Comins-coch, the newspapers of the border country were reporting that David Davies had fulfilled his promise to complete the line by 1 May and that 'the uniting of the valleys of the Dovey and the Severn by an iron band is a fact accomplished.' There were flattering remarks about the contractor's 'indefatigible energy and perseverance' and confident prophecies that the Talerddig cutting would for ages be considered the wonder of Wales.[32] Incredibly, in spite of its plunge into the chasm the *Llandinam* was in good enough shape for a reporter to ride on its 'footboard' when it was used to test the bridges between Talerddig and Machynlleth — including the one doomed to collapse again in August. He must have been a very trusting reporter indeed, as he did not flinch from an experimental journey which involved the hauling of five wagons heavily loaded with stone and three further wagons crammed with exuberant navvies. The high spirits of the navvies were made higher still by the presence in the front seat of honour of someone known to one and all as 'General Jenkins'. This 'Llanbrynmair celebrity' sat there proudly, 'with his soldier's cap and plume and alder whistle.' At Machynlleth David Davies was carried shoulder high on a chair into the town, and there he announced that the train would be returning in half an hour, 'but whether the engine got drunk, or the engine driver got tired, we know not,' wrote that same reporter, 'one thing is certain, that about 4 o'clock in the morning, the shouts of the previous night were revived, and shortly before five, the whistle's scream and puff of the engine announced its departure, with a living freight considerably more intoxicated than they had been on the previous night.'[33]

The contractor was true to his word, rewarding the gangers who had performed outstandingly. This convivial evening was reported at length in the *Oswestry Advertiser*,[34] which was effusive in its praise:

> It has frequently been our duty to refer to Mr D. Davies, the eminent contractor of most of the Montgomeryshire lines, as an enterprising man of business, and as an exceptionable employer; but in the present instance all his former deeds have been completely eclipsed, and firmly deserves the extra meed of praise.
>
> So far as we can learn, Mr Davies is a man who attaches an inviolable sacredness to every promise he makes; and if there be any deviation displayed, it is, as in the present instance, to exceed the terms originally made. Mr Davies's promise, at the Metcalfe presentation, was to the extent of 100 guineas, the sum actually distributed amounted to £203.

The dinner was held at the Aleppo Merchant in Carno, 'in a tent adjoining the inn', entertainment being provided by mine hostess, Mrs Wilson. 'The proceedings were conducted with that decorum which would have done credit to meetings conducted upon the more aristocratic scale' the writer patronizingly observed. 'It may be truly said that there was a refinement in the manners of the parties assembled which is not always to be found amongst the humble sons of toil.'

David Davies, a son of toil who had put humility behind him, delivered his usual homilies.

I think I may say that I always feel a pleasure in the well-being of my work-people, and am at all times desirous to do them the greatest amount of good that I can. I deem it to be the duty of the employers to take the highest interest in the well-being of the workmen; and, on the other hand, the duty of the employed to sympathise in the efforts and undertakings of their employers, and when things are so all will go on well.

He was making the awards 'to assist them to start in life', and he hoped they would not spend the money on drink, for which he had a great aversion. The man from the *Advertiser* thought it 'amusing to hear the parental way in which he talked of these stalwart fellows, every one of whom seemed to listen to his fate with the greatest anxiety.'

> For John Hughes, he said that a more noble fellow never trod upon a shoe of leather, that he had the worst cutting on the line, but he got through it. Of Daniel Pryce he said, I consider him my own boy, and thought to have made him the highest present, but I heard one thing against him, so I lowered him £10 for it. It is true that he had a bit of a quarrel with the clerk, poor David, who is now (a clerk) no more, and that is the way I forgave him, but after all I think I am doing him no injustice, as I pay him more wages than any of the rest, and I think he is satisfied. For John Watker, he said when he came to me, those English fellows said, 'He is only a bit of a boy from the cart tail, and cannot do anything,' but in the short time he has learnt so well, that he can teach any of them now (cheers).
>
> For John Pugh, he is ever ready when a bridge falls down to lay the foundation again, and so I give him £7. For another he said, he is a good fellow, but some time ago he was given to drink, but of late he has got better, so I give him £5 in the hope he will continue to improve; if he had not mended I would not have given him any. None of my money shall go for drink if I know it. . .

Davies reminded them that he had been 'up early and down late' so felt quite justified in being the sole judge of their merit. The highest award of £25 went to Joseph Roberts, 'as much for his kindness and attention to his men as for his other good qualities,' the *Oswestry Advertiser* listing the payments as follows:

> Mr [sic] Joseph Roberts £25; David Hughes £20; John Roberts £20; David Evans £20; Daniel Pryce £20; David Owen £10; Thomas Jones £10; Thomas Davies £5; John Jones £5; Richard Manuel £5; David Manuel carpenter £10; Thomas Humphreys mason £7; John Pugh mason £7; Evan Hughes £7; John Pryce overlooker of the permanent way £10.

The 'overlooker' was given an additional £10, to be shared out among his platelayers.

The cordiality of the evening was in keeping with the spirit of the enterprise. After all his tussles with Whalley, it must have been a relief for David Davies to work for directors more appreciative of his efforts. There was praise for 'the energy with which he had carried on the works, and the astonishing progress which had been made' through the previous autumn and winter, and he was seen as 'a tower of strength' who 'bore up amid difficulties which would have filled most men with dismay,' a man of 'indomitable spirit' ever ready with 'fresh resources for every difficulty'.[35]

One reason why the directors were keen to finish the line as soon as possible was the advantage to be gained from the summer trade to Aberystwyth, but they had no intention of running the trains themselves. They jumped at an offer from the powerful Great Western Railway to work the line for forty per cent of the gross earnings, with a guaranteed dividend of five per cent for the shareholders. The offer, however, was eventually withdrawn, and to Davies's chagrin it was the Oswestry & Newtown that leased the line, optimistically for one hundred years, and Savin's engines that ran along it.[36]

In the closing months of 1862, however, as the day of the official opening of the railway drew closer, the prevailing mood was one of satisfaction and benevolence. The night out for the 'humble sons of toil' at the Aleppo Merchant was followed by a treat for Newtown chapelgoers arranged through the town's temperance committee, David Davies laying on a special train to Comins-coch: not the most exciting of prospects today, but one viewed differently at a time when a twenty-mile trip was like a journey into another land. At Comins-coch there were buns to be had for a ha'penny and teas for a penny, and thus strengthened the excursionists walked the hills or, more morbidly, 'went to the Glyn, the scene of the unfortunate disasters on the line.'[37]

Three weeks later, the contractor laid on another trip for the people of his home village – a 'pleasure excursion to Machynlleth, the old city of Glendower',[38] where the railway had already brought about a significant social change. So many non-Welsh-speaking people had moved into the area that 'for their sakes' the Wesleyan Methodists were holding services in English.[39]

On 3 December it was reported that Captain Tyler of the Board of Trade had inspected the line, travelling along it in a train 'with two very powerful engines of about 80 tons weight . . . minutely examining every point, and severely testing every bridge', and declaring himself satisfied at the end of the journey.[40] The company's balance sheet at 31 December showed that a total of £117,328 had been spent on the works, the minor expenses including £299 for advertising.[41]

In Llandinam, the completion of the line helped Kinsey to expand his business interests still further. 'David Kinsey (Self) had a Truckload of Flags and Slates from *Machynlleth by Rail, the first load that ever came (by rail)*', he noted in the summer of 1862,[42] and in the following October he recorded the big day when 'the Llandinam People & Schools children had a free trip to Machynlleth given by Mr Davies Contractor.'[43]

But it was a different story three months later, when Mr Davies Contractor was in very bad odour.

8 One of the Gentry

The entry in David Kinsey's diary dated 3 January 1863 says it all:

> Newtown & Machynlleth Railway Opened, and David Davies
> Contractor acted *scandalous* to all the Navvies, in deceiving them
> of a Treat, he issued Tickets at Stations on the line, afterwards
> drove through and left all behind, including some Hundreds of
> persons. He was and is, much blamed for his Action.

After writing these uncompromising words, Kinsey drew a heavy border
around the entry in black ink, and put a wavy line in the margin to make
it stand out even more. He was clearly very angry.

By then, however, David Davies was no longer simply a successful
farmer and contractor. He had become one of the landed gentry, a fact
noted by Kinsey on 28 August 1862: 'Mr David Davies Contractor,
Bought Trewythen, Tynpwll, Cwmygath, Cwmdiewyd, Hornby,
Gwernerin, Garnlas & Broneirion for nearly 20,000 pounds.'

It was less than seven years since he had obtained his first railway
contract, and the first time Kinsey had ever called him 'Mr' in his diary.

The purchase meant that Davies now owned many farms, but not —
as Kinsey implied — Gwernerin itself, as he continued to farm it as a
tenant of the Crewe-Reads. (Smaller farmsteads in the vicinity appear on
the census returns as 'Gwernerin Schedule No 13' and 'Gwernerin
Schedule No 16,'[1] so possibly Kinsey meant either or both of these.)
Later he was to acquire more estates in Kerry and Llanwnog, and to
become one of the biggest landowners in Montgomeryshire. It was the
fulfilment of a long-held ambition, and he entered into his new role with
relish. Not least, it enabled him to enjoy to the full the country pursuits
of the wealthy. The shooting of game ranked high on his list of this
world's pleasures, and thanks to his encouragement his grandson David[2]
grew up to be a squire who hunted with a zeal that suggested centuries
of family tradition.

It was with this purchase of the Trewythen estate in the parish of
Llandinam that the gentrifying of the Davies family began. Although he
continued to go to the same chapel, to share hymnbooks with his
deacons and to be — almost ostentatiously — a good landlord, David
Davies was, for ever afterwards, a man apart. By possessing the land
people farmed and the homes in which they dwelt, he had crossed an
invisible barrier. Physically he remained rooted in his native village, but
socially he breathed a different air. The sometime sawyer, grandson of a

The ceremony at Machynlleth to celebrate the opening of the Newtown & Machynlleth Railway, 24 January, 1863.

pauper, was now a man to whom people duffed their caps. He was branded with the stigmata of wealth and possessions, and the power they carried to rule others. Inevitably, he bequeathed to his progeny not only a fortune but a social position. It was to be confirmed by a peerage two generations on, when his grandson David became Lord Davies and his granddaughters Gwendoline and Margaret were to agonize on the use to which inherited wealth should be put in a small nation crucified by unemployment. In marking a black border around that diary entry, Kinsey − unknown to himself − played the part of prophet, for the David Davies who left his navvies stranded on the platforms was to be a man of the people no longer.

It was not so clear-cut immediately; even the most virulent poisons take a little time to work through the system. But the sturdy, rabbit-catching boy who had happily wandered the muddy lanes of Llandinam had grown into a man who looked in the mirror and saw someone to admire. He was no longer simply a man; he was a 'self-made' man. The dislike of public speaking he had displayed when the Clwyd line was opened melted away like the snows on Plynlimon. Henceforth he would address any gathering, not with polish and elegance but certainly with vigour. He would confess to being 'no orator', but even this was something of a boast.

It must have been a subject of some amusement in Llandinam when it became known that he was going to Sardinia to give advice on the construction of railways on the island. The drinking pals of that self-taught scholar David Kinsey may well have asked him for maps so that they might see precisely where Sardinia was. The thought of Davy Davies of Gwernerin going to such an outlandish place looking like a farmer setting out on market day was irresistibly comic. Yet this was to be the forerunner of other excursions to far-distant places: in time David Davies was to be present at the opening of the Suez Canal, to tour the Holy Land and to spend several weeks in Russia as the guest of the Grand Duke Constantine, brother of the Tsar, who believed him to be a practical man whose impartial advice on railway making was worth seeking.[3]

That first trip abroad to Sardinia was reputedly made in 1862 with Benjamin Piercy, the engineer with whom he shared the triumph of the successful completion of the Newtown & Machynlleth line. The probability is that he went as Piercy's sidekick, the engineer having first been consulted. Sardinia was at that time in the throes of radical change, having only just lost its status of independent kingdom to become part of Garibaldi's newly unified Italy. There were 250 miles of railways to be built on the arid, rocky island, but the plans that had been prepared were so daunting − involving twenty miles of tunnels as well as other heavy works − that no contractors could be found willing to take on the job, given the limitations of time and money. Piercy justified the faith placed in him by carrying out his own survey, which enabled him to put forward a much cheaper plan with fewer tunnels, and a firm of British contractors carried out the work. It turned out to be a long job interrupted by the war between Italy and Austria, and was not completed until 1881, but at the end of the day Piercy was made a Commendatore of the Crown of Italy. This is understandable when one considers his achievements there, for apart from bringing railways to the island he is said to have converted deserts and swamps into beautiful gardens, planted eucalyptus trees in abundance and made 'hot-beds of fever perfectly healthy'.[4] Davies's contribution was more modest, as he does not appear to have returned to the island after that initial visit.

He had, however, plenty to occupy him. He had yet another railway to make, the Pembroke & Tenby, and a mansion to build — Broneirion.

The site he chose faced the morning sun. It was on the far side of the river from the village, on the lower slopes of the hill bearing the name of the woodland upon it, Coed Mawr. The romantic in him dictated the setting; he wished the view to take in the chapel he attended, the railway station that symbolized his worldly success and his birthplace, Draintewion.[5] The station was only a few hundred yards away, the chapel a little further distant and Draintewion just about visible through the trees and scrub on Cwmffrwd Hill. There was never any thought in his head of leaving Llandinam in the days of his prosperity. He was rooted in the place, and would play out the role in which he had cast himself.

The house is handsome enough. It stands, square and honest, overlooking a lawn of modest size, with the drive curling downhill to the inevitable lodge. Around it are huge Wellingtonia trees, and the hill behind rises steeply. There is a fine view from the front of the house — it looks over the Severn Valley to the table-top hills to the east. It was the valley he had overlooked as a boy, only now he saw it from the opposite direction — a fact which may well have struck him as symbolic of his change of fortune.

The name Broneirion was there already — it applied to the land on which he built his mansion — and the fact that he did not abandon it for something more Anglicized and grandiloquent tells us something important about David Davies.

So, too, does a detail in the architecture which it is possible to miss. It can be seen above a first-floor window on the northern side of the mansion: a frieze showing five cherubic figures, a locomotive with steam pouring out of its funnel, a tall-masted ship and a girl holding with her right hand a shield bearing the inscription 'DD 1864'.

Broneirion, built by Davies as his family home and later extended by his grandson, the first Lord Davies.

A detail above one of the windows at Broneirion showing the initials 'DD' over the date.

One wonders what the lads in the village thought of that.

When David Davies moved out of Gwernerin, brother Joseph moved in. For thirteen years he had been farming Neuaddfach,[6] and in his elder brother's estimation – by no means an indulgent one – he had thoroughly proved himself. He was now thirty-one, and ready for the challenge of running a farm twice the size of the one he had left. It meant, however, that someone else had to be found to farm Neuaddfach, where their mother and sister Elizabeth were still living, and when the next census was taken in 1871 this role was being filled by Thomas Evans, a 45-year-old widower who went down on the form as a 'general farm servant'.[7]

At this point we must note that according to Matthew Humphreys, David Davies's motivation in building Broneirion was to allow Joseph to farm Gwernerin. In one of the articles he wrote for *Y Brython Cymreig* in 1893, he recalled how the story had gone around that Joseph was about to marry and intended to emigrate to New Zealand. Elizabeth Davies, mother of David and Joseph, was upset by the thought of her son going so far away. 'He [David Davies] feared that this would foreshorten her life so he went up to his brother and told him not to go, that he could go to live at Gwernerin instead of him', writes Matthew Humphreys. 'This is what happened and Mr Davies built Broneirion mansion for himself but as that was not ready for some time he moved to live at Trewythen and stayed there until Broneirion was ready.'[8]

The testimony of Humphreys is not to be taken lightly, but it is far more likely that these family concerns precipitated David Davies's decision to build a mansion for himself in his home village rather than provided the sole reason for doing so. There was undoubtedly a close bond between the brothers; in many ways they were kindred spirits, although Joe lacked David's driving ambition. They looked alike, with their square faces and firm jaws, and shared a taste for the outdoor life and the rugged pursuits that go with it. What the brothers enjoyed most was shooting woodcock, a bird which poses a challenge even to crack shots because of its erratic flight. In his youth David Davies had enjoyed a spot of poaching as much as anyone and Joe had joined in many of these escapades. One of Joe's favourite tricks was to torment a gamekeeper by firing his gun into the air from different points to set the poor man haring hither and thither. Joe had a mischievous streak and once offered to swap bags with a friend who had shot a hare at Gwernerin, saying he had 'black game' in his. The friend complied, only to discover that the 'black game' was a crow.[9] Joe was to outlive his brother by thirty-three years. When he died in 1923, aged ninety, he was said to have been 'one of the best-known patriarchal figures in the county . . . a sound and progressive agriculturist and a well-known naturalist ... Seldom seen without a gun under his arm, he developed a degree of marksmanship which perhaps has never been excelled by any sportsman in Montgomeryshire.' Shortly before his ninetieth birthday he had been seen ferreting — sign, perhaps, of a misspent youth — and an endearing aspect of his character is that he had persistently refused to act as a judge at agricultural shows, as he 'did not like the idea of a man judging his neighbour's exhibits.'[10]

The year of 1864 was an eventful one for Llandinam: it saw not only the building of Broneirion but the beginning of George Edmund Street's restoration of the parish church that resulted, among other things, in the removal of its gallery.[11] The masons started work on what Kinsey called 'David Davies's New Hall on Broneirion field' on 14 March, the very day it was 'Agreed to pull Old Church down and rebuild'.

There was a good deal of stubbornness in the people of Llandinam, and Edward Owen and Jane Benbow were not going to be denied their church wedding. On 20 May they were married at St Llonio's, the ceremony taking place just inside the church door, 'the whole of the other parts being pulled down'.[12] It was the hottest May on record,[13] but in the farmhouse at Neuaddfach the blazing sun served only to increase the distress of David Davies's brother Richard. His once sturdy frame had now turned skeletal as the tubercle bacilli ate his lungs away. Too weak for farm work any longer, he had gone home to die, and as all the quack remedies failed it became painfully clear that he had seen his last harvest. He died on 24 June at the age of thirty-seven, and this time the death certificate baldly gave the cause as 'phthisis'[14] or tuberculosis.

Elizabeth, bereaved of her husband and at least three of her children — four if the elusive Thomas had also died by then — lived on in Neuaddfach. Joseph eagerly set about the task of farming Gwernerin. And David and Margaret began to accustom themselves to being thought of as 'gentry'.

9 The Cross-way

David Davies had not yet finished with railways, but his thoughts were turning elsewhere. At forty-five he was in the prime of life, and although he had the means now to set up as a gentleman farmer and spend the rest of his days living off his investments, it is doubtful if he ever seriously considered this. He was keen for a fresh challenge, something to absorb his energies and zest for commercial adventure. He found it in the coal industry of south Wales, which with improved mining techniques and an expanding railway network was attracting increasing amounts of outside capital into the region.[1] Between 1840 and 1860 the annual output of the coalfield rose from 4 million tons to 10 million tons,[2] and entrepreneurs willing to risk their capital in new ventures did not generally find it difficult to obtain leases from landowners who stood to gain handsomely from royalties on the coal raised.[3]

David Davies's decision to become a coal prospector in the Rhondda Valley could not have been a sudden one, and one can only guess at the doubts that he and his wife may have harboured about it. It involved not only a financial risk but a radical change of direction: if the gamble succeeded, Davies would have to make a long-term commitment to a part of Wales far distant from Llandinam. Margaret may well have reflected ironically that she might lack for nothing in Broneirion save the company of her husband. She was used to his being away from home, making railways; but railway contracts came to an end, whereas a colliery seemed at that time to be as permanent a part of the industrial landscape as any. No matter how staunch his promises to return home to Llandinam every weekend, she must surely have felt some sorrow that his pleasure in her society must still take second place to his driving ambition.

The clinching factor appears to have been a letter that John Osborne Riches wrote to Thomas Webb, an old friend and colleague; in their youth they had worked together on the *Hereford Times*. In his capacity as mineral adviser, Riches had urged Samuel Thomas, owner of the Ysguborwen Colliery in the Aberdare Valley, to develop the rich coal resources of the upper Rhondda Fawr. Thomas declined to do so because he thought the risks were too great, so Riches wrote to Webb asking if his 'chief' might be interested. Davies was, and with a touch of gallows humour invited Samuel Thomas's brother-in-law, the mining engineer Morgan Joseph, to make a more detailed survey.[4] Joseph advised Davies to lease land from Crawshay Bailey, thus setting the stage for a meeting between two men who, in their different ways, came to have symbolic significance.

Davies was the archetypal self-made man, Bailey the archetypal capitalist: he is the 'Kosher' Bailey of the song fervently rendered on social occasions when the enjoyment of the singers is in proportion to the alcohol consumed.

> Kosher Bailey had an engine,
> But the engine wouldn't go,
> So he pulled it on a string
> All the way to Nant-y-glo!

It makes him sound very jolly, but few took liberties with Crawshay Bailey in his lifetime. A Yorkshireman, he was a nephew on his mother's side of Richard Crawshay, founder of the Cyfarthfa ironworks in Merthyr Tydfil.[5] Richard Crawshay, who apparently thought nothing of belabouring idle workmen with his walking stick,[6] had died in 1809, leaving his twenty-year-old nephew £1,000. The young man put the money to work in ways of which he would thoroughly have approved, developing ironworks in Nant-y-glo and Beaufort and at Aberaman in the Cynon Valley.

By the time David Davies built Broneirion in 1864, Crawshay Bailey was an old man of seventy-five living in a mansion in Aberaman, just over the mountain from Merthyr Tydfil. He had been the Tory MP for Monmouth Boroughs — which included the towns of Monmouth, Newport and Usk — since 1852, having been returned unopposed three times after contesting the first election against a Liberal. He knew all about David Davies, and was not averse to having a bit of fun at his expense when the self-made man from Llandinam made it known he wished to do business with him.

To appreciate Crawshay Bailey's shrewdness — or cunning — and David Davies's enterprise, we must remember that at this time the coal reserves of the upper Rhondda had scarcely been touched. The Bute Merthyr Colliery sunk at Cwm-Saerbren, Treherbert, by the Bute Trustees on the advice of the far-sighted agent William Southern Clark had been in existence since 1855,[7] but for the most part the region invited the brush of the landscape artist rather than the attentions of industrialists. There were small mining villages near Pontypridd, but the upper Rhondda was still 'a wild and mountainous region where nature seemed to reign in stern and unbroken silence.'[8] Further south the Taff Vale had changed little since the poetically-minded Lady Charlotte Guest, making the first trip along Brunel's Taff Vale Railway in 1840, had eulogized the 'brilliancy' of the scenery.[9] The railway had been built principally to carry iron from Merthyr to Cardiff, the Glamorganshire

Canal having become inadequate for that purpose, and for the men who had brought the Industrial Revolution to Wales, coal was first and foremost a vital ingredient in the making of iron.

Crawshay Bailey, however, was perceptive enough to foresee that the hills and vales still steeped in tranquillity would soon be ripped apart by speculators. He had bought huge tracts of land in the Rhondda, as well as in the vicinity of Mountain Ash and Aberaman – where he had sunk some small pits in the 1840s – and having made his pile was content to await the arrival of a man with the zeal to exploit the coal seams of the upper Rhondda and so enable him to become richer than ever. He must have known that David Davies was that man, but it was not in Crawshay Bailey's nature to make things too easy for anyone. Moreover, at the age of seventy-five even wealthy old men need diversion. So when Davies presented himself to him as a symbol of success, a 'self-made man' who had risen from nothing to command a fortune and a newly-built mansion, Bailey blandly informed him that he did not enjoy dealing with 'speculators and adventurers'. True to form, Davies bridled and retorted that he was no adventurer but 'an honest trader' who would match Bailey guinea for guinea.[10]

It was probably the toughest deal David Davies ever made in his life, for under an indenture drawn up on 15 June 1866 – one year and nine months after the original lease of land – Bailey ensured that he would be paid a rent of up to £2,000 a year for sixty years and royalties of 8d. for every 2,520 lb of coal taken up from Davies's first mines in the Rhondda.[11] But before that coal was struck, there would be an epic struggle – and the self-made man from Llandinam would all but admit defeat.

David Davies now had a new partner – Ezra Roberts, of St Asaph in Flintshire. In 1861 they had made a bid for the contract for the Anglesey Central Railway, and David Davies had impressed the directors. His reputation for being a practical, no-nonsense sort of fellow was enhanced when he bluntly informed the directors that £3,000 would be enough to spend on stations as 'it was very wrong to spend the shareholders' money in elegant stations instead of making them useful and permanent.' He was described as

> ... the stalwart Mr Davies, formerly of the firm of Davies & Savin, and now of the firm of Davies & Roberts ... a thoroughly respectable and practical man [who] offers to construct the line, including the cost of obtaining the act, lawyers' and engineers' charges, purchase of land, stations, sidings, signals and everything complete, except rolling stock, at £6,000 per mile. Or he will make the line at £5,000 per mile, leaving the company to pay preliminary and parliamentary expenses, and to purchase the land.

In either case, he will take a large proportion of the shares, and also the company's debentures at par, thus reducing the actual amount to be raised in the district, including purchase of land, to £43,000.

This directors' report, which won the thorough approval of the chairman, Sir Richard W. Bulkeley MP, continued: 'We have no recollection of so liberal an offer ever having been made to any company; and we may mention that Mr Davies, as a guarantee of good faith, offered to deposit £6,000 until such time as the contract should have been executed to the satisfaction of the directors. The financial difficulty which seemed at first to beset the project is, by Mr Davies's offer, reduced to a nutshell . . .'[12]

After all this praise, it seems a shame that Davies & Roberts did not make the line after all, but left it for the firm of Russell & Dickson to carry out.

They did, however, go west together – to Pembrokeshire. There they made lines which eventually linked Pembroke and Tenby with the South Wales Railway (later the GWR), to the great relief of the hoteliers of Tenby, who had feared they might lose out to seaside resorts fortunate enough to have been brought into the new age of communications.[13]

The junction with the main south Wales line was at Whitland, by means of an extension of their Pembroke & Tenby Railway. The survival of a ledger showing the expenses incurred by David Davies and Ezra Roberts in constructing this line makes intriguing reading, as it shows how railway contractors at that time set about the job.[14] First of all there was the task of obtaining the necessary printed material, and the connections both men had with north-east Wales – Roberts through birth and Davies through making the Vale of Clwyd line – probably accounts for the fact that in July 1862 Thomas Gee of Denbigh obtained the order for printing 500 contract sheets at £1. 7s. 6d. and fifty-two timekeeper books at £3. 5s. A month later Robert Jones, ironmonger, supplied two 'railway shovels' for 4s. 8d., a spade for 3s., a pound of six-inch nails for 3d., and two padlocks – a large one costing 2s. and a smaller one at 8d. Margaret Lewis, dealer, of Pembroke Dock, charged the contractors 17s. for a ton of coal, while Edward Tracy, a Pembroke saddler stocking 'a superior assortment of hunting-whips, London bits, spurs and stirrups, always on hand, at moderate prices,' charged them 5s. for a pair of leggings and 3d. for a 'silklash and binding gig whip'.

In November that same year John Ormond, chemist and druggist, Pembroke ('prescriptions dispensed with greatest care, with Drugs of the purest kind') sent an invoice for the supply of horse powder, sweet oil, physic balls and soft soap! Ten shillings went on hiring a fly to take someone important from the Lion in Pembroke to Tenby.

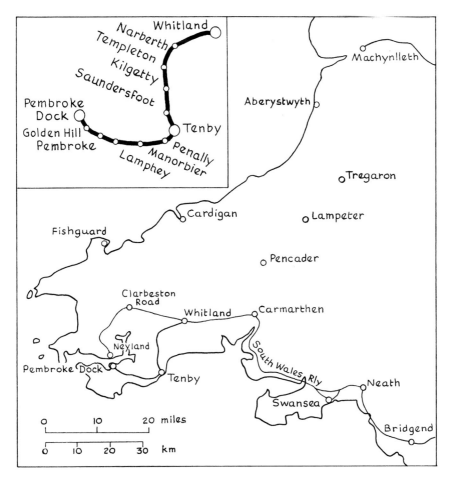

The Pembroke & Tenby Railway, constructed by Davies in partnership with Ezra Roberts, was conitinued to Whitland to provide a link with the main South Wales Railway in 1866.

There are several bills for gunpowder bearing various dates in 1865 — Curtiss & Harvey, trading at the 'Gunpowder Office, Swansea', provided twenty and a half barrels for a grand total of £22, roughly half the price charged by a rival firm. By then the Pembroke & Tenby line was open and in September 1866 the forging of the link with Whitland was celebrated in style.

The bill for this feasting survives among the Llandinam family papers. It shows that although David Davies was a teetotaller and non-smoker, he and Ezra Roberts were happy to foot the bill for a night of self-indulgence on the part of their guests. Eleven people — almost certainly including Davies and Roberts themselves — sat down to dinner at the

Royal Gate House Hotel in Tenby on Monday 3 September, the night before the line was formally opened. The bill for the dinners and desserts came to £3. 11s. 6d., and in addition there was a charge for sherry, 14s.; port, 8s.; ale, 2s.; champagne, 30s.; claret, 12s.; Seltzer, lemonade, gin and brandy, 11s., and cigars, 4s. 6d. 'Beds and attendance' cost the contractors £1. 2s.

More sherry, gin and brandy were consumed, and cigars puffed, the following evening, and the last guests did not depart until the Thursday morning, when Messrs Davis (*sic*) and Roberts picked up the bill for a grand total of £13. 18s.

Apart from this private entertainment there was a public banquet on the day of the railway's opening, when the directors and contractors were the guests of the Tenby authorities. The tributes were as lavish as the feasting, *The Welshman* noting that no expense had been spared in ensuring the safety of the passengers. Two rival schemes had foundered before Davies and Roberts had come along to complete the line in only three years, thus 'uniting by rail' all the important towns of south Pembrokeshire. The newspaper optimistically hoped that the local lines made by the contractors in south-west Wales would eventually form part of the grand plan of a Milford to Manchester railway: 'This was at last a business-like and easy method of accomplishing that which others had failed to do.' The immediate advantage for Tenby of being linked with the main South Wales line was that holidaymakers would be spared the vexation and fatigue of completing their journey by means of a tortuous route involving the ferry from New Milford (Neyland).[15]

Once again the weather dismally failed to match the optimism of the occasion, so instead of delivering his address in the rain-swept station — itself an uninspiring temporary structure — the mayor of Tenby, George White, spoke his resounding words at the banquet. It was full of Pickwickian flourishes, with praise for the 'liberality and untiring energy' of the contractors.

'After so many disappointments,' he declared, 'we thought we had reason to fear that Tenby, in spite of its many claims and attractions, was doomed to remain still in its state of distant isolation. It is to you, Gentlemen, to your enterprise, your abilities and perseverance, that we owe the accomplishment of a work so long and so much desired by us.'[16]

The speech David Davies delivered at the public banquet at the Gate House Assembly Rooms in Tenby was in the style he was making peculiarly his own. Since he could not compete with the polished phrases and scholarly allusions of the educated, he presented himself as the plain-speaking common man unashamed of his lack of cultivation. There was a good deal of humour in these speeches, and his colloquialisms delighted audiences usually rendered comatose by after-dinner clichés. In time this style of address would become a parody of itself, but when it first enlivened public occasions it came as a breath of fresh air.

'I know well that you are all noble hearted and true,' he said that day, 'and I feel that you believe we are the same. Then I would say, remember one thing, and that is, we went into this railway as a pure speculation, let there be no mistake about the point. I do not therefore see that we can run away with all the honour and the money too, that would not be fair by any means. I agree with the Mayor that the directors should have the honour, and we shall be satisfied to go away with our pockets full of money and leave the honour here. I know which is worth having and I repeat, let the directors have all the honour . . .'[17]

Only a very self-confident man, secure in his sense of himself as one of high reputation, could risk this gentle teasing of local dignitaries.

It is no wonder that David Davies was in such sparkling form that day, because by then coal had been struck in the Rhondda.

The story of the proving of the coal seams has become one of the legends of the South Wales coalfield. It is impossible to tell now where fact ends and fancy begins. The indisputable facts are that David Davies of Llandinam 'and others' took a sixty-year lease 'of mines and minerals under the Maendy, Ton and Gelli Farms, in the parish of Ystradofodwg, in the Rhondda Valley,' from 29 September 1864.[18]

By the summer of 1866 they were trading as 'coalmasters' in Ystrad under the title of David Davies & Co. On 15 June that year they signed an indenture listing a scale of royalty payments to Crawshay Bailey in respect of coal 'both great and small', iron ore, fireclay and building stone, as well as an annual rent of £1,500, rising to £2,000.[19]

The legend is that by the beginning of March in the year 1866, David Davies had all but given up hope of reaching the coal he knew was there. The sum of £38,000 had been spent on the sinking of two shafts, without success. David Davies called the men together and told them he could not afford to go on.

After he had left, they held a meeting and decided to give him a week's work for nothing. Before the week was out, the Two Feet Nine seam of steam coal was struck at Maindy at a depth of 215 yards.[20] David Davies, farmer and railway contractor, thus became Davies the Ocean, for with a flair for salesmanship well in advance of his time he decided to call his product Ocean Merthyr coal: a marketing ploy, pure and simple. His collieries were known as the Ocean collieries, and eventually the entire undertaking became the Ocean Coal Company Ltd.[21] This was no ordinary coal but steam coal of the finest quality, precisely the kind for which the maritime nations were crying out at a time when shipping was rapidly going over from sail to steam. 'Ocean Merthyr' coal became famous the world over, and the riches it brought David Davies gave him the reputation of being a kind of Welsh Croesus.

'The fact is that you are believed to be so fabulously wealthy that a few thousands are less than nothing to you . . .' John Gibson of the *Cambrian News* would write to him during the election campaign of 1886. 'If you were to give half a million to something few people would be surprised at the amount as they believe you possess millions.'[22]

Yet those millions did not automatically fall into Davies's lap with the cutting of the first coal. There was a hard road to travel before then. Indeed, the event which by the turn of the century had assumed such epoch-making proportions seemed so insignificant at the time that the few newspapers existing in Wales failed to report it. The Maindy Colliery opened in May 1866 without a single fanfare, and although it became received wisdom to say that the Ocean company was 'born under a lucky star',[23] its light was decidedly dim at the outset. Gibson acknowledged Davies's steadfastness of vision when he wrote with a typical vividness of phrase: 'In the sinking of the collieries he never wavered. He saw the coal, so to speak, as if it had been won, and he persevered whoever faltered.'[24]

All the perseverance in the world, however, would not have been enough to save David Davies from financial ruin in his very first days as a colliery proprietor, had he not possessed the support of a friendly banker. In the month that saw the first coal hauled up the shaft at Maindy Colliery, the world's biggest discounting house, the Overend and Gurney Bank, collapsed with liabilities of £11m, and for years afterwards 10 May 1866 was remembered as 'Black Friday' on the Stock Exchange.[25] This financial earthquake undermined even the strongest. One of the biggest of all railway contractors, Samuel Peto, was brought down by it; so was David Davies's old associate, Thomas Savin. Davies himself was in Carmarthen when the news broke, and although he had feared for years that something of the kind might happen he was shaken to the core; foreseeing disaster is one thing, enduring it another. As calmly as he could, he sat down and calculated his liabilities and assets, filling page after page with the sprawling figures which were the language he knew best. The stark fact facing him was that he had sunk so much of his capital into the search for black diamonds in the Rhondda that if he were called to account at that moment, he would be £70,000 in the red. It meant he would have to start again, not only at the bottom but, as he put it, 'lower than the very bottom.'

Even the grimmest events moved more slowly in the 1860s. In the absence of telephones, the quickest way of doing business was by telegram. Davies promptly despatched one to George Rae, general manager of the North and South Wales Bank in Liverpool, who wired back: 'Go on STOP we will back you up STOP.' This was, Davies would say, 'the cross-way, the turning-point in my career.'[26]

The men who, like him, breathed more freely after Rae's intervention were his business associates in the Rhondda: they are listed in Crawshay Bailey's indenture of June 1866 as Abraham Howell of Welshpool, Morgan Joseph of Ystradfechan, John Osborne Riches of Aberdare, Ezra Roberts of Tenby, and Thomas Webb of Llandinam. With David Davies of Llandinam, they were described as 'carrying on business at Ystrad, in the said county of Glamorgan and elsewhere, as coalmasters, in company partnership under the name, style or form of David Davies & Co.'[27]

It is tempting to see the Rhondda of 1866 in terms of the Wild West, a cowboy country where frontiers were being steadily rolled back by brave pioneers. The absence of any identifiable Indians, however, makes this a dubious exercise. There was a small native population, but it shared a common culture with what today would be called the 'incomers', who were Welsh like themselves: some years were to pass before the rapid growth of the coal industry enticed people from the West Country and other parts of England into the region. There was, however, a sense of great change in the offing, and this is reflected in the pages of the *Cardiff Times*. The newspaper was strongly in favour of a police station in Treherbert, 'some of the men employed in the steam coal pits being the scum of other places.'[28] The coal trade had 'increased greatly in the valley during the last two years,' new pits having been opened and shafts sunk at collieries which had hitherto consisted only of levels. The Rhondda's coal output in 1865 was given as 478,377 tons — an increase of nearly forty-five per cent in two years — the most productive collieries being named as Troedyrhiw, Cwmclydach and Dinas.[29]

In August 1866, when David Davies's second colliery, Park, came into production, the *Cardiff Times* renewed its call for a lock-up in the upper Rhondda to cope with the young men of the 'labouring classes' who caused trouble on pay-day.[30] By the following month 'hundreds of men' were at work sinking pits 'and some hundreds of masons are employed to build houses'. The report added: 'In a short time this place [Ystrad] will be a second Aberdare.'[31] The new houses were badly needed, for many of the colliers and their families were forced into insanitary hovels for want of anything better. They were breeding grounds for disease, and before the year was out there was a cholera epidemic in the valley. In October nine people died overnight in the tiny village of Abergorci: 'The deadly malady filled every one with fear, and about three-fourths of the inhabitants immediately fled.'[32] Quacks were quick to cash in with 'cures,' which included 'Kernick's Anti-Cholera Mixture ... useful in all cases of Bowel Complaints and Spasms.' It was being offered for sale in bottles costing 1s. 1½d. and 2s. 9d., but was unlikely to have been much use to the victims of a disease characterized by violent retching and diarrhoea.[33]

This 'visitation' — the word was often used when epidemic struck a community — strengthened David Davies's resolve to see his miners properly housed. In October 1866 the *Cardiff Times* said a piece of land near Ystrad station was being let for the building of 300 houses. 'Messrs Davies and Co, Park and Ton Collieries, are lending money on mortgage, at a low interest, and they will also supply stones at a low price for the buildings;'[34] twenty years later the company assets included 494 cottages,[35] and eventually there were more than 1,300 Ocean Coal houses, 'apart from those financed by certain directors personally.'[36]

Typically, David Davies showed concern not only for the health of his workmen's bodies but the state of their souls as well. By December 1866, work had begun on a Calvinistic Methodist Chapel in Ystrad, the Wesleyans having just completed their own chapel in the village.[37] 'Rhondda Valley. — It is very gratifying to state that this locality is in such a prosperous state,' the *Cardiff Times* told its readers just before Christmas. 'During the summer several new collieries have been sunk, and others enlarged, hence a vast number of fresh hands have been employed ... Ordinary cottages are now charged from 13s. to £1 per month, which, two years ago, were let at 8s. per month.'[38] A collier was being paid 8s. to 10s. a day (six-day working was then the rule), about twice as much as the miners working away from the coal face, who were classified as mere 'labourers'.[39] Output in the Rhondda rose to 649,828 tons in 1866 — a thirty-five per cent increase over the previous year — but David Davies's new collieries amid the bare mountains in the upper reaches of the valley naturally accounted for only a fraction of this: a mere 8,890 tons had been mined at Maindy and Park in their first months of operation. A third pit, however, was being sunk at Cwmparc — the Dare Colliery — and coal was already exacting its price. On his twenty-third birthday, one of the 'sinkers', Thomas Ashton, was killed by a fall of stone.[40]

10   A Fightable Man

David Davies was now a public figure in Wales — 'Davies Llandinam', a man whose opinions were valued. In 1865, the year before his first collieries opened, he was invited to make a speech at the National Eisteddfod of Wales in Aberystwyth. It might be thought that the organizers showed singular lack of tact by asking Thomas Savin along as well, but although they were no longer partners the names of Davies and Savin were still automatically linked together, and since it was Savin who had completed the line to Aberystwyth in 1864 it would have been rank ingratitude on their part to exclude him. In the event Savin rose to the occasion, referring to David Davies as 'his esteemed friend', and observing that 'under Providence' they had together been the means of improving communications. He could not resist adding that 'soon they would have an uninterrupted line of communication from Tenby in the south to Caernarfon in the north,'[1] and if Davies resented this coupling of his Tenby initiative with the visionary coast railway scheme over which he and Savin had quarrelled so bitterly, he did his best not to show it.

In the 1860s, the Eisteddfod was a far different festival from the one it became later, most notably in the fact that much of it was conducted in the English language. One of the specially invited performers, Lewis Thomas, was able to sing the 'fine buffo song, O, Ruddier than the Cherry'[2] without the risk of being bombarded with over-ripe fruit, and the only fault which the correspondent of the *Aberystwyth Observer* found with Miss Edith Wynn was not that she sang in Italian but that 'her pronunciation of the liquid tongue was somewhat harsh and cramped.'[3]

David Davies's speech came at the close of the fourth day, during a week in which the pavilion was crowded in spite of stiflingly hot September weather.[4] He stepped forward 'in response to enthusiastic calls from the audience, and addressed the meeting in Welsh.' This turned out to be one of his seminal speeches, encapsulating his attitude to the Welsh language with characteristic honesty. The account of his speech in the *Aberystwyth Observer* runs as follows:

> He said this was the first Eisteddfod he had ever attended, but he hoped it would not be the last. He was himself a great admirer of the old Welsh language, and he had no sympathy with those who reviled their country and language (applause). Still he had seen enough of the world to know that the best medium to make money by was English; and he would advise every one of his

countrymen to master it perfectly (applause). If they were content with brown bread, let them of course remain where they were; but if they wished to enjoy the luxuries of life, with white bread to boot, the way to do so would be by the acquisition of English. He knew what it was to eat both (cheers).[5]

When the language of white bread and 'luxury' came to threaten the very existence of the mother tongue, speeches like this would be despised for their shameless philistinism and lack of foresight. Yet the fact that it won cheers and applause proves that Davies was not alone in failing to see the cultural quicksands ahead. Perhaps a man so perceptive in other ways should have been more alert to the dangers, and taken more pains to hedge his robust arguments with some qualifications. That he failed to do so (unless, of course, he voiced qualifications which went unreported), tells us something about him, and even more about the status of Wales and her language in mid-Victorian Britain.

The fact is that Wales was seen, even by many Welsh people themselves, as a backward region of the British Isles badly in need of such 'civilizing' influences as the English tongue and the increased trade that came in the wake of the railways. 'A few years ago,' wrote the editor of the *Carmarthen Journal* when trains first steamed into the town in 1852, 'the Principality was an isolated and unknown country. Its language and mountains formed an impassible [sic] barrier to the enterprising Englishman . . .' The word 'England' was at that time used to denote both England and Wales, the lack of national institutions in the 'Principality' confirming the generally held view that Wales scarcely existed as a separate entity, except in the romantic sense of being a mountainous and rather quaint region offering the wealthy a cheaper alternative to the Grand Tour of Europe. Wales was not merely disregarded, but despised. The Government-appointed commissioners of 1847 had produced the notorious Blue Books blaming the Welsh language and Nonconformity for what they saw as widespread ignorance and immorality. Wales had no defenders in the House of Commons, according to Henry Richard, who in his successful election campaign of 1868 told an audience in Aberdare that Welsh MPs felt 'no sympathy with your principles, no pride in your national history . . . and when you were assailed again and again in the House of Commons . . . not one man ever stood up to defend his calumniated countrymen.'[6]

In the twentieth century 'Anglicization' came to be seen as an evil, but this represented a complete reversal of attitude. The 'progressive' view of the mid-nineteenth century was succinctly expressed by Enoch Gibbon Salisbury at the opening of the Vale of Clwyd Railway in 1858.

Although a Welsh-speaker, Salisbury — a barrister who the previous year had become an MP for Chester — quite shamelessly declared:

> Gentlemen, I am a Welshman, and I love my country ... How is the renovation of the Welsh race to be brought about? By the promotion of railways. I, for one, am not ashamed to say — and I say it here boldly — that I shall be delighted to see the Welsh people anglicized. I am quite sure that the way to Anglicize the Welsh people is by the promotion of railways and commerce among them, and making the English and Welsh thoroughly and completely one people.[7]

In this climate it is not surprising that in 1866 *The Times* felt disposed not only to ridicule the National Eisteddfod, but to abuse the Welsh language in the most violent terms. The immediate cause of this eruption was an article by the poet and educationist Matthew Arnold, who had attended the Eisteddfod and dared to suggest that the Welsh in their culture, morals and intelligence, 'had the same superiority over their conquerors, the English, as the Greeks had to the Romans.' The outraged editor of *The Times* replied:

> Now, we are quite willing to believe that this effusion from the Professor of Poetry at Oxford may have been too absurd even for the bards and other enthusiasts who assembled under the banner of the Red Dragon ... Nevertheless ... these Eisteddfods are intended to preserve not only the memory of old Welsh customs, but the Welsh language, and Welsh literature. They are intended to assist, and they do assist, in inducing the Welsh people to cherish their ancient tongue, and to believe that it will still be understood and 'honoured' in this country.
>
> Now, from this point of view we must protest against such proceedings as one of the most mischievous and selfish pieces of sentimentalism that could possibly be perpetrated. The Welsh language is the curse of Wales. Its prevalence and the ignorance of English have excluded, and even now exclude, the Welsh people from the civilization, the improvement, and the material prosperity of their English neighbours. It is, perhaps, little known to what an extent this unknown tongue still keeps its hold upon the Welsh population. There are villages in Wales where there are no more than two or three persons, including the parson, who habitually speak English. The Government have done all they can by providing that English shall be taught in the schools, but as it is not spoken in the cottages it is soon forgotten. The result has been that the Welsh have remained in Wales, unable to mix with their English fellow-subjects, shut out from all literature except what is translated into their own language, and incapable of progress ...

Their antiquated and semibarbarous language, in short, shrouds them in darkness. It both prevents them from finding their own way into the world, and excludes the light of day from themselves.[8]

Such were the insults Wales had to endure when David Davies first aspired to be a member of the Mother of Parliaments.

His decision to contest Cardiganshire in 1865 has wrongly been seen as having been partly inspired by his parents' supposed links with the county. In fact, as we have seen, both his parents had been born in Montgomeryshire.[9] He did have strong business interests in the county, however, for by then he was engaged in constructing a railway between Pencader and Aberystwyth for the absurdly-named Manchester & Milford company.

His partner in this venture was Frederick Beeston, who as a Llanidloes man was practically one of his neighbours. For some years Beeston alone had been the company's contractor, but little progress had been made in that time. In the four years between 1860 — when Beeston received his first payment of £2,200[10] — and 1864, four miles of single track had been laid from Llanidloes to Llangurig, but that was all.[11] Beeston had accepted the awesome commission to take a line through the Cambrian Mountains from Llangurig to Pontrhydfendigaid via Devil's Bridge, an engineering nightmare involving a viaduct standing on piers 280 feet high and two tunnels totalling a mile and a half in length. At their meeting in Cannon Row, Westminster, on 2 February 1864, the directors abandoned this plan and decided to concentrate on 'the southern end of the company's line, commencing at the authorised junction with the Carmarthen & Cardigan Railway at Pencader.' With great relief, they noted that

> after careful consideration of all the bearings of this question . . . they have entered into a contract with Messrs Davies (Llandinam) and Beeston (Llanidloes) for the whole of the works from Pencader to Pontrhydfendigaid, nearly 27 miles . . . and the Directors are of opinion that in the present state of the money market, and the probability of Public Works being influenced thereby, the Company may be considered fortunate in this engagement with two gentlemen, one of whom is well known in the Principality as a man of energy and character.[12]

Having paid David Davies such a handsome compliment, the directors tactfully added that they had every confidence in Mr Beeston, too, and when the contractors asked for an issue of £10,000 in shares two months later, under the terms of their contract, it was provided without argument.[13] Further amounts in paid-up shares rapidly followed — £10,000 in May, £20,000 in June and another £20,000 in August, when the directors congratulated the shareholders on the 'materially improved prospects of the company' and happily noted that their 'expectations as to the energy and resources of the contractors have been fully justified.'[14]

Much was made of David Davies's commercial investment in Cardiganshire in that election campaign of 1865. In his election address, when he put himself forward as a Liberal candidate, he boldly stated: 'I am connected with Lines branching from Aberystwyth to Llanidloes, to Rhayader, and to Carmarthen, representing a capital of nearly a million. I also intend to promote Railway extensions to the Coast. It must be manifest, therefore, that few can have a greater or an equal interest in the general improvement and welfare of the county.'[15] On nomination day, 15 July, in Cardigan, his proposer, William Jones, JP, of Llwynygroes, described him as 'a thorough and practical man of business, who had raised himself by his own downright energy and merits to a high position in the world; a position second to none in the railway interest.' In his view, 'Mr Davies was just the man Cardiganshire wanted to open its ports for trade, draw the attention of capitalists to the capabilities of its quarries, carry lines of railways through its towns and villages and make its trade in every branch prosperous.'[16] The argument was neatly turned around by his opponents, however, J. Pugh Pryse declaring that 'twelve months ago Mr Davies was totally unknown to them, and he never would have come into the county had he not had his own interests to serve in making them a railway.'[17]

The odd thing about this election is that both Davies and his opponent, Sir Thomas Lloyd, were Liberals. They were, however, Liberals of a very different stamp. Lloyd was one of the old Whig brigade who had the support of the aristocracy, whereas Davies was a 'new man' who in spite of his wealth was seen as being of the people. There were arguments throughout David Davies's political life over the precise nature of his Liberalism, but no disputing the fact that his appearance on the scene fundamentally altered the political landscape. It posed a challenge to the old landed families' monopoly of political power in the county, for with a restricted franchise and no secret ballot (this would not be introduced until 1872) the squires had until then ruled the roost: Sir Thomas indisputably belonged to the county set, as one of the Lloyds of Bronwydd in south Cardiganshire.[18] The two dominant families were the Pryses of Gogerddan, Liberals of decidedly Whiggish inclination, and the Powells of Nanteos, Tories all.[19] The picture was complicated by the fact that there were then two Parliamentary constituencies in Cardiganshire: the county seat which David Davies was contesting, and

Cardigan Boroughs (a situation which would change by the time of the climactic election of 1886).

The sitting member for the county seat in 1865 was the doddering Colonel William Powell of Nanteos, whose health was so poor that he was being taken into the chamber of the Commons in a wheelchair.[20] He was a Conservative in a predominantly Liberal House, Palmerston having achieved the Premiership for the second time in 1859 at the age of seventy-five. Nobody was surprised when Powell made known his intention of resigning, and the Liberals of Cardiganshire looked forward to his replacement by their own nominee, Sir Thomas Lloyd: a cosy arrangement, since the marginal differences in politics between Powell and Lloyd did not prevent their being close friends. To their chagrin, however, Powell changed his mind and decided to contest the seat after all at the general election. Lloyd immediately declared that he would not contemplate opposing the sitting member, but then came the news that Henry Richard and David Davies were interested in contesting the seat. Richard, who at fifty-three was six years older than Davies, had been actively engaged on the margin of politics for some time, having been secretary of the Peace Society since 1848.[21] He would be known, in time, as the Apostle of Peace, and would have his statue placed in the square in his home town of Tregaron. As a native of Cardiganshire and a Congregational minister into the bargain, his credentials for the seat were impeccable. David Davies, however, was not seen as a political figure at all; his energies appeared to have been entirely absorbed by the world of industry in which he had performed so astoundingly. Little wonder that the ill-organized Liberals of Cardiganshire, who lacked even a properly constructed Liberal Association at the time, were thrown into confusion. The dramatic — and sometimes hilarious — events of that first week in July were vividly recreated in a letter which a leading Aberystwyth Liberal, John Matthews, wrote to his son when the electoral dust had settled. He recalled how the Liberation Society — a pressure group campaigning for the disestablishment of the Anglican Church and other causes dear to the hearts of Nonconformists — had brought Henry Richard forward as a candidate, and sent two of its officers to Aberystwyth to help plan the campaign. He was talking to them in the front parlour of his house on Tuesday 4 July when there was a rap on the door. There he found the Machynlleth solicitor David Howells and Davies's partner Ezra Roberts, and assuming they were there on railway business he took them to the back parlour and told them he was in the middle of discussing 'electioneering business'.

> Well, well. After a very short prologue they told me that they had also called on similar business, that their candidate was in the field

and that he was there in Aberystwyth. I asked, Is it Mr Savin?
'No. Mr Davies is our candidate, and he is prepared and
determined to go through with the contest.' Here was a mess … I
at once told them my opinion, that it would never do to have two
Liberal candidates to oppose so popular a man as Colonel Powell,
that the best way for them was at once to meet manfully and try
to arrange which of the two was to stand and which to retire …
The next morning it was rumoured that Mr Davies had deposited
£10,000 in the bank: all ready for the battle. The upshot was, Col.
P retired quietly rather than fight. Mr H.R. had not yet arrived
and I am not sure that the Col. had heard that he was in the
field; however I have been told that the Col. has said that it was
Davies that drove him away.[22]

Henry Richard arrived in Aberystwyth by the six o'clock train on
Wednesday evening, and made his way to the chapel where Matthews
was attending a prayer meeting. He scribbled a note which was handed
to Matthews in the *sêt fawr* as the service ended. This was simply a
request for an immediate meeting with Matthews and a fellow-Liberal,
Richard Roberts, but the gossips made a meal of it: next day the rumour
flew around the town that the mysterious stranger had been 'a lawyer
from London' serving Matthews a writ.[23]

The meeting to decide which of the two should stand, Henry Richard
or David Davies, was called for Aberaeron on Thursday 6 July — as it
happened, the day on which Parliament was dissolved. By then,
however, there was a third potential Liberal candidate — for on hearing
that Colonel Powell had finally quit, Sir Thomas Lloyd had the gall to
come forward again as the man of the hour. Henry Richard promptly
withdrew from the contest, pleading that his 'London friends' had told
them he must not oppose another Liberal.[24] David Davies, however,
took a different view, as John Matthews explained.

Mr Davies had more pluck: he would not do so. As Sir Thomas
had so completely sold us to the Tories without once consulting
our feelings or asking our opinion he thought there was no
obligation on him to give way. He had rescued us from the
clutches — the talons of the tories — he was in no way convinced
that Sir Thomas had any right to step forward and snatch the
victory out of his hands without a struggle. He had money —
plenty of money — and that his own money to carry on the
Campaign and he was determined to fight it out. I wish [Henry
Richard had retired] with a better feeling. He appears to have been
sadly disappointed. He and his friends are bitter beyond expression.
Why they should be so, I cannot understand.[25]

The rift between Henry Richard and David Davies remained for the rest of their days, and the rights and wrongs of the affair were the subject of fiercely partisan letters in the press two years later, when Henry Richard was pressing his claims to be MP for Merthyr Tydfil — a status he achieved in the 1868 election. For John Matthews, however, writing just after the July poll in 1865, the issue was clear-cut:

> The newspaper press is a glorious institution, but it is very sad to think that men otherwise respectable should debase themselves so much as to make use of papers like the Banner and Nonconformists to propagate falshoods [sic] in order to lower men like Mr Davies, who had pluck enough to contest the County of Cardigan against the whole body of Tories and Whigs, together with all the Lawyers and nearly the whole of the Aristocracy combined.
>
> They appear to have another object in view — that is to break the fall of my old friend Henry Richard.[26]

The smear campaign hinted at by Matthews was in full swing by 15 July, when the *Aberystwyth Observer* carried a letter signed 'A Welsh Landowner' posing the following questions:

> 1. How long has Mr Davies been a Liberal and an admirer of Lord Palmerston and his Government?
> 2. Did he not at the County Election for Montgomeryshire, where he lives, support the Tory Candidate, Mr Wynne, against the Liberal, the Hon. Mr Tracey?
> 3. Was not Mr Wynne a declared supporter of Lord Derby, and Mr Tracey of Lord Palmerston?
> 4. If, as in truth Mr Davies must answer the two last questions in the affirmative, then when and how was he converted into a Liberal?
>
> If Mr Davies will disclose to the public the process by which, in a few years, he became a convert from Conservatism to Liberalism he will probably confer upon them greater benefits than he ever is calculated to do as a Member of Parliament, more especially if he will do so in his own natural straightforward way, and without the aid of his clerk; for he must bear in mind that he will not be allowed to perform his duties of legislator through his clerk.

The clue to the identity of the author of this barbed — not to say malicious — epistle lies in the next few paragraphs, in which the writer questions David Davies's claim to have railway interests in Cardiganshire 'representing a capital of nearly a million'.

> 1. Whose money is this million? and if it is not all Mr Davies', what part of it is his?

It is pretty well known that railway contractors are generally only in the shadow of men of capital, to whom they hand over scrip for about double the amount of money advanced.

2. How long will Mr Davies hold this valuable property? for it is well known that he parted with it in other lines that he made as soon as they were finished, and the shareholders were left to the mercies of the speculative men of capital without protection from any guardian angel in the person of Mr Davies.

I beg to assure you that I ask the foregoing in no spirit of ill feeling towards Mr Davies, for whom, as a railway contractor, I have a very great respect; but as he presumes upon one of the highest positions in the country, and one requiring high education, learning, and varied accomplishments, he must expect to have his qualifications for a legislator tested, before he shall become one.

There is little doubt that this letter was written by the Squire of Rhiwabon, George Hammond Whalley, who was clearly a long way from forgiving 'Contractor Davies' for the independence of mind he had shown in their railway dealings some years earlier. David Davies does not appear to have answered the charge that his conversion to Liberalism was of a recent date, even when it was repeated in the newspaper correspondence of 1867. Henry Richard then not only declared that Davies had previously voted for the Tory candidate in Montgomery, but actually alleged that at the meeting they had both attended in Aberaeron in 1865, he had boasted of having 'secured promises of support from some of the greatest Tory landowners in Cardiganshire'![27] This conflicts curiously with the observation in John Gibson's *Cambrian News* that in the fight between Sir Thomas Lloyd and David Davies 'the former represented the Whig section, and was supported by the aristocracy – and notably the Gogerddan family – while the latter represented the more advanced section of the Liberal Party.' [28]

What is beyond dispute is that David Davies threw himself whole-heartedly into the campaign. He showed a flair for public relations far in advance of his time by travelling around the county in style in an open wagonette drawn by four horses, two of which were ridden by postilions.[29] This not only enabled him to go quickly from meeting to meeting, but made a huge impression on the country people. 'Never did a candidate receive from a people a warmer, a more enthusiastic reception, than that with which Mr Davies was honoured in Cardiganshire,' observed *The Montgomeryshire Guardian and Cardiganshire Advertiser*. 'Scarcely did he enter any of the towns or villages, but that the people, meeting him in scores and hundreds, would persist in taking the horses from his carriage and drawing it themselves . . . Sir Thomas also moved about, but silently like death, and scarcely anywhere could he command a hearing.'[30]

Elections in those days were rumbustious affairs in which people heartily took sides, even if they weren't all entitled to vote. They were public entertainments, and all the better for being free. There were elections songs, making up in enthusiasm what they lacked in sophistication. At an earlier election, the Liberals of Cardiganshire had gone around bawling:

> Pryse Pryse of our woodlands comes forth with his good hounds,
> To solicit the votes of all good men and true;
> 'Tis for freedom he fights, and those national rights,
> Which real sons of Cambria have ever in view.
>
> This true Patriot Pryse, the good man of our choice,
> To our beautiful hills brings the gay sporting world;
> Strangers flock to his Race & they join in his Chace [*sic*],
> Then Electors hurrah! for the flag he's unfurled.[31]

Meetings often turned rowdy, but David Davies was prepared for this. According to his grandson, he 'hired pugilists . . . to do some of the chucking out,' which Lord Davies believed 'was common form in those days.'[32] In his younger days David Davies had not been averse to a spot of fisticuffs, but now he was eager to present a different idea of himself. During the course of a muddled and inauspicious speech delivered on nomination day in Cardigan, he declared that he 'was not a fightable man, although some of them said he squared his fists in the committee that met at Aberaeron, but all he did there was to tell them that he had an old engine that when 70 tons was put on, went majestic — and he showed with his arms how it pulled, so they spread about that he was fightable.'[33]

This robust explanation provoked roars of laughter, and the editor of the *Aberystwyth Observer* took a malicious delight in publishing Davies's exact words, warts and all, without the discreet tidying-up he would have accorded a political ally. Some thought he had made a 'ridiculous spectacle' of himself on this occasion,[34] when even his supporters felt obliged to make apologies for the fact that he did not possess the elegant style of address expected of prospective Members of Parliament. 'An objection had been raised to Mr Davies, that he was no speaker, that he would never do for the House of Commons,' his proposer, William Jones, was reported as saying. 'Well, his had been a busy, useful life, and he had not had time to acquire the polish of the honourable gentlemen on the other side, but the great want of Parliament was not speakers, but thorough men of business in the committee rooms, where, after all, the real business of the nation was transacted.'[35] This did not satisfy a former mayor of Aberystwyth, T.O. Thomas, who in seconding the nomination of Sir Thomas Lloyd said that in canvassing the county he had met people 'who unhesitatingly said they would consider it a disgrace to have an uneducated man, and one unable to speak properly, sent to the great senate of the land.' He himself thought it 'required a man of education to make laws for the country.' This brought the retort from David Davies that 'the gentleman who had just said he couldn't make a speech need not have said it for he was not so very fluent himself after all.'[36]

Sir Thomas's proposer, J. Pugh Pryse, had nothing to say about Davies's capacity as a speaker, but thought it 'would never do for them to look for a stranger to represent them, and such Mr Davies was' — a point taken up by Sir Thomas himself. After 'acknowledging that his opponent had 'raised himself from a humble station to one of fortune and influence', he rather snidely observed that apart from being a stranger to them, he 'of course expected, very properly and reasonably, a return for all the capital he laid out amongst them.'[37]

The printed address which David Davies laid before the electorate had undoubtedly been drafted by his amanuensis Thomas Webb. It expressed approval for Lord Palmerston's financial affairs and foreign policy, which in his opinion had 'aided considerably in producing our present state of prosperity,' and contained promises to abolish Church rates and to support 'any well considered measure for the extension of the Franchise.'[38] It did not, however, advocate the introduction of the secret ballot, although the squirearchy in many parts of Wales was notorious for its application of 'The Screw' — the word used at the time to describe the pressure put on tenant farmers and others to vote Tory rather than Liberal.

Amazingly for someone supposedly in the 'more advanced section of the Liberal Party', Davies went along with Sir Thomas Lloyd in opposing the ballot, arguing that 'it was only needed when people suffer for their opinions; and I believe the nation is too far advanced and enlightened in this age for the need of the ballot.' Having voiced these exalted thoughts, however, he effectively demolished his own argument by admitting that The Screw was a fact. 'But one thing I'll tell you,' he added, 'if this election goes against me, it will go far to make me an advocate of the ballot.'[39]

Polling day arrived in Aberystwyth with a sense of foreboding in the air. The authorities feared that David Davies's navvies, busily at work on the M&M line south of Lampeter, might take their enthusiasm for his cause to the point of threatening the town 'with disturbance and disorder,' so more than a hundred special constables were sworn in before the mayor. In the event, however, they were not needed.[40] 'The first vote polled here was that of Dr Williams, of Bridge Street, and he, of course, voted for Sir Thomas Lloyd,' reported the *Aberystwyth Observer*,[41] the public nature of the poll before the passing of the Ballot Act making individual support a matter not of speculation but of observation. Thus 'a majority was gained by the worthy baronet which he never lost' in Aberystwyth, which voted 461–390 for Lloyd. The squire of Bronwydd also won hands down in Cardigan, 360–65, and Llandysul, 200–63, and more narrowly in Aberaeron, 299–215.

David Davies, however, triumphed handsomely in Tregaron, 290–96, and comfortably won the day in Lampeter, 126–94. When all the votes were added up, however, Sir Thomas Lloyd was declared the victor by 1510 to 1149 – a majority of 361.[42]

Supporters of David Davies were by no means downcast. In their view he had polled well in spite of being 'an almost perfect stranger, a man who had nothing but his character, talents and enterprising spirit to recommend him,'[43] while in the opposite camp the Tory *Aberystwyth Observer* acknowledged his 'earnestness and pluck', but considered he had made a fatal mistake. 'He threw himself bodily into the arms of the extreme dissenters, and he thereby alienated from the good wishes of the Church people, and of all men of liberal and enlightened mind.'[44]

Relaxing after the struggle, John Matthews analysed the causes of defeat and found grounds for optimism.

This has been a more hotly contested election than any I have seen in Cardiganshire. Intimidation has done its work most efficiently. Landlords have frightened their tenants – lawyers their clients – Mine Captains their workmen etc. So that several hundreds of votes that were promised to Mr Davies were polled by the other party. After all Mr D. polled a greater Number than anyone else ever did before this election. Well done the poor Methodists. They stood almost alone and nevertheless polled more [than] 1100 votes. We have hundreds more that can be put on the register – and this we shall do by and bye. Mr D. is determined to spend a little money in that way. The whole country [sic] from one end to the other was enthusiastic in his cause; and had we the ballot he would have been the conquering hero with an overwhelming majority. We can afford to wait a little longer. He is sure to win his way ere long. I might mention to you that he is going about it in a way that will tell powerfully in time to come. He has promised to subscribe £100 to Borth new chapel & another £100 I am told towards the English Independent Chapel at Aberystwyth. He promised me last Thursday to subscribe £300 towards the British School room here and if it will be necessary he will raise the amount to £500. He is anxious to do something for the people along the coast.[45]

This blatant buying of votes raises doubts about the honesty of David Davies's intentions when he sat down to write some of his 'charitable' cheques. But not a hint of vulgarity was allowed to enter the elegant public letter of thanks to his supporters composed on his behalf by Thomas Webb.

> Although in a minority on this occasion, my coming forward has been the means of gaining a seat for the Liberal party ... there is not the remotest chance that Liberal Cardiganshire can ever again be subject to the stigma of such a compact as that which I have been instrumental in defeating.
>
> It has been said that my opponent is a freeholder in the county, and I am not. I am sure, however, that you will not need to be asked whether the freehold on which I am engaged in putting down an iron road, is not occupied to greater advantage than that held by Sir Thomas D. Lloyd and his tenants. A man may expect to be paid for his honest labour, and yet be a public benefactor; while my experience tells me that a man may inherit many broad acres, and yet be insensible to any interest but his own. You are the best judges as to whether I am a stranger amongst you or not. At any rate I will do my best to cure this defeat; and I trust by the time I next ask for your suffrage I shall not be unknown to a single elector, while to many I hope to be known as having contributed to their prosperity and happiness.[46]

So the fever and the shouting died, and the election song of '65 became history. Decidedly pro-Davies in character, it included the following rousing verses:

> In July Eighteen Sixty five
> As well as I remember,
> Cardiganshire was all alive
> To return a County Member.

> Colonel Powell had resigned,
> A Parliamentary Beauty,
> Feeling in his feeble mind
> Unfit for public duty.

> They soon began to look about
> For a Gentleman and Tory,
> But though they made a great Rout out,
> The Reds had gone to glory.

> But while they slowly talked and thought,
> Up started the 'Contractor,'
> Who soon determined, as he ought,
> To be a public Actor.

All in a flurry and a heat,
Poor Lloyd looked round the corner, —
'Oh dear, indeed, I might be beat,
By Davies the Reformer.'

'Lord help you,' cried Mr Pryse,
'Put a bold face upon it;
I'll set a trap and catch the mice,
With a Patent Screw above it.

I'll canvass all the County side,
I'll make the men go with me;
And all my tenants, far and wide,
Shall vote for Lloyd of Bronwy.'

'Oh, Mr Parry,' county swell,
'I ask your Vote of you!'
'Yes, yes,' cries Mr Parry,
'And all my tenants too.'

'My eye,' cries Lloyd. 'I'm better now,
I think I breathe more free,
Ne'er thinking that a Tory
Would vote for such as me!'

Here ends my tale of '65,
And long we'll all remember, —
How hard the Screw the Tories drive,
To Poll a Liberal!!! Member.[47]

11 Across Cors Caron

There was no time to sit and brood over that election defeat, even if Davies Llandinam had been the sort of man to do so. There was the iron road through Cardiganshire to complete, and in the Rhondda his men were driving their shaft ever deeper in their search for the steam coal.

It was, perhaps, his confidential secretary rather than himself who spotted a letter in *The Times* on 14 August 1865, from John Henry Scourfield, MP for Haverfordwest. We can picture Thomas Webb — that 'pure Englishman' in the eyes of Matthew Humphreys[1] — pointing it out to his employer, and the angry scowl on David Davies's face as he took in its import. It followed a *Times* leader a few days before on the subject of the Wensum Valley railway in Norfolk, a modest line running between Norwich and East Dereham which had provided a notorious example of profiteering by a railway contractor. According to the leader writer, the cost of making the line had been so wildly exaggerated that the contractor had been made 'a clear present of £146,000 stock' under financial arrangements involving the Great Eastern company[2]. Scourfield, an old Harrovian who had changed his name from Philipps after coming into the estates of his maternal uncle in 1862,[3] recalled in his letter that he had been chairman of the Parliamentary committee hearing evidence on the Wensum Valley line. He said he 'suspected that a large number of railways were founded on similar financial operations', and suggested that if there were closer scrutiny by Parliament 'our railways would be better designed and more carefully and economically constructed, and an improvement made in financial morality, which is very much to be desired.'[4]

It was the reference to 'financial morality' that touched a raw nerve with David Davies, especially as it came from a dilettante scribbler and part-time politician whom he regarded as never having done an honest day's work in his life. He felt honour bound to answer the criticism of such men as himself, who had accepted payment for railway contracts partly in shares and debentures but who, in his view, were honest traders and not the kind of rogues who had infested undertakings when 'railway mania' was rife. We must remember, too, that he would have been sensitive to accusations of excess profit-making as railway contractors were supposed in some quarters to be vulgar little men on the make.

His reply, carefully ghosted by Webb and curiously addressed from 'Llandinam, Shrewsbury,' appeared in *The Times* of 18 August 1865 under the headline Railway Legislation and Welsh Railways. It ran:

The case of the Wensum Valley Railway may be more representative than exceptional in that part of the country ... but with reference to Wales (Mr Scourfield's own country) I can speak with confidence and I have no hesitation in saying that Mr Scourfield's conclusions are not borne out by the facts.

Almost all the railways which have been made in Wales of late years have been made by contractors who have provided nearly all the capital, and have taken the shares of the different concerns at their own risk. The country has in this way had the benefit of something like 700 miles of railway which would not have been made for at least another century if we had waited for the localities to subscribe the necessary funds.

If, therefore, Parliament had done what Mr Scourfield suggests it ought to have done, refused its sanction to these lines, the men who have made them would have taken their knowledge and capital to distant countries, and at least £8,000,000 of money would have been lost, as far as Wales is concerned; to say nothing of the advantages which arise from the expenditure of that sum of money for increasing the means of communication to a portion of the kingdom which was before singularly inaccessible. In Mr Scourfield's own neighbourhood he has two railways which have been made on this plan − I mean the South Wales and the Carmarthen and Cardigan. Your readers will be better able to judge whether these have been 'better designed and more carefully and economically carried out' than those lines which have been made by contractors when they hear that the South Wales cost £28,000 a mile, and the Carmarthen and Cardigan £50,000 a mile. I have myself made about 150 miles of railways in Wales during the last seven years, at a cost (in shares and debentures) not exceeding £10,000 a mile ... As to contractors' lines being 'ill considered', I think when there are no petty local interests and small subscribers to be consulted, and when the only object is to construct the line through the best traffic-producing district, the line is much more likely to be made in its proper and natural course.

David Davies's old ally R.S. France, his staunch supporter in those brushes with Whalley a few years earlier, followed up with a letter in *The Times* in which he remarked that 'Mr Scourfield's dictum that the capital ought first to be subscribed would, had Parliament adhered to it, now find Wales the same blank on the map so far as railways are concerned as it was in 1855, when local parties took the construction of Welsh lines into their own hands, and called in the aid of contractors whose financial connections enabled them to supply that very large proportion of the capital which it was absolutely impossible to raise in the district.' Writing from Monkland Hall, Shrewsbury, he observed that the big companies had failed to build a single mile in mid Wales, 'allowing powers of doing so obtained in 1845 to lapse,' and continued:

> Such was the state of things up to 1852; then ensued a Parliamentary fight between two companies — London and North-Western and Great Western — as to which company should obtain possession of this large district.
>
> The result of this Parliamentary fight was that both failed — the one in the Commons, and the other in the Lords. Then, in 1853 . . . both companies came to a truce for two years. May I ask what became of the unfortunate people during all this warfare? Why, Sir, they hoped against hope until this truce, and then they determined no more to trust to either of these great companies, but to take the question in hand themselves, and, with the aid of contractors, endeavour to place themselves on a par with those more favoured districts possessing railway communications.
>
> The result has been, as Mr Davies states, that something like £8,000,000 has been spent in the district in the construction of these much-coveted lines of railway, and when Mr Scourfield talks and writes about contractors' lines, let us, in common fairness, ask him to point to any district in England where anything like the same amount of railway communication has been given for the same money — even when that money has been expended by his adopted allies, the great companies, whom it is well known he so warmly espouses.[5]

Against this special pleading, however, we must set the undoubted fact that successful railway contractors like David Davies did enrich themselves enormously in a short space of time, and that the morality of profit-making on so huge a scale had been a matter of public concern for over a decade. Writing in 1855, the sociologist Herbert Spencer had characterized them as 'insatiate millionaires' in a pamphlet bearing the high-minded title *Railway Morals and Railway Policy*:

> Railway enterprise has given to this class of men [contractors] a gigantic development, not only in respect of numbers, but in respect of the vast wealth to which some of them have attained. Originally, half a dozen miles of earthwork, fencing, and bridges, were as much as any single contractor undertook. Of late years, however, it has become common for one man to engage to contract an entire railway; and deliver it over to the company in a fit condition for opening. Great capital is necessarily required for this: great profits are made by it: and the fortunes accumulated in course of time have been such that sundry contractors are described as being able to make a railway at his own cost. But they are as insatiate as millionaires in general; and so long as they

continue in business at all, are, in some sort, forced to provide new undertakings to keep their plant employed. As may be imagined, enormous stocks of working materials are needed; many hundreds of earth-waggons and horses; many miles of temporary rails and sleepers; some half-dozen locomotive engines and several fixed ones; innumerable tools; besides vast stores of timber, bricks, stone, rails, and other constituent and permanent works, that have been bought on speculation . . . The great contractor . . . is . . . under a pressing stimulus to get fresh work, and enabled by his wealth to do this.[6]

David Davies was never as great a contractor as those who made the lines uniting the principal cities of England, but he was great enough for the cap to fit when the morality of railway profit-making was being discussed. Replies to letters, however – even letters in *The Times* – were mere diversions from the immediate task of completing the railway between Pencader and Aberystwyth with his partner, Frederick Beeston.

Originally conceived merely as a branch line of the Manchester & Milford Railway, this was to be the only line operated by the company and a suitable target for jesters, who designated the M&M the 'Meek and Mild.'

The construction of this 41½-mile line through rural Cardiganshire seems a modest enough achievement today, but that is to mistake the size of the task and the importance of the undertaking. The decision to carry the line through the very heart of the county was a bold one, for the terrain through which it travelled was isolated and wild. There were roads near the coast wide enough to take waggons, but inland the tracks were so narrow and rough that according to David Davies, it was impossible to get lime or coal in or the agricultural produce out.[7] Economically and socially, the railway was of immense benefit to the county, opening up its trade and giving isolated communities a new perspective.

One of the greatest tasks was crossing Tregaron Bog, Cors Caron, a place of haunting beauty at some seasons and brooding malevolence at others. A reporter from *The Welshman*, visiting the spot in 1866, spoke of 'hundreds of tons of earth' being thrown into the 'soft, brown, saturated fibrous matter.'[8] More ingeniously still, the contractors hit on the idea of buying all the wool the local farmers could provide and laying it beneath the track bed to soak up the water.[9] Their cunning was at least the equal of that shown by Robert Stephenson at Chat Moss near Manchester in 1826, when he covered the marshland with hurdles of brushwood before making a firm surface of sand, earth and gravel.[10]

In spite of these difficulties, Davies and Beeston set an amazing pace for themselves and completed the project in half the allotted time. [11]

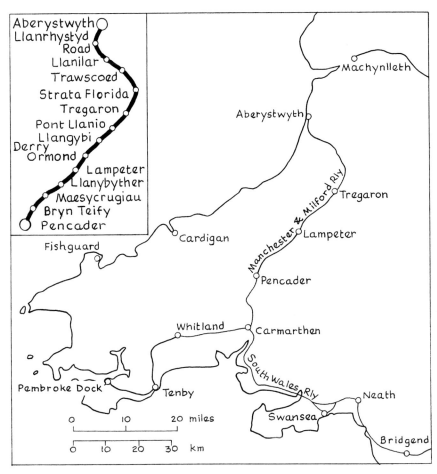

The route of the Pencader–Aberystwyth line, originally called the Manchester &
Milford Railway and later absorbed in Cambrian Railways. Opening day was in
August 1867.

The 12¼ miles of single track from Pencader Junction to Lampeter were
ready for inspection by the end of 1865, when Colonel Yolland of the
Board of Trade travelled up from Carmarthen to arrive at 9.40 a.m. at
Pencader, where he was greeted by the contactors and engineer, James
Szlumper – who was later to be knighted – and a director, J.W.
Armstrong.[12]

Yolland 'ordered two of the Manchester and Milford engines to be
placed funnel to funnel, so as to get the greatest possible weight per foot
on the rails; and the party proceeded slowly towards Lampeter, testing
the bridges that carry the railway', reported the *Aberystwyth Observer.*

'The results were all most satisfactory, the large girder over the Teifi (seventy-eight feet span) only deflecting five-sixteenths of an inch under the severest test.' At seven o'clock that evening, Yolland declared himself satisfied. 'The line throughout has been thoroughly well constructed, being inferior in no respect to the older railways, although only a contractor's line,' the report continued.

> The cuttings are well finished, and the whole line is admirably ballasted ... The latest improvements in the details of railway construction in signals &c have everywhere been adopted; and it is plain that there has been no buttoning up of the pocket when efficiency of any kind has been in question. On the other hand, the experienced eye is conscious of no waste of means in anything. Messrs Davies and Beeston and their engineer have done their part in making a first-class railway with the least possible outlay.[13]

The M&M directors' minutes for February 1866 formally record the fact that 'the line from Pencader to Lampeter is now open for public traffic', and they also note: 'Debentures amounting to £40,000 for five years to be issued to David Davies.'[14] A further £5,100 in debentures followed in October, as well as £15,300 in preference shares.[15] It was around this time that the Carmarthen-based weekly *The Welshman* decided to make a progress report, having got wind of the fact that the 15¼ miles between Lampeter and Strata Florida had been completed. 'There was an entire absence of any show or demonstration in opening an important portion of the Manchester and Milford Railway last week,' its readers were informed.

> This was in perfect keeping with the quiet and unobtrusive way in which the works on the railway have been carried out ... This great undertaking has been very nearly accomplished by the almost unaided efforts of Messrs Davies and Beeston, who have themselves found the capital, with the exception of a few paid-up shares amounting to a very small proportion of the whole. Indeed, we may with perfect truthfulness say that the line has been altogether made by them, and on sound commercial principles, which have stood the test of the severest monetary panic of the present century.[16]

This was a reference to the collapse of the Overend and Gurney Bank on Black Friday, 10 May 1866. It reminds us of David Davies's amazing capacity for survival at a time when so many apparently well-established businessmen went under. *The Welshman* observed that 'by avoiding immature speculations and Lloyd's bonds' Davies and Beeston had been able to continue their works 'even with the Bank rate of discount at 10 per cent.'[17] What is more, never once did they suspend the payment of wages to their workers.[18]

It is a remarkable fact that in spite of the crash of '66, Davies managed not only to continue work on the Pencader–Aberystwyth line but to complete the Whitland Extension in Pembrokeshire. In the course of that speech at Tenby on 4 September 1866, quoted in the previous chapter, he admitted to having 'held back for a bit' after obtaining powers to make the Whitland Extension because money had been so tight.

> I had for six years been prophesying a desperate monetary panic, and I assure you that I was preparing for it all that time. Of course, I was anxious to see it over before we began the works ... well, at last we began and worked hard at it in the hope that we should tide it over before the panic came, but it began when we were in the middle of it. I saw clearly the panic was severe, and had an ugly appearance, but said, 'There is nothing for it; we must go on.' Having been anticipating for it [sic] the last five or six years, we were better prepared for it than many other contractors. Happily we had three good banks to draw upon in the emergency. The first, and best, was our own pockets. The next was our personal friends, who knew nothing of the railway and cared nothing for it. But they knew us, and they came out like bricks. Then there were friends of the railway, and Tenby ought to be proud of her people.[19]

At the celebrations marking the opening of the entire length of the Pencader–Aberystwyth line in August 1867, he returned to the same theme.

> People were spending money where there was no value. I saw them spending 20s. where there was not 10s. in value, and I knew the panic must come ... The greatest difficulty about a railway always is making the first half of the line. Properly speaking, there should be no difficulty in doing the last half, but it was not so with this. We spent our own money in making the first half ... This railway cost £488,000 ... Well, when we had half made the railway, and our difficulties should have been at an end, there was wanting some £160,000 or £170,000 ... I felt very anxious after paying up a great deal of money and opening all the way to Lampeter and Strata Florida. The panic was just coming ... Well, it was as bad as I expected, and a little worse too. Indeed, it had been staved off longer than it should have been, in consequence of those joint stock and discount houses and finance companies formed in 1863. They tided it over and delayed it longer than it would have been

in its natural course ... consequently the panic in the railway world became much greater; the speculation was so great that the debentures became of no value ... But I am happy to be able today to know that the men never went away without some money every Saturday, and on the second Saturday they were paid every shilling that was due to them.[20]

The complexities of railway travel in the 1860s can be appreciated when one considers that those making the comparatively short journey from Carmarthen to Aberystwyth were the patrons of two separate companies: the Carmarthen & Cardigan Railway as far as Pencader, and the Manchester & Milford thereafter. (Both eventually became absorbed into the GWR.) A further complication was that the railways had different gauges: the Carmarthen & Cardigan company had adopted the 7 ft. broad gauge then still in use on the main South Wales line, whereas the M&M directors had opted for the 'narrow' gauge of 4ft. 8in. (which was to become the standard). The writer of that progress report in *The Welshman* in August 1866 found the M&M 'narrow-gauge' carriages far superior, all but the first-class broad gauge carriages being 'shamefully filthy and disagreeable'.[21]

The intermediate stations between Pencader and Aberystwyth were shown in the early timetables as Maesycrugiau, Llanybyther, Lampeter, Bettws, Pont-Llanio, Tregaron, Strata Florida, Trawscoed, Llanilar and Llanrhystid Road.[22] Llanrhystid (later Llanrhystyd) Road was in the village of Llanfarian and the naming of Strata Florida station after the ruined Cistercian abbey three miles away gave rise to such resentment in the locality that a petition was sent to the M&M directors. They were asked to change the name to Ystrad Meurig, but refused.[23]

'The line has been unfortunate in its name,' observed *The Welshman*, 'which gives those who are not familiar with the country no idea of its whereabouts.'[24] According to the writer, one million cubic yards of earth had been removed between Lampeter and Strata Florida, and 12,000 tons of iron used between Pencader and Strata Florida — a section of line where the crossing and re-crossing of rivers had entailed the construction of sixty stone and iron bridges:

> The over-bridges are built of large blocks of stones, giving them a massive and solid character. The bridges across the rivers are elegantly designed, and of wrought iron, and have a very striking appearance ... No permanent stations have yet been erected. The small wooden structures will answer that purpose for a while, and will not be removed until the traffic is to some extent developed, and it is known what kind of buildings are required. We notice that provision has been made at every station for a spacious yard

to accommodate the mineral traffic, which is sure to be
considerable ... There is neither lime nor coal in the whole
district traversed by this line, and these minerals are prime
necessities in an agricultural county where the spirit of
improvement has begun to disturb the people.

It was noted that the contractors had 'met with great encouragement
from many of the landowners, some of whom behaved with most
commendable liberality.'[25]

There was a grand opening of the entire line on 12 August 1867, when a
ceremonial train swollen with dignitaries struggled out of Aberystwyth
station, across the bridge over the Rheidol, around the hill fort of Pen Dinas
and into the Ystwyth Valley. It returned from Pencader a good deal faster
than it went, however, hurtling out of control down a 1 in 41 gradient to the
'inconceivable astonishment of the crowds collected on the Trawscoed
platform,' who had been hoping to get on it. The train went far beyond the
station before it was at last brought to a halt by the shaken driver, for whom
the *Aberystwyth Observer* found an excuse: he had 'never driven on that line
before.' Although disaster had been narrowly avoided nobody was held to
account, the assurance that 'a greater number of powerful breaks [*sic*]'
would be provided on each train apparently being enough.[26]

It was the height of the season in Aberystwyth, and for once the
sunshine was as bright as the hopes of the shareholders. The windows
were thrown up at the Belle Vue Hotel on the sea front to admit a sea
breeze into the stifling banqueting room, where in a bantering speech
David Davies made an uncharacteristically rash promise. He said he
would like to see a railway from Llanilar to Aberaeron and New Quay
and that, if the people living along the coast 'exerted' themselves, 'I
would be very happy in my humble way to assist them in everything I
can' − a promise never fulfilled. He was on firmer ground when
reminding the company that the M&M debentures were fast being taken
up. 'There are only a few left, and if any of you want some now is your
time. I shall be glad to part with them. But if you will not buy them I
must keep them myself, and do no more work.'[27]

The idea of Davies of Llandinam resting on his laurels gave some
amusement to his listeners, for they knew well enough that with his
colliery output expanding daily in the Rhondda, he had work enough to
last him a lifetime. It was a jest he avoided the following day, when he
treated fifty of his navvies to dinner at the Belle Vue, for with the end
of this contract men who had been in his employment for fifteen years
were being thrown out of work. He made excuses for himself:

I know many contractors who have taken care of the men, and
have wasted them all the winter about the country. Consequently,

they have never received value for the men, then everything went wrong. I have endeavoured to select whatever is worth the money I give for it. I have taken care not to waste my own money or anyone else's. I must get 20s. in the pound; and if everybody did that we should not have had this panic.[28]

This was small comfort for men who had drawn their last week's wages, but the select fifty (probably all gangers) invited to dinner were in no mood for a public upsetting of the apple cart. They voiced their gratitude to their employers in terms which later generations would find uncomfortably ingratiating: 'Gentlemen,' said that doughty old faithful, ganger David Evans, 'we have the pleasure of meeting here this day to show our kind love for our worthy masters ...' David Davies was presented with a clock (to help him 'get up at six every morning') and he chaffingly recalled that they had once given him a watch.

I felt at first a little nervous for fear I had been abusing you working too much overtime ... I have no objection to reduce the time, for it may be that I shall have to work for you some time, and then everything will balance itself. I have been working for people before now, and I may do so again, so we are all brothers together.

He went on to develop the now familiar theme of himself as a working man on a par with those he employed, a theme which would appear increasingly artificial in years to come, when his accumulation of wealth made it plain beyond doubt that there was not the slightest fear of Davies the Ocean having to bend his back as a navvy once more to earn his daily bread.

If Providence should ever call upon me to work for you I shall be happy to do so. I do not despise workmen, I am a humble worker myself, and I have been in much more humble employment than many of you are in today. I want you to understand that I do not want any compliment paid to me higher than any of you would pay to one of yourselves, because I remember that I once worked as you are working now. I do not work for myself for anything more now than I used to, except that more important duties devolve upon me than I formerly had to perform.

It is unfortunate that, having plucked the string of harmony, he should then sour the occasion by reprimanding those who had committed the cardinal sin of wasting his money.

One of my great duties now is to take care not to pay to any one of you more than you are entitled to, but at the same time to take care to pay you all you are really worth. This is a very important

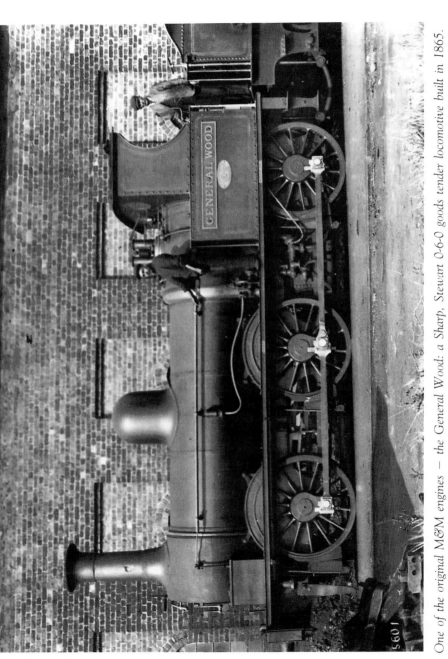

One of the original M&M engines – the General Wood: a Sharp, Stewart 0-6-0 goods tender locomotive built in 1865.

point, a point which many have gone wrong upon. For instance, supposing that one of you, in consequence of incapability of doing your work, were to put ten men on a job when nine men could do. What effect would that have upon Mr Beeston and myself? It would just have this effect, it would cost us £40,000. That is, it would be 2s. in the £ on the amount of our contract ... I have seen some men now in this room using eight men to do the work of five men. I do not say it is done all the year round, but I have seen it done, and when I have seen it, what have I been ready to do? Why, to take up a stone, and shy it at the fellow's head. I felt so angry at him, because there were other men actually working harder than they ought, for the want of putting men in their proper places.

He followed this up with a crass and jingoistic comparison between the ending of the contract and the settlement of 1856 that had brought the Crimean War to a close.

I feel just like the English army felt at the time when the Russian War came to an end and you know how angry we all felt then, because we were just in the right trim to get at them in style. Well, here we are, we have finished our contract just as we are in the right trim to go at a good one.

These banal sentiments show that there were limits to his imagination, but he was not alone in failing to comprehend the horrors of warfare. He was also able to dispose of his workmen's livelihoods with what appears to be no more than a cursory wave of the hand, but perhaps his jauntiness of expression concealed the depth of his feelings.

We must work one in one place and one in another. I have already done something for some of you. There's Joseph here, he has gone to burn lime, and has become an important man. Then Watkins says he has bought a mill for £200, and is going to build houses for £80 and sell them for £100 − and he will go on well, I have no doubt. That is the way I did, and that is what John Watkins is going to do. There is no reason why you should not be as independent as I am, if you think I am independent, and I do not want you to think so. I can very well remember the time when I had very much less troubles than I have at present. However, I live in hopes that a better day is coming, and it will come too, if we only have patience to wait for it.[29]

With these boisterous words on a summer evening in Aberystwyth, David Davies bade farewell to the men who had played such a big part in his destiny.

12   Strangers in the Valley

David Davies's refusal to 'take care of' his railwaymen by finding them work through the winter, when this was not economically justified, reminds us that he never allowed sentiment to deflect him from good accountancy. The interesting question arises, however, of whether he experienced any conflict between his religious beliefs and his stern business ethic. The probability is that he did not, for one of the intriguing things about him is the way that so many apparently disparate strands in his nature were woven into a harmonious whole. David Davies was sometimes at odds with the world, but he never appears to be at odds with himself.

The fact that he was a Calvinistic Methodist is of crucial importance. Calvinists believed they were of the elect, predestined by God for salvation.[1] Davies would have regarded his life's work as a glorification of God and his success as a sign of His approval.[2] It was, no doubt, a convenient belief, but convenience does not invariably imply hypocrisy.

The Calvinistic Methodists in Wales in Victorian times were highly disciplined people who could be suspended from membership of their church for working on Sundays or even courting on Sundays.[3] Although predestined to the life eternal, they were expected to apply themselves vigorously to the concerns of the life temporal in a spirit of honest endeavour. Their rules of discipline specified that they 'must not be idle, nor make a habit of wandering from place to place.' They must trade honestly, abstain from usury or miserliness, avoid lotteries 'or any other games of chance' and 'be merciful, compassionate and generous, giving according to their ability to every good cause.' They were even instructed not to shorten the Sabbath 'by indulging in too much sleep'.[4] In such words we seem to hear the very voice of David Davies, yet these rules had been adopted by the Welsh Calvinistic Methodists in 1823, when he was barely five years old. They provided a theological basis for his most vigorous prejudices.

It is as well, perhaps, that the rules did not forbid the making of any image of a person, or we would have been denied a remarkable portrait of David Davies painted in 1873 by Ford Madox Brown. It shows Davies seated in a leather armchair, gold watch-chain prominent. He looks steadily at the artist, who has captured in him something not seen either in the later photographs of him or in the statues of Davies that stand in Llandinam and Barry. The face seems narrower, the eyes more sensitive. This is Davies the visionary rather than Davies the businessman; it is the face of a man with the capacity to win trust and affection, and capable of being hurt if he feels himself misunderstood. A decade later the painter might have seen a different subject; a man not only older but coarser, the mouth harder, the eyes more calculating. It is no accident that the years between were those in which the primary concern of David Davies was coal; a mineral which, innocent in itself, was the cause of much cruelty and strife. It made some people very rich and kept others in poverty. It broke bodies, widowed wives, orphaned children, set brother against brother. Such was its power to corrupt, one might well have considered it to have been made black by act of God rather than accident of nature.

It was coal that made the name of David Davies known far beyond his native land; and it was the stress and strife it carried within itself like a curse that brought his life to a premature end. For although at seventy-two he had gone two years beyond the allotted Biblical span, he had the constitution to have lived much longer had it not been undermined by the cares that coal inflicted on him.

The portrait was one of a pair, the other being of his wife, Margaret. They were the gifts of the shareholders of David Davies and Co., who in August 1872 had set aside £500 for the purchase of a 'fitting testimonial' to their chairman. The presentation was made on 13 February 1874 'as a friendly offering from friends to a friend and as a pleasant remembrance of their regard and esteem for himself and his estimable wife.' In reply, David Davies 'feelingly expressed the pleasure it gave him to receive in so pleasant and agreeable a form the proof of the friendly relations which existed between the proprietors and himself.'[5]

By this time David Davies had established himself as one of the most powerful coal-owners in the rapidly developing south Wales coalfield. His three Rhondda collieries, Maindy at Gelli and Park and Dare at Cwmparc, were together known as the Ocean collieries, and he had plans for more. Maindy had begun producing coal in May 1866, Park in August 1866, Dare in April 1870.[6] In the south Wales coalfield as a whole, production had increased by fifty per cent in nine years, rising from 10,970,000 tons in 1864 to 16,180,000 tons in 1873.[7] Coal exports from Cardiff Docks had soared from two million to three million tons annually between 1861 and 1870, two-thirds of this going to foreign ports, and the Roath Basin was being constructed to help cope with the vastly increased trade.[8] It was a time of rapid change, of expansion on an unprecedented scale. But it was a time of misery too, of hunger and deprivation.

The coal owners were few in number, and they held in their hands the destinies of the many. The owners might have said that they too were in thrall, to market forces and to the ability of those they employed to combine against them. For the miner and his family, however, the power appeared to be all on one side. The master (a term still in use although fast disappearing) owned the pit shaft, the winding gear, the machinery above and below ground, the colliery buildings; he owned the coal the miners cut; he owned the very walls that gave them shelter. The master fixed the wages, often in association with his fellows; in a dispute the master could lock the miners out, and if necessary the law would come to his support.

It was a hard and unyielding world, different in kind and in temper from that of the railway makers. There was no chance here of maintaining that 'comradeship in labour' that David Davies had relished in the great outdoors, although at first he had hopes of forging the same kind of bond with his men that he had hitherto enjoyed. He would often be seen underground in the early years, and in the disputes of the 1870s that gave a depressing foretaste of things to come in the coalfield he would visit the collieries to make personal appeals for a compromise.[9] By the 1880s, however, disillusion had set in and what he regarded as generous settlements — in particular the Ocean sliding scale of payments — were thrown back in his face. He would speak bitterly of 'the men we had to deal with'[10] and would write: 'They are like the Irish the more you give them the further they are from being satisfied until they have had all and more than all.'[11] They, for their part, saw in him no semblance of a man in a navvy's shirt but a boss like any other, and his argument that they should see themselves as partners with common interests seemed as false as the smile of an executioner.

By the 1870s there were combinations both of masters and men in south Wales. The Aberdare Steam Coal Collieries Association, founded in 1864, was the first attempt at joint action by the south Wales coal owners, and the membership included David Davies and Co.[12] This was succeeded in 1873 by the Monmouthshire and South Wales Coal Owners' Association, a much more powerful organization which controlled seventy-five per cent of the total output of the coalfield.[13] The miners, for their part, were slowly learning that unity was strength, but historic fears had first to be overcome: the Combination Laws of 1799–1800, drummed up by a ruling class fearful of revolution crossing the Channel, had made anything resembling trade unions illegal. These laws had been repealed in 1824, but a judge was still able to find legal grounds for transporting the Tolpuddle Martyrs ten years later, and well-founded fears of victimization were a formidable obstacle in the path of organization.

It was the great strike of 1871 that saw the beginnings of a miners' union in south Wales. There were meetings addressed by Tom Halliday, president of the Amalgamated Association of Miners, one of the fledgling unions which were to lead in time to the Miners' Federation and, later still, to the National Union of Miners. When he arrived in Pontypridd for a meeting he was greeted by Dr William Price of Llantrisant, a lifelong radical who had been a Chartist in his younger days. The *Western Mail* reported that Dr Price, 'with his flowing white beard, fine white linen smock frock with its "scolloped" collar and cuffs, and the inevitable huge fox-skin cap,' had heartily shaken Halliday's hand at the railway station.

'I hear you are the colliers' friend,' said Dr Price. 'Mind that you are. Lift them up!'[14]

'I am doing my best with them,' replied Halliday sagely, before expressing 'great pleasure in meeting the doctor.'

The strike was caused by the decision to cut the men's pay by five per cent, the excuse being the trade recession that had set in after the conclusion of the American Civil War. It was a decision jointly made by the Merthyr ironmasters and the steam coal proprietors of Aberdare and Rhondda, who were not always on the best of terms with each other: the ironmasters had actually increased the production of steam coal from their own collieries in competition with the Aberdare and Rhondda coal owners. They were able to undercut them because they paid landowners lower royalties and their men lower wages. There were hopes of bringing about what was called 'equalization of wages' but no positive steps towards this had been taken when the strike began on 1 June 1871. It dragged on until mid-August, the men showing great determination and heroic self-restraint when strike-breakers were brought in from Staffordshire and Cornwall.[15]

In trade-union terms, this has every right to be regarded as a classic struggle. It throws a lurid light on the power of the masters to coerce their men, and the limitations of that power. The original proposal had been for a ten per cent pay cut all round, and although the Aberdare and Rhondda coal owners held out for this reduction they followed the lead of the ironmasters in cutting wages by only half this amount at first. 'The action of the ironmasters,' wrote Alexander Dalziel of the South Wales Steam Coal Collieries Association sternly, 'was not as firm as that which should have characterized the conduct of employers of 20,000 workmen.' He had found 'a positive buoyancy of spirit among the workmen' because 'they could not fail to perceive the split in the masters' camp' and lamented: 'Agitation was rife, professional unionists came into the district and roused the workmen to a state of insubordination and dissatisfaction with the existing state of affairs. The Union spread its seed in the Aberdare and Rhondda Valleys, but it made no progress either in Monmouthshire or Merthyr.'

In the end, the owners lost in the short term and to some extent in the longer term. The arbitrators appointed to settle the dispute awarded the men a two and a half per cent pay increase immediately, with a further ten per cent the following February. What is more, the men learned lessons in combined action and mutual support they were able to put to good use in later disputes. In a sense they learned from their masters, who had banded together in the hope of reducing wages. There was a recipe for further trouble, however, in the clause stipulating that after the payment of the ten per cent any general rise or fall in wages paid at the ironworks should be followed by a corresponding rise or fall in wages at the collieries.

David Davies's three Ocean collieries — Maindy, Park and Dare — remained closed throughout the strike. They employed 1,192 men and boys, who produced 290,299 tons of coal in 1870. Davies's company was in fact the largest employer in the Rhondda and Aberdare districts, followed by the firm of Nixon, Taylor and Cory, whose Navigation and Deep Duffryn pits employed 1,112. A curiosity is that some of the men on strike were able to find work at neighbouring pits where production continued because their owners were outside the employers' organization: towards the end of June the manager of the strike-bound Ocean pits was asked if he would lend pit ponies to a neighbouring colliery which was going at full stretch with the help of Ocean strikers![16]

Although David Davies played a key role in the settlement of the strike, he had no compunction in agreeing to take on 'scab' labour from Staffordshire. These strike-breakers were recruited by Paul Roper of Bilston after he had travelled to Cardiff to meet the masters on 21 July. He agreed to find three hundred men and boys — two hundred by 1 August and the other hundred by 8 August, 'the men to be good, practical miners, to be brought to Aberdare and Rhondda as shall be ordered . . . their wages to be 6s. per day for good and practical colliers; 3s. about for lads . . .' Roper, who signed the agreement with his mark, was to receive a commission of 6s. for each workman he brought from Staffordshire into the Aberdare and Rhondda valleys. The first batch of men were to be sent to the Navigation Colliery, and in the Rhondda Valley the Ocean collieries would be the first to reopen.[17]

The importation of these 'strangers' — it was the politest of the terms applied to them — made the strikers angrier still. They simply did not believe the employers' tales of being hard hit by the recession, noting that the owners of the small steam coal collieries had actually found the cash to give their men a pay rise, although they had to compete in the same market as the large firms. 'When the next election comes for Parliament, Board of Guardians, Board of Health, School Board &c, turn your enemies out, and substitute them by your friends — you have the

---

DAVID DAVIES & CO.,

𝔓roprietors of the well-known

OCEAN (MERTHYR) STEAM COAL,

At present working upwards of 400,000 Tons per Annum.

USED BY THE PENINSULAR AND ORIENTAL AND THE PRINCIPAL STEAM NAVIGATION COMPANIES.

The **Ocean Coal** makes little or no smoke, ignites readily, possesses an evaporative power unsurpassed by any Coal yet discovered, makes little ash or clinker, requires no stoking, and is not destructive to the fire bars; while it likewise possesses the immense advantage that the SMALL *made in process of transit, will burn more readily than the* LARGE *of the drier or more anthracitic descriptions.*

REPORTS FROM CONSUMERS AND ALL INFORMATION SUPPLIED ON APPLICATION.

OFFICES (Chief)—Britannia Buildings, Bute Docks, CARDIFF ; J. Osborne
Riches, Manager.

   ,,   LONDON—1, Leadenhall Street; Fletcher, Parr & Co., Agents.

   ,,   LIVERPOOL—Oriel Chambers, Water Street; Goodwin, Barnes & Co.,
Agents.

   ,,   SOUTHAMPTON—Hickie, Borman & Co., Agents.

---

*Davies's commercial flair is shown in this advertisement of 1871 — the word
'Merthyr' was simply a marketing ploy, as Merthyr Tydfil was famous the world
over and the Rhondda still relatively unknown.*

power, use it,' urged the Amalgamated Association of Miners, in a
statement printed in both English and Welsh and addressed 'To the
workmen in general, and to the colliers in particular.' It continued:

> Dear Brethren and Fellow-Workmen — should we be obliged to go
> to work at the reduction, you may depend upon it, that all those
> who are now working on the advance will be reduced also; and
> where reductions may end no one can say. The Union that has
> lately been established is what our employers want to scatter to the
> winds — although they have a Union themselves, they do not
> want the men to be united ... Therefore, we sincerely call on you
> to help us to win the battle by levies and subscriptions. There are
> many families in want of bread — let us give them to eat.
> Remember, that is the weak place in our ranks. The masters know
> it well, and are doing all they can to starve us ....'[18]

By now many colliers living in company houses were being evicted for joining the strike, the *Western Mail* — although no friend of the miners — regretting the fact that they were thus being denied the fruits of their labours in the gardens in which they had worked so hard in the spring. 'Some of the gardens are worth at least £7 to £8. This is a great deal for a working man to sacrifice . . . All shifts are being made by their fellow-workmen living in private owner's houses to take them in.'[19] The paper reported that scores of families were leaving the Rhondda. 'Between the Star Inn (Ystrad) and the Ifor Hael (Llwynypia) I saw as many as seven waggons and carts full of furniture leaving the valley,' wrote a correspondent. 'At one place a workman's wife stood at the door calling after her friends "Good luck to you!" '[20]

This report appeared on 1 August, the day when Paul Roper, true to his word, brought the first quota of blacklegs to south Wales. They arrived by special train at midnight, to be greeted with hisses and groans at Mountain Ash station.[21] They had been provided with free stout on the journey[22] and were promised 'good lodgings' on their arrival, but from the moment they stepped off the train they were treated as pariahs. The firemen handed in their lamps and refused to go down the pit with them, and the shopkeepers put up the shutters. Within a fortnight the *Western Mail* was reporting that a large number of the Staffordshire men had gone home after 'fraternising with old colliers', the shopkeepers having 'refused to supply them with a single article.'[23] Dalziel admitted that 'only the roughest and unskilled Staffordshire men came to Wales, the better class of men being afraid to trust themselves in small numbers in the strike district.' What is more, they were no good at their work. Dalziel doubted whether any of them possessed genuine mining skill, and their coal production was 'wretched.'

Of these 145 so-called 'colliers', sixty-six were sent to Nixon's Navigation Colliery and seventy-nine to Powell's Lower Duffryn.[24] Although the Ocean collieries were listed to receive them, there is no evidence that any of them actually ever reached the Rhondda. Within a few days of their arrival in south Wales, David Davies was acting the part of peace-maker. A letter drafted at the Ocean Steam Coal Offices in Cardiff strongly supported arbitration and contained a piece of special pleading: 'As to ourselves, we have had no stoppages during the two years preceding this dispute, except such as have been caused by the men themselves.'[25]

One hundred miners from Cornwall and Devon arrived on the steamship *Diana* from Burnham-on-Sea on 9 August to work in the strike-bound pits,[26] but by now the forces for conciliation were irresistible. In a second letter to the press, David Davies and Co said a meeting between the owners and the men could be arranged without difficulty if the strikers sent 'an authorised deputation to their respective colliery managers,'[27] and this suggestion was taken up so promptly that the meeting between the two sides actually took place at the Royal Hotel in Cardiff three days later.[28] The men went back to work and the process of arbitration began, Alexander Macdonald of the National Association of Miners — a rival to Tom Halliday's Amalgamated Association of Miners — piously expressing the hope that 'we have seen the very last strike that will ever take place in our day in these valleys.'[29] Macdonald was one of the arbitrators who made the award that vindicated the miners' fight for a pay rise, and three men from the Ocean management — David Davies himself, J. Osborne Riches and Thomas Webb — were among the twelve-strong delegation representing the owners.[30]

'No good will come of this unionism,' a seventy-year-old collier told a meeting of miners in Llantwit Fardre as the strike ended, 'but as you will all join the union, I suppose I must do the same.'[31] His words reflect the sea change that took place in the strike of 1871; the Union, as an idea, firmly took hold of the miners' imaginations, and an industrial army was in the making.

13 A Ghost at the Feast

The decade had begun miserably for David Davies, with the death of his mother. Elizabeth Davies died at Neuaddfach on 10 July 1870 aged seventy-five. She was buried in the parish churchyard, where she had chosen her last resting place: the grave of her husband and sons Edward and John to one side, that of her son Richard on the other. It is indicative of the times that not a word of Welsh appears on her tombstone, although the Latin phrase 'Memento Mori' appears around the carving of a Bible. The main text is in English: 'Jesus said unto her: I am the resurrection and the life: he that believeth in me, though he were dead, yet shall he live.'

It is difficult to know how much significance we should read into the fact that although her eldest son's wealth had by then become legendary in Wales, the probate certificate issued by the district registry in Shrewsbury shows that she died intestate, and that her personal estate and effects were 'sworn under One Hundred Pounds'.[1]

One of the mourners at her graveside was her grandson Edward — now eighteen years old, coming to manhood. He was destined for great things, whether he wanted them or no — some day he would inherit, if not the earth, then that part of it that lay within the domain of Ocean collieries. His father would say of him that 'he did not go to Cambridge because he preferred coal to college.'[2] The truth is that he had no real choice in the matter.

It is hard to see Edward other than as a victim, in spite of all his riches. By nature shy and studious, he entirely lacked his father's bravura and ability to mix freely and happily with all manner of men. He was most at home in the laboratory, for he was a born scientist with a flair for invention. Yet his fate was to be head of the family business, and the unwanted responsibilities drove him to an early grave. It is in his treatment of Edward that we see the less attractive side of David Davies's nature: the will to dominate and urge for self-aggrandizement, qualities he did not recognize in himself, least of all in his relationship with his only child. There is no doubt that he loved Edward, and imagined himself always to be doing his best for the boy, but ultimately he denied him the self-expression and happiness he had gained for himself.

In her study of Edward's daughters, Gwendoline and Margaret Davies of Gregynog, Lady (Eirene) White observes that Edward was 'a studious man who by inclination might have won academic distinction in science, his special interest being chemistry.' She quotes a letter Gwendoline sent to Thomas Jones — Lady White's father — in which she recalled 'the terror of the night, in her sixteenth year, when the family realized that their father had crossed the line between mental stress and mental breakdown.'

> His great ambition had been to go to Cambridge, but to his bitter disappointment he had to give up his dreams as things were going badly at the collieries and had to plunge instead into the vortex of industrial struggle. He had an almost overwhelming sense of honesty and justice; he was always tortured by the fear that the small investor, who put his money into the collieries because he trusted him, might in the uncertainty of pioneer undertakings, lose it. It was this fear, coupled with the mental strain and stress of the collieries and Barry Dock in those early days which killed him.[3]

Edward joined the management of Ocean collieries just before the strike of 1871, having been placed fourth out of 400 candidates in matriculating at London University.[4] There was another strike early in 1873, when 60,000 men and boys resisted a ten per cent pay cut enforced by the ironmasters and coal owners:[5] so much for Macdonald's hope of industrial peace in the valleys. The strike had been in progress for nearly four weeks when a *Western Mail* correspondent reported seeing 'poverty in its most loathsome form' in Merthyr Tydfil:

> Would that I could so direct the gaze of the public to these dark recesses in the by-lanes of what is proudly designated the metropolis of the iron kings of the principality, so as to bring about a reform . . . The miserable hovels which are inhabited by many hard-working men . . . could hardly be anything else but dens of misery.[6]

This time the men lost, going back to work in March at the ten per cent reduction.[7] This was the year in which, according to the London *Star*, David Davies had a personal income of £95,000 and refused an offer of £375,000 for his interest in the Ocean collieries.[8]

It was also the year of Edward's coming-of-age. The occasion was marked by a feast in Llandinam which, while purportedly being in Edward's honour, was in effect a celebration of the unprecedented success of the 'rich man in a navvy's shirt' who lived in Broneirion.[9] It was like all the gala railway openings rolled into one, with a huge marquee and four special trains of twenty coaches apiece bringing between 3,000 and 4,000 miners with their wives and children from the Rhondda. There were floral arches all over the village displaying such mottoes as 'A Man Diligent in Business Shall Stand Before Kings' and 'Success to Old King Coal, for He is a *Dear* Old Soul.' Some were in

Welsh — 'Hir Oes a Llwyddiant' and 'Parch i'r Hwn y mae Parch yn Ddyledus' among them. The one thing the occasion lacked was a suitable liquid to put in the glasses. Although David Davies had quite happily provided his railway navvies with ale at their celebratory suppers, here on his home patch nothing stronger than lemonade was allowed. There were 12,000 bottles of lemonade, each guest being allowed a maximum of three bottles, and the reporter for *The Welshman*, who wrote the fullest account of the proceedings, noted how 'the constant popping of corks and the fizzing of the effervescent fluid was a source of amusement not unmixed with alarm where any fine clothes were in danger of being spoiled.' The miners' views went unrecorded.

There had been various collections for Edward Davies, the farmers of Llandinam parish raising between £200 and £300 and the Ocean colliers £150, 'which will be given to Mr Jones of Merthyr, who has to paint Mr Edward Davies's portrait.' Llandinam Sunday School purchased 'a magnificent Dore Bible value £15 to present to the young man, the Calvinist Methodist churches in the Rhondda Valley procured a Welsh Bible and Hymn Book, and the owners of the Ocean Colliery a silver dessert service worth £300.'

David Davies's old friend Captain Robert Davies Pryce was there, recalling their railway-making days on the Newtown & Machynlleth line in a hearty speech in which he spoke of their host's 'gigantic operations'.

> Once upon a time my friend Mr Davies may have been an
> ordinary individual like myself or any of yourselves, but I don't
> believe he ever was. I am going to tell you now the ingredients of
> which this giant is composed . . . in the first place, strict integrity.
> Great energy, great perseverance, and a resolution that whatever
> his hand found to do, do it with all his might . . .

Did a shiver pass through the 'giant' as he heard these words, presaging as they did the epitaph that would be etched on his tomb?

It is hardly surprising that Captain Pryce made scarcely a mention of Edward Davies in his speech, as the young man was like a ghost at his own feast. It was his father's day and he knew it. His carefully-prepared words seemed too slippery to grasp as he sat beside his mother, waiting his turn to speak. He knew his speech would be no match for his father's.

When David Davies stood up, the crowd gave him roar after roar of acclaim. Theoretically he was there to celebrate his son, but all was designed for his own greater glory. It was a speech full of homilies and the kind of pithy observations that people had come to expect of him. To call it 'untutored', however, is to ignore the fact that by now he had thoroughly tutored himself in this kind of public speaking: a style of address in which self-aggrandizement masqueraded as humility, and a reputation for down-to-earth speaking became an excuse for delivering patronizing lectures to working men and their wives. In this respect, he had become as moralizing as any bishop.

'It is my opinion,' he said sententiously,

> ... that a great amount of the misery and poverty that we have in this country is caused by the wives ... A girl ought to be able to mend her husband's stockings before she has any right to be married ... She should be able to put a neat piece on her husband's trousers ... A wife should be able to make a nice white loaf of bread with good heaving in it, not like a lump of clay ... A wife should be able to cook well, cook a joint ... A wife should keep her house neat and clean. A wife should have her house ready for the man when he comes home from work. And that isn't all. A wife should meet him at the door with a smile on her face, and say to him, "I'm very pleased to see you back once again, my dear" ... In short, what I mean is this, that a wife should make her husband's home the best place he can find. And if the husband after that goes to a public house and spends his money there, he is a monster, he is not fit to be called a man.

This was paternalism on a grand scale, and one wonders what comments passed between the colliers and their wives on the way back to the Rhondda that evening.

In the course of this sermon − delivered entirely in English, despite cries of 'Cymraeg' from some of the miners − Davies professed himself ready to 'try the trade unions':

> If there is one part of the business more unpleasant than another it is the bargaining and agreeing to what the wages shall be. Well, you know, if trade unions do anything at all they do that, and I hope they do it effectually, and that when it is settled all of us abide by what they do. I will answer for myself as one individual. I always will abide by what they do. I advise you, all of you, to give it a fair trial, and if it answers, stick to it by all means.

He claimed they had the second largest colliery company in South Wales,[10] raising 'more coal than anybody', and grandiloquently wondered what might have happened had they not gone to the Rhondda.

> I believe that old England would have had to shut up. And I don't know, if old England had to shut up, what would have become of the rest of the world ... I cannot conceive what the rest of the world would be worth if it was not for old England.

With this characteristic mixture of sentiment and absurdity, shrewd observation and banter, David Davies ploughed on with a speech that must have taken a full hour to deliver, and held a good measure not merely of self-praise but of self-justification.

> Now I have satisfied you that we are an important company, I should like to know how we could keep that coal without capital. How could we sink those deep pits through those hard rocks and get rid of all that water? How could we have built all those cottages without money? And how could we have spent all these hundreds and thousands if we had not had them? If we had borrowed it, things would not have been so satisfactory. But we have got our own capital — and I can assure you we can look after it too. Well now, what becomes of that capital? It goes to you, and I am happy to see you all, as fine specimens of working men as England could produce. You have proved it in your work; you have done your duty as nobody else did in the same time. That is a proof that you are the right people in the right place.

How could poor Edward follow this? His speech revealed, most of all, his discomfiture. 'I am conscious of the fact,' he said, after being showered with gifts, 'that it is not I myself who have earned them, but I regard them chiefly as an outburst of your feelings towards those whom I am happy to say I have always found pleasure in honouring and obeying.'

He too had some words for the miners and their families, though less didactic than his father's.

> I sincerely hope that we shall always remember that it is our bounden duty to consider your interest as well as ours, that we may always endeavour to treat you justly and fairly and liberally, to do all we reasonably can to make you comfortable and happy, and to assist you in improving your position in that respect. And whilst we continue to do this, we shall expect too that you, as workmen, will not forget that we expect your actions to be a reflection of ours, that whilst we take care of your interests you will take care of ours ... and that as one happy family we may entertain that affectionate goodwill and regard for each other which alone can make us prosperous and happy as a community ...

Listening to these pretty sentiments, one might almost have forgotten that this 'happy family' had, in the best traditions of families, been busily engaged in tearing each other apart in the strike so lately concluded.

It must not be thought that David Davies had altogether neglected to mention his son as he stood on that platform transfigured by self-congratulation. It was wholly in keeping with the spirit of the day, however, that he should apologize for doing so.

'Now, if you will excuse me, I will ask to say a very few words about Edward ...'

What he said, basically, was that the boy had been no trouble. They had always been 'very good friends' and he had never had occasion to 'threaten the rod' on him — no small boast in Victorian times. What is more, he had cost 'very little to nurse' and — a tiny joke, no doubt — 'I think if I had been blessed with twenty like him I could have nursed them without missing the money.'

One might fairly reflect that had Edward been a little more difficult he might have ended up a happier man. How he must have inwardly chafed as he heard words which, while designed as a compliment, renewed his sense of injury at the sacrifice of the Cambridge education that would have meant so much to him. They were words written in pencil from his sick-bed by George Rae — the banker who had come to David Davies's rescue in the 1866 crash, and who was now (not entirely coincidentally) deputy chairman of the Ocean company.

'We respect and honour him,' said Rae of Edward Davies, 'because although his tendencies are purely scholarly and intellectual . . . he has not hesitated, ever since he left college, to devote himself to the Ocean Colliery as a voluntary assistant to the chief engineer, and has daily descended and daily shared the dangers of the pit, equally with the bravest and hardiest veterans of the mine. And he has done all this without the slightest remuneration, or the idea of such a thing entering his mind.'

This was easier to take, perhaps, than the song specially composed for the occasion by Mrs St Clair Williams, and sung by a choir to the tune of *Men of Harlech*:

Edward! Manhood now hath crown'd thee,
Dear friends by thy side aye found be,
Wisdom, wit and worth surround ye,
And thy footsteps guide.
Rejoice! thy sun hath risen in splendour,
Dawn hath fled, may Day yet render
Deeds, that will kind thoughts engender
And yield honest pride.
Virtue, thee caressing,
In thy heart still pressing
Every gift she hath, to charm, be thine her purest blessing.
Strong men — toilers 'neath the earth
Stand here today to honour worth
On this fair spot that gave thee birth
Near Severn's silv'ry tide.

'Just one word more I will say before I leave Edward,' said David Davies that day, 'and it is this. I trust and hope that he will live long to do a deal of good things in his old country. But one thing I want to ask you. Don't expect him to do for his country and for his people and for his friends more than I have done because if you do, you may be disappointed.'

They were scarcely words calculated to boost the self-confidence of a young man painfully aware of his own shortcomings. One's heart goes out to him. To be the son of a famous man is always difficult; to be the son of David Davies was impossible.

14 Where Are The Rich Men?

If he took stock of himself on that warm summer evening, as the trains carried the colliers back south and the empty lemonade bottles clattered into the rubbish sacks, David Davies could look back on eighteen years of amazing success. The one-time sawyer had made a fortune out of railways and was in the process of making another out of coal. And he had a sense of obligation that was new and intriguing. Some of the greatest ironmasters and quarry owners hoarded their wealth, as if to part with a sovereign were to lose a pound of flesh. But Davies of Llandinam was beginning to give on the grand scale, and religion and education were the causes nearest his heart.

The ceremonial silver trowels that were given him on the opening of the chapels raised with his money have survived the succeeding century better than the buildings themselves. Shut away from the world and the social upheavals that have lain waste the chapel culture he cherished, they shine still with the hope and confidence of late Victorian Wales. They show his importance not only in Wales but in Welsh communities in England, for he laid the foundation stones of chapels in London, Liverpool and Manchester. He kept a cheque book especially for the building funds of chapels,[1] and did not limit his support to those of his own Calvinistic Methodist persuasion. Once he sent a cheque to help a young man through his final term in college before ordination in the then still established Anglican Church in Wales.[2]

Like other rich people he had begging letters by the thousand, but he was − need one say it − no soft touch. 'Mr David Davies once sent me a list of what he had paid in a year and what he had refused to pay. The two lists were sad really,' John Gibson of the *Cambrian News* remarked in a letter to Stuart Rendel.[3] In his obituary of Davies he noted how he had 'allowed himself to be bled pretty freely, but no man ever more thoroughly understood the harpies that preyed upon him than he did. He knew how to deal with them too, and if they thought he did not see through them they were woefully mistaken.'[4] The cunning learned when best to tap him for money. According to a chapel deacon who knew him well, if he walked around very quickly it showed he was feeling irritable but if he approached in a leisurely way, with his hands in his pockets, he was in a benevolent mood.[5]

It was fortunate for Wales that the creation of the Davies fortune coincided with the fulfilment of a long-standing dream: the establishment of a Welsh university. It had been a long time coming; nearly 500

Ceremonial trowels presented to Davies on the many occasions when he laid the memorial stone for a new chapel.

years had passed since Owain Glyndŵr had proposed a university in the south of the country and another in the north. The creation of St David's College in Lampeter by the Anglican Church in the 1820s was a small but important advance, and at one time there were hopes of its developing into 'a small Welsh utility-model Oxbridge.'[6] Theological colleges were set up in other parts of Wales, but the idea of a university remained only speculative until a national campaign was launched in the 1860s. Two of the leading figures were Hugh Owen, a civil servant who had long been an advocate of a Welsh university,[7] and Dr Thomas Nicholas, a tutor at Carmarthen Presbyterian College.[8] In 1863 Nicholas drafted an Address to the friends of education in Wales in which he lamented the fact that 'Wales, with nearly a million and a quarter inhabitants, remains to this day without a single High Class College,' whereas Scotland had four universities receiving £20,000 a year in public funds, and Ireland three Queen's Colleges as well as Trinity College, Dublin.[9] The Goverment had, in fact, spent over £100,000 in establishing the Queen's Colleges, which had been federated into the Queen's University. Nervous of Westminster's reaction to the radical notion of a Welsh university, Nicholas rejected 'all fanciful ideas of nationality' and predictably promised that the university would 'spread a knowledge of the English language and literature among the people of Wales.'[10]

The story of the Welsh university movement is fully told in Dr E.L. Ellis's *The University College of Wales, Aberystwyth 1872–1972*. He explains how there had initially been hopes of raising a national fund of £50,000 by public subscription.[11] By mid-1865, however, only £5,000 had been collected in hard cash, while 'a slightly larger nominal amount lay exasperatingly in unfulfilled promises.'[12] In the following two years sites at Llantwit Major in Glamorgan and Menai Bridge on Anglesey were considered, and Aberystwyth came to be chosen simply as the result of Thomas Savin's bankruptcy in the wake of the collapse of the Overend and Gurney clearing bank. Savin had built a huge hotel on the sea front in Aberystwyth around an existing building, Castle House, with the intention of offering what would now be called package holidays, rail fare and accommodation being included in the price. After spending £80,000 on this architectural eccentricity – built in a style designated 'early marzipan' by a wit – he went under, and the university committee was able to buy the site for a mere £10,000 in 1867.[13] In view of David Davies's involvement with Aberystwyth, the fact that it was his late partner's fall from grace that led to the creation of 'The College by the Sea' has a special irony.

'The course of instruction contemplated will be of the highest order . . . special attention will be paid to natural science, on account of its bearing upon the important mining and manufacturing industries of the principality,' the *Cardiff Times* reported. 'No privileges will be withheld on account of religious distinctions – the members of all churches being placed on an entirely equal footing. The best men available, whether churchmen or nonconformists, will be elected to the professorships.'[14]

This shows at once a curious narrowness of academic vision and an admirable absence of religious prejudice. There was at first a widespread feeling that the prime function of the college would be to fit young men for the world of commerce and industry, and this was a view held by David Davies.

'My object in assisting this College,' he wrote in 1876, four years after its opening, 'was to give the Welsh poor or lower middle class a higher standard of education than they could get elsewhere on account of its cheapness . . . to fit the young men of Wales for better situations in the mercantile world to compete with the English & Scotch . . . I understood it to be pure and simple a mercantile College or school purely Elementary.'[15] Ellis notes that some of the first students had no clear idea of the difference between a school and a college, and that even the principal, the Revd Thomas Charles Edwards, believed that for years the institution would have an indeterminate status somewhere between that of a school and an authentic university college.[16]

The misunderstanding did not prevent David Davies becoming the college's greatest benefactor. He is believed to have given between £5,000 and £6,000 to its funds,[17] and in the view of Ellis he 'saved it from extinction more than once'.[18] For eleven years he was its treasurer, resigning in the wake of the disastrous 1886 Parliamentary election in protest at his treatment by the students, whom he said had 'kicked him nearly to death' in their pro-Gladstone enthusiasm.[19] The family support of the college continued, however, first through his son Edward and then through his grandchildren, Lord Davies and the Davies sisters of Gregynog.

David Davies's initial contribution was a modest £100,[20] the first subscription list being headed by the MP for Lambeth, William Williams, a Welsh Radical who had for years been urging the Government to spend more money on education in Wales. He contributed £1,088, and another generous benefactor was an Englishman, Samuel Morley, the Liberal MP for Bristol.[21]

The University College of Wales was officially opened on Tuesday 15 October 1872, students having been admitted for examinations the previous Wednesday. There was great enthusiasm in the town of Aberystwyth and a public holiday was declared. The *Cambrian News* under its campaigning editor John Gibson had zealously fostered a sense of occasion among the townspeople, and in a leading article he saw the college as a means of improving the 'moral, social and intellectual position of the country.'[22]

When David Davies arrived in Aberystwyth for the opening ceremony he might justly have reflected on the way his efforts had increased the town's importance. He had laid the first rails of the iron road that now connected the Cardigan Bay coast with the English border, and without the railway he had built from the south the choice of Aberystwyth as the site of the college would have been laughable. He was by far the greatest benefactor Cardiganshire had ever known, and he hoped before long to play a bigger part in the life of the county than ever – as its MP.

He had good reason, then, to feel a sense of destiny as he passed through the festive-looking streets, bright with flags and streamers, on his way to Savin's folly on the sea front. The Promenade Band and the Aberystwyth Choir had been engaged to provide music for this public breakfast, the band playing on an open space then intended as the college lawn. On the platform David Davies found he had to endure the company of Henry Richard, now MP for Merthyr Tydfil, towards whom he still felt bitter as a result of the 1865 election. Richard, in fact, spoke before him,[23] but it was Davies who made the speech of the day, building up to a climax that showed his sense of the theatrical was by this time reflected in his public speaking.

He began by confessing that he had harboured serious doubts about the viability of the college, which he had regarded 'as a sick child.'

> I was afraid that he was consumptive. If he was consumptive he would have died. However, I am happy to know now that he is not consumptive, but I think I have found out the mystery of his dragging along in the way that he has been, and waste so much valuable time. He was born in an unfortunate time; he was born just before the great Parliament of 1866, and that was very likely to have killed him. I watched him very closely, and I made up my mind I would give him only £100 because I never like to put my hand on anything that is likely to be a failure. Looking on quietly, I found by-and-by some small, idle dogs begin to bark at him, and by that time I was aware that there was some life in him. He revived, and then I promised him £300. But I am not here today to regret that; I am very pleased — I am only sorry I did not promise more. But now . . . some of my friends have thrown out a hint that we ought to have done something more . . . My only failure has been that I am rather disposed when I am a little elevated like I am today, to promise sometimes more than it is convenient for me to pay. However, I don't think I shall do so on this occasion . . .[24]

It was a teasing address, by means of which he kept his audience wondering up to the last second whether in fact he meant to promise any more money at all. Eventually, however, he brought the rabbit out of the hat.

> I will tell you what my opinion of this institution is. We ought to have a fund of at least £50,000 in the hands of the committee. I should like to see interest on some of it given as scholarships to this institution. I can't help feeling that before we have the roof on this building, to talk of scholarships is like putting the cart before the horse, and showing its spare ribs[25] to everybody who comes. But we may safely leave that to the committee. I for one am willing to give, say, £1,000 towards this building. [Great applause.] When the £50,000 is complete, I will give another £2,000 towards the scholarships. ['Long continued applause' greeted these words, according to the *Cambrian News*, and the 'waving of handkerchiefs.']

In the course of this speech, Davies voiced the hope that the 'men of good common sense' who would be educated at Aberystwyth would 'become good commercial men'. With so many influential people present, he also took the opportunity to speak out plainly on a subject close to his heart: the lack of confidence which the Welsh had in themselves, and their failure to realize the wealth of their own country. His words are important in our assessment of David Davies, for they reveal that for all his blustering praise of 'old England' on so many occasions, he had a pride in Wales which should not be discounted.

> It has gone abroad that we in Wales are very poor. I am here today to contradict that. I say we are not poor; we live in the finest country in the world — and not only the finest, but the richest ... a great deal has been said with reference to this university, about getting an endowment from the Government ... I am not one of those who are over-sanguine about getting from the Government what we can do for ourselves. What I say is this — let us do what we can first, then let us go to the Government ... Let us see whether we have done our best for this institution. I say we have not. Where are the rich men of Wales? Have they come forward and done their best? I don't think they have ... No-one knows better than the Government that we in Wales are not poor. Government got alarmed in 1867 I think ... They instituted an inquiry, and we find that we have a vast amount of coal, and not only that, but we have one-third of the coal of the whole United Kingdom. I say, therefore, Wales is rich.[26]

Perhaps it is not surprising that, with such appeals for self-help receiving widespread publicity, no support for Aberystwyth was received from central government until 1884.

David Davies was by now a man who had travelled far, and not just metaphorically. His visit to Sardinia with Benjamin Piercy early in the 1860s had been followed by a trip to Egypt for the opening of the Suez Canal in the autumn of 1869. He was invited there as a director of the Cambrian Railways, fellow-director James (later Sir James) Falshaw going with him,[27] but he was not over-impressed. He found fault with the way the canal had been constructed, believing it should have been both wider and deeper, and thought that as a financial speculation it would never pay.[28] What excited him far more was the journey he made through the Holy Land immediately afterwards. On his return he was much in demand as a lecturer, and chapels were filled to the doors as he described his journey through Palestine. They were very long lectures lasting up to two and a half hours, but we are told that 'the attention of the audience never for a moment flagged.' He had a good deal to say about the 'character and manners of the people' and showed specimens of stones, trees and vegetables.[29]

This visit to the land of the Bible made a lasting impression on David Davies, and the men who attended his Sunday school class in Llandinam learned how to exploit it craftily. On a hot summer afternoon, when they were not really in the mood for Bible study, one or other of them would casually mention Egypt or Palestine and like Pavlov's dogs Davies would instantly respond, launching into yet another account of his travels.[30]

A few months after his return from Palestine, David Davies spent some weeks in Russia giving advice on railway construction, taking Edward with him.[31] It is disappointing that there is so little information on these overseas journeys, made at a time when such travel was a comparative rarity.

David Davies had become a director of the Cambrian Railways in February 1867, the shareholders voting him on to the board at their half-yearly meeting at the Langham Hotel in London. He replaced a retiring director, Swinton Henry Boult, who had put himself up for re-election.[32] The company was then in its third year, having been created in July 1864 as an amalgamation of the small concerns which had played such a large part in Davies's life – the Oswestry & Newtown, Llanidloes & Newtown and Newtown & Machynlleth. The Oswestry, Ellesmere & Whitchurch Railway was also part of the grouping, and the line which was to prove Savin's downfall, the Aberystwyth & Welsh Coast, was absorbed in 1865.[33]

The first meeting Davies attended as a director was on 8 March 1867 – when, ironically, one of the points under discussion was Savin's failure to complete his contracts on the coast line.[34] Later that month he was appointed to a committee charged with the task of 'conferring with Mr Savin's inspectors upon the present condition of the coast works', Savin's affairs being then in receivership.[35] In April, he was made a member of the finance, works and traffic committee.[36]

For twelve years, David Davies would remain a board member – and when he quit he would do so in style, after an almighty row with his co-directors over what he regarded as dangerous penny-pinching by the company. For the time being, however, all was sweetness and light. The company valued his experience, and he appeared to fit in well with these men of business. With his well-known keenness for saving the shareholders' money, he enthusiastically went along with a decision made in August 1869 to reduce the directors' remuneration from £2,000 a year to £1,000[37] – and he did not demur, either, when it was resolved a month later that the £1,000 should be inclusive of expenses.[38]

Early in the 1870s, David Davies built the last of his railways: a modest little line, only six and a half miles long, just over the hill from Broneirion. This was the Van Railway, named after the village of Van, an Anglicized corruption of Y Fan. Its purpose was to link the lead mines at Van with the main Newtown-Machynlleth line at Caersws, and it came about as the result of a change of heart by Davies: he had declared himself done with railway making, but relented because this one was 'so near to his doors.'[39]

Although short, its route was picturesque, running west from Caersws along the valley of the River Cerist. The company was registered on 9 June 1870 and within a month the *Cambrian News* was reporting that the work of constructing this 'short but important' railway had begun at 'wonderfully small expenditure', the paper having every confidence that Davies would 'no doubt display his usual energy.'[40] The promoters were Davies himself and Earl Vane, whom he had come to know through Vane's chairmanship of the Newtown & Machynlleth Railway.

The lead mines at Van had known their ups and downs since first being opened in 1850, and prospects looked good when Davies was enticed into the railway scheme. The shares leapt in value from £5 to £86 in 1868, when the Van Mining Co took them over, and they provided work for 700 men. This proved to be something of a swansong, however, for the mines were fated to suffer badly from the slump in world prices in the 1870s and intense overseas competition.[41]

Some of the land over which the railway ran was owned by David Davies and Earl Vane themselves, another landowner being Capt Offley Malcolm Crewe-Read of Plas Dinam. The railway rose 120ft. from Caersws to its terminus among the spoil heaps at Van, with Bryn y Fan rising 1,580ft. to the west (today, the Clywedog Reservoir lies on the far side of this mountain). The line was opened for freight traffic in August 1871 and when passenger trains began running in December 1873 no high hopes were entertained of any 'gentry' booking a seat; only second and third-class carriages were provided![42] The journey took up to forty minutes and in 1871 engine driver John Aldridge was being paid 5s. a day and fireman William Roberts 3s. 4d. a day.[43]

The railway's chief interest lies in the fact that its manager was the poet Ceiriog, John Ceiriog Hughes. He went there from Llanidloes, where he had been stationmaster since 1865, having returned to his native hills after pining for them while serving as a clerk in a railway goods office in Manchester. Like many a poet he was a man of unpredictable habits, who thought nothing of wearing his best frock coat and top hat on duty one day and a shabby old overcoat and cloth cap the next. He called his two store rooms at Caersws 'Machynlleth' and 'Llanrwst' for no apparent reason, and when his eldest daughter was married he had the loco shed at Van cleaned and whitewashed and hung with Chinese lanterns, and staged an all-night dance there in her honour.[44]

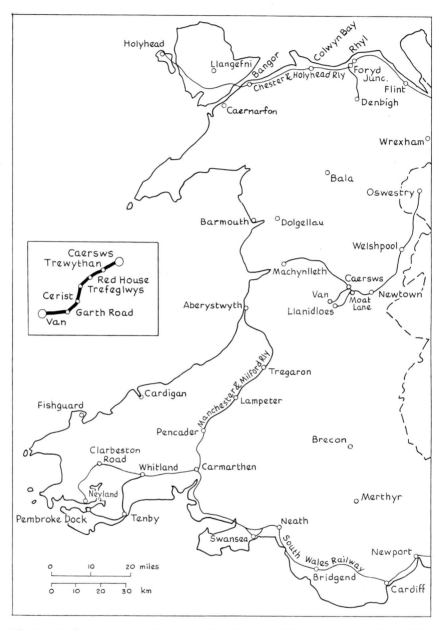

The Van Railway: the last of the lines built by David Davies and opened in 1871. This map shows all of Davies's lines and their links with other railways.

When Ceiriog died in 1887 the line practically died with him; passenger traffic had ceased in 1879 and the railway closed entirely in

1893. It was reopened for freight traffic three years later, being worked first by the Cambrian Railways and then by the GWR until its unremarkable history came to an end in 1940.[45] Between the wars services had become so infrequent that David Davies's grandson, Lord Davies, was able to ride along it following the hounds, safe in the knowledge that trains would be encountered only two or three times a week.[46]

In Llandinam, David Kinsey had duly recorded the creation of the Van Railway in his diary — although, curiously, he called it the Trefeglwys Railway when he noted the cutting of the first sod by David Davies on 5 July 1870.[47] In spite of his increased responsibilities — he was now assistant overseer as well as postmaster and stonemason — he continued to make daily jottings on village life. He noted the advent of penny readings in the schoolroom in 1865,[48] the provision of a new lich-gate for the church in 1867[49] and a change of name for the village local in 1868: a new sign went up showing it was now The Lion instead of The Mermaid.[50]

He also recorded the death in Llanidloes of the old Chartist leader John (O'Connor) Lewis in 1869, aged 65,[51] and a practical joke the following year:

> February 24 1870. — Old "Tom" Breese and Edward Savage play'd the Fool with. Some Wags invited them to Newtown to Measure for a Suit of Livery to attend the Assizes this all being a "Hoax." They returned to Llandinam Crestfallen, no-one attended to Measure.

Kinsey had not forgotten how the grand man of Broneirion, now being listed among the 'Gentry and Clergy' in the directories that circulated among the well-to-do,[52] had once been a poor village boy hunting squirrels and playing marbles as if his life depended on it. He thought it uproarious when the one-time sawyer added to his estates by purchasing a property with extensive woodlands:

'July 9 1874. — David Davies Esq MP bought the "Gwernygo" Property at Kerry for the sum of £74,000. The Timber to be valued !!!'

Kinsey was rich in one thing only: a sense of humour.

15 Into Parliament He Shall Go!

Kinsey's droll observation reminds us that by the time he bought that Kerry estate, David Davies had achieved his ambition to become a Member of Parliament. Writing the magic letters 'MP' after his name was, in fact, still a novelty: he had been returned unopposed for Cardigan District – the Boroughs seat – in the general election of February 1874.

Nearly nine years had passed since he had fought Sir Thomas Lloyd and there had been an intervening election, in 1868, when he had firmly declined the invitation to stand again for the county seat. His refusal to do so surprised those who considered that he had an excellent chance of being elected this time, and he felt obliged to explain himself.

'At the last election,' he said in a public statement printed by the *Aberystwyth Observer*, 'I was strongly opposed by the Gogerddan family; and they succeeded in turning the scale against me. I have no reason to believe that I should be more fortunate in this respect if I came forward on this occasion.'[1]

The Gogerddan family were the Pryses, who had thrown their weight behind the blue-blooded Lloyd in 1865 rather than the upstart sawyer.

'Their objections to me, I take it, were of a personal nature; and there is now a likelihood of a Liberal candidate coming forward, as to whose perfect fitness to represent the Liberal interest of the county I believe there cannot be a single doubt.' He had therefore 'decided to sacrifice my own wishes rather than imperil the seat' by risking a division.

The candidate was the Swansea industrialist Evan Matthew Richards, whom David Davies generously acknowledged would make an 'excellent member'.[2] Davies was clearly not exaggerating the influence of the Pryses, as several months before the election a staunch Liberal, Thomas Harris of Llechryd, had written to the influential John Matthews in Aberystwyth suggesting they should ask 'the House of Gogerddan' to name a candidate, as 'they have much influence, and it would not do to offend them.'[3] Richards was in fact the Pryses' nominee, and with their support he won the seat, polling 2,074 votes against the 1,918 cast for the Tory, E.M. Vaughan – one of the Vaughans of Trawscoed (Crosswood).

Although he stood aside from the hustings David Davies may have played an indirect part in this campaign, as he is said to have marched on Tregaron from Pencader with a band of his railway navvies after hearing that the Tories had barricaded the streets of the town to prevent the Liberals going to the polls. 'As soon as the Tories heard of this they fled and DD entered the town and took possession,' Lord Davies wrote to Ivor Thomas, author of *Top Sawyer*, in 1937.[4] There was some debate between the two on the precise year of the march, Thomas eventually settling for 1868, 'at which time,' he wrote to Lord Davies, 'your grandfather still had a number of navvies at work on the Manchester and Milford'[5] — which had been completed the previous year. The evidence is by no means conclusive, however, as one cannot ignore the fact that Richards, on being elected, remarked that they had 'not done so well in Tregaron.'[6] Lord Davies himself believed that the march may well have taken place in 1865, although his grandfather had then been a candidate: 'It was just the sort of thing he would do.'[7]

The election of 1868 is chiefly remembered for the spirit of independence which voters displayed in the Welsh countryside, when in spite of 'The Screw' of Tory landlords they voted Liberal in large numbers. This has been seen as a symbol of national awakening, and the historian Kenneth O. Morgan has reminded us that to Lloyd George forty years later 'it woke the spirit of the mountains, the genius of freedom that fought the might of the Normans.'[8]

Even without the advantage of historical perspective, contemporary newspapers realized the significance of the voters' defiance. In a leading article, the *Merionethshire Standard* expressed the hope that 'the spectacle of large bodies of men earnestly contending for a great principle is one that . . . will not be lost upon English constituencies.' It saw the battle with the landlords in military terms:

> The men of Wales have been fighting like very brave volunteers in the political battles — not waiting to be cajoled into voting, but coming forward gladly to do their duty as citizen soldiers in the great contest.[9]

There were casualties among the soldiery, however, for many tenant farmers who dared to vote Liberal were evicted from their holdings. A Political Evictions Fund was set up to help them, and the sense of grievance was still strong when the Welsh Land Commission took evidence from 1893–95.

A letter sent to Richards after one of his first speeches in the Commons gives fine expression to the sentiments of 1868.

> The landlords in Cardiganshire have come out with a vengeance . . . Some of the landlords, Crosswood among others, have given notices to their political supporters as well as their opponents, most likely as a cloak . . . We are all very proud of the high position gained by the Member for Cardiganshire in the H of C. We now begin to think we are somebody, and can venture to raise our heads up. We shall not henceforth suffer ourselves to be

trampled upon and ignored by such arrogant incapables as the Cardiganshire tories.[10]

'The Screw' as an open method of intimidation was consigned to the past with the introduction of the secret ballot in 1872. The general election of 1874 was the first to be conducted under the new rules, but it saw the defeat of the Liberal administration that had brought about this historic advance. Having gone to the country with a programme which included the abolition of income tax, Gladstone was astonished to find himself rejected, the Conservatives winning 350 seats to the Liberals' 242 and the Irish Home Rulers' 60. 'Is it not disgusting,' Mrs Gladstone wrote to her son, 'after all Papa's labour and patriotism and years of work to think of handing over his nest-egg to that Jew?'[11] This took 'that Jew' Disraeli to the top of the greasy pole for the second time, as he had first kissed the Queen's hand when taking office briefly in succession to Lord Derby just before the 1868 election. It was, however, his first taste of real power.

The election address which David Davies put before 'the electors of the United Boroughs of Cardigan, Aberystwyth, Lampeter and Adper' showed his willingness, at this stage, to follow his leader. 'I am prepared to give a cordial but independent support of Mr Gladstone's policy and am consequently ready to vote for the Abolition of the Income Tax,' he declared. He was also in favour of 'every measure conducive to Perfect Religious equality' and concluded:

> Being personally known to most of the electors and largely interested in the material prosperity of the County I need hardly assure you that, if honoured with your confidence, I shall give my best attention towards promoting the welfare of your respective boroughs.[12]

'It is an extraordinary thing. I am seldom beaten,' he said at an election meeting in Aberystwyth, looking back to the 1865 campaign. He believed that then, he had been regarded as 'one of a class who were not thought respectable enough to be sent to Parliament,' but now he was looked upon with less suspicion as 'it was admitted by nearly everyone that the working man had a perfect right to be represented in the House of Commons.'

One of the interesting things about this speech was his definition of the rich as people 'with incomes above £150 a year.' He contrasted their revenue of £450m annually with the £500m combined income of the working men, who had the right to be represented 'to the same extent as the other class.'

'He looked at the nation as a big waggon,' reported the *Cambrian News*, 'with a Locomotive in front and a break [sic] and van behind . . .

The Conservative break was too heavy, and could do with a little lightening, for it took too much trouble to drag it uphill before it was useful.'

Davies promised, rather confusedly, that 'if he did not make any speeches in the House of Commons he would try to make one. He would perhaps break down but he would try again.' He was confident that he could make himself understood, and 'perhaps he knew as much about real practical work as any of the members of the House.' At any rate, he would represent them honestly and fairly and 'shrink on every occasion from acting shabbily.'[13]

Davies's candidature received strong support from John Gibson of the *Cambrian News*, who was to remain a staunch ally until the fateful election of 1886. In a leading article Gibson observed that Davies's election address was 'like himself homely, outspoken and to the point,' and paid him the compliment of saying that he did not use language to disguise his thoughts.

All that is required to silence Conservatism in Cardiganshire as it has already been silenced in Merionethshire is to return Mr Davies for the Boroughs and . . . to double Mr E.M. Richards's majority in the county . . . The farmers of Cardiganshire know their own rights and wrongs far too well, and have too vivid a recollection of the oppression to which they were subjected in 1868 to reverse their opposition in favour of that party which helped, by the now notorious evictions, to give the electors the protection of the ballot. There is much yet to be done before the vaunted freedom and equality of which we hear so much becomes a reality, and we confidently appeal to the electors of Cardiganshire to remain true to those great principles of freedom for which they have fought in the past — principles which have been hindered by the Conservative Party on every possible opportunity. [14]

Gibson's hopes were only half fulfilled, David Davies being returned unopposed but Richards losing his seat to a Tory squire from the south of the county — Thomas Edward Lloyd of Coedmore, a mansion romantically set above a wooded precipice on the Teifi, opposite Cilgerran Castle. Lloyd, a man of studious tastes — he was a classical scholar who played the cello[15] — polled 1,850 votes to Richards' 1,605, and made a modest notch for himself in Welsh political history by being the last openly Conservative candidate to represent Cardiganshire, up to the time of writing.

David Davies's star was then at its height. To the Welsh he had become the supreme success symbol, and for years to come the words 'Davies of Llandinam' were to be a synonym for untold wealth. Long before the days of television, he was a celebrity whose face was familiar to everyone. A 'Life Like Portrait of David Davies Esq MP Llandinam' was offered for sale for 5s. in the columns of the *Cambrian News*, with a quotation from *The Welshman*:

> Everywhere in Wales his name is mentioned with pride, and we have no doubt that this portrait of him will soon adorn hundreds of homes in the Principality ... No one can look on those bright eyes, and that broad forehead, without a consciousness that there lies beneath that wealth of power which has enabled him to reach unaided the high position he now holds.[16]

On his return to Llandinam he said he would not regard himself as the Member for Cardiganshire alone, but would try to serve his native country and be 'a Member for Wales and England, and endeavour to do all the good he could in his day and generation.' A dinner was laid on at the Lion for the men of the village, the women having to content themselves with taking home slices of meat from an ox which was divided up during the course of the week.[17]

Davies was one of nineteen Welsh Liberal MPs, four fewer than in 1868, the Tories having increased their representation from ten to fourteen. The Liberals took a shade under 61 per cent of the votes cast in Wales, polling 57,768 to the Tories' 31,574. The Liberals were in fact the majority party in terms of votes cast in the UK as a whole, taking 52.7 per cent of the poll but finding themselves with 108 fewer seats than the Tories. The Home Rule candidates, fighting as such for the first time and winning sixty seats, accounted for the Liberals' representation in Ireland being drastically reduced from sixty-six to ten.[18]

The new Parliament − Queen Victoria's ninth − opened on 5 March 1874. By half-past one the floor was densely crowded, the more knowing members of this most exclusive of gentlemen's clubs having reserved their seats by placing their toppers on them. David Davies could be forgiven for feeling a little daunted as he entered the Commons for the first time, for this was elevated company even for a top sawyer. It did not help matters that for some time he tended to be mistaken for a workman come to do a job about the House. 'Davies's early Parliamentary life was much chequered by conflicts with the attendants in the lobby,' wrote Henry W. Lucy, who provided lively accounts of Parliamentary proceedings for readers of the *Daily News*. 'There are a good many of them there, and it took some weeks to convince them individually that he was not a carpenter come to ease the door or nail down the matting.' The Member for Cardigan District appears to have taken it all in good part. 'Davies was never offended at this mistake, only feeling the inconvenience of having to explain it to so many.'

It was a gaslit Commons of bewhiskered MPs, only two of whom were without either beards or moustaches. The dominant figures were those two old antagonists, Benjamin Disraeli and William Ewart Gladstone, but there were minor characters who caught the eye such as Major O'Gorman, a mountain of a man. Sitting in a London cab one day, the floor collapsed under him, 'and he had to trot along at the same rate as the horse – luckily not too fast,' recalled Lucy. He once voted against his own party, explaining that it was a hot night and he ' knew there would be more room in the Aye lobby.'[19]

Disraeli and Gladstone had contrasting personal styles. Although in his sixty-fifth year, Gladstone was brimming over with energy – a man of quick movements who gesticulated a great deal as he spoke in his fine, resonant voice. As Prime Minister in the previous session he had displayed his restless energy and impetuous temperament to the full, but when he was replaced by Disraeli the picture altered completely. 'With instinctive dramatic art Disraeli personally assumed an attitude and manner in marked contrast with the feverish haste of his predecessor. Silent, impassive, almost sombre in mood, he sat looking on through the sittings, rarely interposing save in response to questions directly addressed to him.' He would sit right through even relatively unimportant debates, the tail of his frock-coat draped over his crossed leg and his arms folded.[20]

All this was new to David Davies, but there were several familiar faces in the House – among them the not altogether welcome face of George Hammond Whalley, his old adversary from railway-making days in mid Wales. He could take comfort in the fact that Whalley, also a Liberal, had become something of a figure of fun, 'a flesh-and-blood Don Quixote . . . quite as addle-pated as the immortal knight of La Mancha.'[21]

The session was only seven weeks old when Davies lived up to his promise to 'try to make a speech' even though he might break down. In the event he did not break down and his maiden speech made a considerable impression. It was on the subject of drink, a fact ironically noted by Kinsey in his diary.[22] Joshua Fielden, a Tory sitting for a Yorkshire rural constituency, moved the reduction of the malt tax, arguing that 'it was not the amount of pure beer drunk that injured the people, but the quantity of adulterated poison sold under the name of beer.' He was anxious to restore the practice of cottage brewing, 'which because of the high price of malt had fallen into disuse in most agricultural districts.'[23]

Davies would have none of this, and in a violent assault on the notion that cheap drink could be good for anyone he treated the Commons to the first of many speeches in which he presented himself as a man who knew what was good for 'working men' because he was one himself.

D. Davies, having been a working man at the age of 14, bespoke the indulgence of the House ... He had never had 6d. that he had not made himself. He had commenced life as a working man, and during the last 18 years had employed on an average 2,000 men, and he therefore claimed to be as good a judge as any Member of that House of the requirements of the working man. Not only had he acted as a working man for a considerable number of years, but he had mixed with them afterwards as the principal partner in a large colliery-owning firm where 2,500 men and boys were employed. He went regularly amongst them every fortnight. He did not object to as much drink as was good for a man if he required it at all; but three things he had noticed all his life promoted excessive drink — high wages, cheap beer and convenient public houses ... While the men were away drinking in the public house the roof of the working was cracking and the buttresses were giving way ... But this loss was not the worst of it. An hon. gentleman was about to propose that the employers should have to pay for injuries done to the workmen; but the fact was that three out of every four men who were killed lost their lives from this cause — irregularity of working. [He claimed that only half the men were at work on Monday, and the output that day was less than half that on Thursdays.] It was not the loss of money that vexed him, but the misery which was brought on the men and their families. He was popular with his workmen; he had never had any trouble with the Master and Servant Act, and no man of his had ever brought him into the County Court. What he wanted was to promote the well-being of everyone in the United Kingdom. But if the malster, brewer and publican drove things too far they would kill the goose which laid the golden eggs.[24]

This highly unorthodox speech, which made up in vigour what it lacked in public school polish, was acclaimed inside and outside Parliament. 'If he takes care he will be a favourite,' observed the *Liverpool Daily Post.* 'If he is not, as he himself put it, "a bit of a statesman," he is evidently a humourist of the sort the House likes, and harum-scarum speeches without beginning or ending, such as he delivered tonight, are always welcome. He has accomplished in Parliament ... by one happy stroke what his indomitable perseverance has won for him in other fields.'[25] The motion, incidentally, was lost by 244 votes to seventeen.

Heartened by this triumph, David Davies managed to catch the Speaker's eye four days later, when he proposed ten o'clock closing of public houses in the countryside so that the 'working classes' might get to work on time after a good night's sleep.[26] He was on his feet again next day, observing that 'a poor railway was the worst security upon which a man could raise money' during a debate on whether the Irish Railways should be acquired by the State.[27]

Six weeks later, he gave only cautious support to a Bill designed to protect the health of women working in factories, recalling that the Mines Regulation Act of 1873 had provided that women should work two hours less than men.

> He had in his mines some 30 or 40 nice girls — intelligent and independent girls — their work was very light, and their pay very good under the old hours, and they were satisfied; but when the new rules came into operation, he asked his manager, 'Where are all the girls?' The answer was, that they had gone because they could not get what (pay) they wanted . . . the Act was there to prevent it. What was the consequence? These girls went to the farmers to make butter and cheese. They had to work 17 hours a day instead of nine, and they were paid 50 per cent less. Some went to the publicans, where their hours were twice as long, and their pay little better, so that the Act of last session, which was meant for their good, had done nothing but harm to these girls . . . His own opinion was that the Government ought to have included a clause to shorten the hours of agricultural labour, and had they done so they would have received his support.[28]

This was all very interesting but unremarkable, and there were cries of 'Divide, divide' during the latter part of a long and repetitive speech which he made in June on another liquor Bill, when again he professed to know the 'working man' better than most.

> I have been rather amused since I have been in this House by the remarks of some hon. members who profess to be so anxious to take care of the interests of the working man. They object to any interference with the liberty of the working classes . . . but how much beer does a working man want? I can tell the House that [when making railways] not 15 per cent of my men took a glass of beer once a month. If beer was of such great importance to the working man, would he not want more than one glass a month? But when men drank, they quarrelled in their drink, and sometimes they killed their partners, sometimes they killed themselves, and sometimes they nearly killed me — for I have been very nearly killed three or four times . . .
>
> There is not one in this House who has the interest of working men more at heart than I have. Last year I built 100 houses for working men, better houses than I was born in, and next year I hope to build 100 more. I am now engaged in working pits, and within seven yards of them there is a public house which I cannot get rid of; and yet if any accident occurred in these pits in

consequence of any of the men ... having drunk too much, I should be held responsible under the present law, until I have proved that I am not guilty. I put it solemnly to the House, whether that public house ought to be allowed to remain there. As the matter stands, I must either stop the pits and throw the men out of work, or else stop the public house, which is killing the men.[29]

He was learning the painful lesson that the indulgence accorded new Members was of limited duration. 'Those who interrupt me,' he remarked rather plaintively during this speech, 'know they have a very bad case.' The lesson was salutary, however, and he was to be more sparing in his contributions after those first heady months in the Commons. Very sensibly, for the most part he spoke only on matters on which he had first-hand knowledge and Henry Lucy was to describe him as 'one of the most modest and most genuine members ...who never sits down without having first imparted to the House some shrewd observation or some humorous notion.'[30]

A pleasing enough compliment, in its way; but it left David Davies a long way short of being a Parliamentary favourite.

In the 1870s, being an MP was far from ranking as a full-time occupation. The legislative programme was light in comparison with later periods, and the job was unpaid. So perhaps it is not surprising that it was nearly two years before Davies felt the need to make his first address to his constituents — a kind of reporting back which gives us an insight into his views on politics and politicians.

The House of Commons was, he granted, composed of men above the average — 'people said there was not much sense there, but this was not his experience;' the Speaker 'knew his business well and performed it in a marvellous way,' while the Prime Minister was 'a most extraordinary man who although he did not work himself, made his men work.'

Sometimes the Conservatives got into trouble, and then the Prime Minister would get up, and with a grave face and most solemn manner would say something most strikingly witty, and conclude that he did not think the House was in a mood to discuss the question. And very likely move an adjournment.[31]

These droll remarks suggest that David Davies was every bit as shrewd a judge of Dizzy as Dizzy was of him. There is, too, a wealth of earthy wisdom in his description of some common weaknesses to be found in the Commons.

One of the most painful things to see in the House was some respectable member trying to say something after he had lost the point. If he would sit down when he had lost the point no harm would be done; but instead of doing that, he tried vainly to regain the lost point, and at last sat down and smashed his hat.

This was greeted with loud laughter, and having thoroughly won his audience Davies gave them his thoughts on the standard of representation in the House. The most important point was 'to send gentlemen who had no purpose whatever to serve, except the good of the country.' Many MPs came into this category, 'but there was also another class, namely men who were anxious to serve their own personal interests. Many of these were lawyers ... There were already too many lawyers in the House of Commons, and he gave that information so that they need not send any more at present.'[32] This was one of many remarks which David Davies made about lawyers, indicating that they were not, to say the least, his favourite people. All the more ironic that he should, eventually, lose his seat to one.

As for his views on the political scene as a whole, he rather naively observed that there had been little activity in the Commons, but this was only to be expected. 'The Liberal Government had worked hard, and there was not much for the Conservatives to do. However, the Conservatives had behaved pretty fairly, and had not done much in the way of altering laws which had been passed by the Liberals.'[33]

The Parliament of 1874–80, however, did bring in measures which have been described as 'the biggest instalment of social reform passed by any one government in the nineteenth century.'[34] These included two Acts strengthening the position of trade unions, a Public Health Act regarded as a landmark in sanitary legislation, a programme replacing slums with new houses for working men and their families, the regulation of the sale of food and drugs, an Act safeguarding the funds of friendly societies, and the enforcement of the Plimsoll line on merchant vessels.

There was also the Agricultural Holdings Act, designed to remove some of the grievances of tenants against their landlords – an issue which would return in the next Parliament, and towards which David Davies, the Liberal squire of Broneirion, would display a curious ambiguity.

16   Despots and Poltroons

By the time David Davies entered Parliament, the Ocean collieries were acknowledged to be among the most successful in the south Wales coalfield. They ran up gross profits of £184,411 in 1873 and £151,878 in 1874, taking their gross profits in nine years to a grand total of £493,823,[1] a sum roughly equivalent to £14m in the mid-1980s.[2] Trevor Boyns has pointed out that the early growth of the firm of David Davies & Co was greatly helped by the booming fortunes of the coal trade between 1871 and 1874, the large profits enabling the company both to pay high dividends and to finance new collieries.[3]

The company had been incorporated in 1867 with an authorised capital of £240,000.[4] It was the only prominent steam coal firm to register as a joint stock company with unlimited liability, the apparent reason being the intention of bringing in new partners and dividing the 240 original shares into 24,000 £10 shares.[5] As chairman of the company David Davies was indisputably the boss, but he had learned the art of delegation. The day-to-day running of the collieries was in the hands of officials, chief among which was the general manager. The first in this role was Morgan Joseph, the mining engineer who had been among Davies's first associates in the Rhondda. He was paid a salary of £700 a year, but resigned in 1871 because of mining difficulties.[6] He was succeeded by another mining engineer, William Jenkins, to whom is credited the admirable dictum: 'Safety first, and then economy.'[7] Jenkins remained in the job for forty-four years, seeing the output rise from 340,000 tons from three pits in 1871 to 1,900,000 tons from ten pits in 1915.[8] He was based at the Ocean offices in Treorchy and lived in some style at Ystradfechan House. To the locals he was 'Jenkins Ty Mawr' and they are described as having 'greeted him with an air which was an amusing admixture of friendliness and reverence'.[9] The company secretary, Thomas Webb, and the commercial manager, J. Osborne Riches, were to be found in what was then the commercial heart of Cardiff: the dockland area. This is where the vital deals were struck with buyers or their agents, a directory for 1871 giving the address of the Ocean (Merthyr) Steam Coal Offices as Britannia Buildings, 131 Bute Street; the company also had offices in London, Liverpool and Southampton.[10] Webb was entrusted with the entire control of the company's finances, David Davies's faith in him being such that they were never submitted to audit.[11] Davies is reputed never to have spoken a harsh word about Webb[12] and he actively involved him in a foreign enterprise: they jointly owned the Port Said and Suez Coal Company.[13]

With his entry into Parliament, David Davies needed men such as Webb, Riches and Jenkins more than ever. He spent much time in London, and his home remained in Llandinam. He ran the Ocean collieries from a distance, scribbling innumerable business letters which made up in forcefulness what they lacked in grammatical precision. His son Edward lived in the Rhondda for many years and bore much of the responsibility for the sinking and equipping of Garw pit,[14] but he himself was essentially an absentee employer whose visits became increasingly like state occasions. Writing in 1933, an old employee recalled:

> Mr Davies would be met at Ystrad Station and there enter his carriage which would be drawn up to Treorchy preceded by Johnny Treharne's brass band and a number of door-boys, who usually bore lighted torches. Those were the happy days so often referred [*sic*] as the days of direct contact between master and man. Mr Davies would address us from an improvised platform on the edge of Ystradfechan grounds, and he would spend the next few days visiting his collieries.[15]

Such recollections give some substance to David Davies's claim to be 'popular with his workmen',[16] but inevitably this popularity was eroded by the industrial disputes into which the Ocean collieries were drawn. One questions, too, whether the doorboys bearing lighted torches were inspired more by affection for the boss rather than fear of the consequences should they refuse to take part in such demonstrations of fealty. Squires were accustomed to such treatment and the man known even to his colliers as 'the squire of Llandinam'[17] was no exception. For all the talk of 'direct contact', it signified the tentative touching of fingertips across a social gulf rather than the firm handclasp of comrades in labour.

Within a year of Davies's entry into Parliament, his collieries were caught up in the most bitter dispute of the decade. The strike in the south Wales coalfield at the beginning of 1875 was the miners' response to a ten per cent reduction in pay, coming less than two years after the ten per cent pay cut of March 1873. Addressing miners of the Bristol district on 'the crisis in South Wales' at the close of 1874, Tom Halliday of the Amalgamated Association of Miners bitterly remarked that wages were always slow to advance, but 'the moment prices gave way' they were reduced by the owners. He was 'afraid the South Wales masters did not mean any good to the men or their union. They had broken faith with the men.'[18] The *Colliery Guardian*, mouthpiece of the owners, predictably accused the men of improvidence. 'During the days of high wages these men, with a few honourable exceptions ... squandered their money in public houses and extravagant living' and were now the very persons who are asking alms from door to door.'[19] A week later, the same journal reported that a lock-out had been 'reluctantly agreed upon' in south Wales, but only after the striking colliers 'had openly boasted of the assistance they were receiving from those men who had accepted the reduction.' Pits belonging to the coal owners outside the masters' association remained in production,[20] but the locked-out miners had a grim time of it.

> Many unfortunate men are employed in stone-breaking, clumsily and slowly doing the work by which none but an experienced and exceptionally diligent hand can realize as much as two shillings per day. So numerous are the stone-breakers that a difficulty is experienced in finding hammers for their use, and every day will swell the list of applicants for public relief ... For our own part, we have little doubt what the end will be. The men will be starved into submission, and will go back to the pits sadder and wiser than when they left them.[21]

The *Colliery Guardian* poured scorn on the proposition that the miners' representatives should have the right to examine the owners' books, saying this was akin to allowing the baker to investigate the miner's pay before fixing the price of a loaf.[22] The growing sense of solidarity among the workers was displayed at a meeting in Birkenhead called by the local trades council 'to express sympathy with the miners' lock-out in South Wales.'[23] The principal speaker was William Pickard of the Amalgamated Miners' Association, who in appearance resembled 'the old English squire of song and story', with 'a real John Bull cast of countenance',[24] but whose opinions the squires detested.

Pickard spoke of the 'moral force of organization' that had brought about the settlement of the 1871 dispute through arbitration, and called the lock-out 'one of the most unnatural states of things that had ever darkened the pages of history.' He accused the owners of paying their men twenty to thirty per cent less than the average pay of English miners, and ironically pointed out that while British people were sending thousands of pounds to stave off famine in Bengal, 'a famine had set in in South Wales, and children were picking the refuse from the dung-hills and eating it.'[25]

David Davies was stung into replying. In a letter to *The Times* sent on behalf of his company, he accused Pickard of an 'inexcusable ignorance of the facts', and portrayed the coal owners as peace-makers in the 1871 dispute:

The iron-masters were then, as now, among the largest of the coal exporters, and it was a recognized fact that they were paying less wages for raising their coal than was [*sic*] paid by those who were only coal proprietors, although both competed in the same market. The coal-masters, finding it impossible to carry on their business with this difference in wages against them, proposed that the question should be referred to arbitration. This the men refused, and struck for 12 weeks, when they at length agreed to the arbitration proposed from the first by the masters . . .

The letter rejected Pickard's claim that wages were only 4s. to 4s. 6d. a day. The average for the past four months, 'after the last two reductions of 10 per cent each', had been 7s. 0¼d. for an eight-hour day, 'which covered the poorest as well as the best workmen.' As for the men's contracts of employment, the 'masters and union leaders' had agreed to set up a joint committee to settle the rules, but 'the men never appointed their representatives because they could not find half a dozen of their own class in whom they could place sufficient confidence to act for them . . . not a very encouraging proof that consultation with the men tends to promote conciliation and immunity from strikes.'[26]

Although he would not himself have written the letter, which would almost certainly have come from the ever-fluent pen of Thomas Webb, it must have been sent at David Davies's dictate. Its tone is unfortunate, since the use of such phrases as 'of their own class' and the sarcastic reference to consultation did not fit well with his own view of himself as an employer of enlightened views who was still one of the *gwerin*. He had, however, been stung by a speech made a month previously by Alexander Macdonald, president of the National Association of Miners, who was now MP for Stafford. Macdonald had put the name of Davies alongside that of the ironmaster Crawshay and others as examples of despotism in south Wales. In his view 'self-made men' grew rich only by exploiting others, and there was an alternative path – that of co-operation.

> The men had been forced to submit at the close of the previous year to a 10 per cent reduction in wages without consultation and without any reasons being given. This showed an arrogant assumption that the working classes could not be too soon put under foot.
>   There were four or five families notably in front – the Crawshays, the Fothergills, the Vivians, the Davies, and a few others, ruling in this despotic manner. What was the position of these men? Not a century ago the dingles and valleys of Wales possessed primeval peace and quietude. One or two entered those

valleys, and began to work there, not with an overwhelming capital, but with small means. By means of the accumulated labour of the workmen they were able to develop their operations still further, but had it been left to the arm of a Crawshay or a Fothergill or a Vivian . . . no wealth would have accumulated in South Wales today. It was the working ironminers, the working coal miners and the navvies that gave those men the capital they now possessed. It had come from the accumulated capital which the working men had foolishly allowed to be drawn from them, instead of dividing it among themselves by means of co-operative production, which they should have done years ago . . .

The wealth of a few great families in Wales had been collected from workmen and produced by workmen; and he questioned the right of men to turn round with that wealth and try to starve the workmen and their families and their children . . . the mineowners of South Wales were making war, not only against the men, who were fair game to fight, but they were infamously attempting to carry their designs by making war and bringing destitution upon the women and carrying misery and starvation to the children . . .

He did hope that when the social history of England was written . . . names like those of Crawshay and Fothergill, Vivian and Davies, and others would go down to posterity with that infamy which poltroons who would attack women and children would ever receive at the hands of an enlightened age.[27]

The lockout continued throughout March, with the men resolutely refusing to submit to the owners' terms. 'The distress continues to increase,' reported *The Times* towards the end of the month, 'as evinced by the returns to the Board of Guardians. In the parish of Merthyr the regular and irregular paupers now amount to nearly 12,000. About 1,000 men are employed upon works of permanent utility in the Aberdare and Rhondda valleys alone. The cry of suffering grows louder, and although the workmen bravely refrain from troubling the authorities . . . yet the privation is far in excess of the means of private charity and relief committees to deal with it successfully. At Merthyr the scheme for supplying poor children with one meal a day works well, and subscriptions have flowed in liberally.'[28]

It was the middle of April before the first moves were made to end the dispute, with a conference between representatives of the coal-owners' association and the miners at the Royal Hotel, Cardiff. David Davies had played a leading part in bringing the two sides together, but although on this and other occasions he proved himself a conciliator, he showed no remorse whatever at the use of the lockout, the cruellest of weapons, against the workmen. All the same, he still presented himself as 'a friend of the workmen' in his speech, which was a blend of the hard-headed — even hard-hearted — and the sentimental. He claimed that more men were being employed than in 1870 to do the same amount of work; that coal was being produced at a price unprofitable to the employers; that it was hard to compete with the Northumberland coalfield because of the 'dead work' in South Wales caused by geological difficulties — roofing and so on.[29] This *cri de coeur* for the owners makes one wonder how Davies was able to justify taking £95,000 as his share of his collieries' profits only two years before. He went on, however, to accuse his colliers of bad workmanship.

> So long as a good price could be obtained for the coal the men were left pretty much to take their own course, although he had been many times ashamed to see the idle and slovenly way in which the work was done. Masters had been accused of doing all in their power to crush the union. He had stood up in the presence of men now present and persuaded them to stick to the union, because it was easier to meet delegates than men individually.[30]

According to Davies, there were restrictive practices in the mines. When wages had been at their highest, 'men had come to him with tears in their eyes and complained that they were not allowed to fill more than a limited number of trams, and that the advance in wages was not beneficial to them.' He returned to the well-worn theme of his own youthful providence, remarking that when the 'youths of 16 or 18' had been earning £1. 13s. a week, 'they could well have lived on 13s. and paid the £1 into the bank, which was the way he had got on himself. It was not by short work, but by making the most of opportunities, that success in life was attained.' He urged the miners' delegates to 'take as long as they liked to decide these questions,' promising that if they stayed until ten o'clock that evening 'he would, if need be, pay the cost of a special train to take them home.'

> He believed that the masters were the best friends the workmen ever had, and certainly had no wish to 'crush the men down to the dust,' as some spurious speculators had ventured to assert. He was sorry to see men in want and poverty, and women and children starving. But it was not the fault of the masters. He had all his life been a friend of the working man, and it was hard, just before he was going into the grave, to have such an accusation made against him, in common with others, as some persons had thought proper to heedlessly indulge in.[31]

Hard it may have been, but it was far harder for the miners, who had to accept humiliating terms as the price of reopening the collieries. They were told that the 10 per cent pay reduction was no longer on offer; they would have to agree to return to work for still lower wages. Even so, there was still some fight in them. When the associated masters tried to browbeat them into taking a 15 per cent reduction, like the men in pits owned by the ironmasters, they resisted. They proposed instead a 12½ per cent pay cut and this was agreed to by the employers in what was risibly called 'a spirit of conciliation'. The owners, however, threw out the suggestion that all future disputes should be settled by a twelve-man committee representing both sides. Instead, they persuaded the miners' delegates to agree that in future any changes in wage rates should depend 'on a sliding scale of wages, to be regulated by the selling price of coal.'[32]

Thus was introduced a system which was to cause endless trouble.

'I think that we have now established a system of regulating wages by the price of coal, without calling in the aid of anybody to say what is right and what is wrong. A good, sound, sensible principle that shall always regulate itself, so that none of these unpleasant differences will arise in future,' said H. Hussey Vivian MP optimistically, at a dinner in Cardiff's Royal Hotel celebrating the end of the lockout.[33]

This 'sumptuous repast' was laid on by the coal owners for the miners' representatives. There was an abundant supply of champagne, which may have clouded the judgements of the delegates. At any rate, they raised a cheer for Vivian when he declared that by introducing the sliding scale they had 'set a pattern which the rest of the world would admire', a bold statement given the fact that even some of those present – David Davies included – had grave doubts about it.

The idea behind the sliding scale was that wages should rise or fall according to the retail price of coal. But Davies contended that this was 'but a very minor element in settling the rate of wages.' He argued that because production costs had increased, the rise in the price of coal from 9s. a ton to 13s. a ton in the space of a few years did not mean that the proprietor was any better off, 'the increased price of coal being exhausted by the increased price of getting it'. Thus, the coal-owner had no more money to spare for higher wages. In his opinion, 'the delegate mind has never studied that question in its wider aspects, and has shown itself radically unable to grasp it.'[34]

One of those who agreed with Davies on this was Lord Aberdare, who as Henry Austin Bruce had been Home Secretary in Gladstone's administration of 1868. He thought that while the price of an article 'might occasionally, and perhaps often, have something to do with the price of labour, in very many cases it had little or nothing to do with it. What should determine the value of labour was the proportion of labourers to the amount of work which could be given to them to do.'[35]

In spite of his reservations, David Davies became the first chairman of the joint committee of employers' and miners' representatives operating the sliding scale agreement. The plan was largely the brain-child of (Sir) William Thomas Lewis, who became Lord Merthyr and a bitter enemy of Davies's. It also had the support of the coal owner John Nixon and of the union leader William Abraham, better known as Mabon, who had come into prominence as a miners' agent during the 1873 strike.[36]

Ironically, Lewis was to cause a split in the employers' ranks by breaking the agreement only two years after its inception. He did so in order to reduce wages by 10 per cent below the sliding scale minimum at the Plymouth (Merthyr) and Aberdare collieries, a proposal for which − by threatening to close the works altogether − they managed to obtain the men's consent. There was an immediate protest from David Davies, to which Lewis suavely replied on 31 May 1877 arguing that there was nothing under the agreement to prevent any owner from 'arranging with his workmen to work at lower wages than is customary in the District − what is prohibited is that no owner shall advance wages or insist upon a reduction so as to produce a strike and thus become chargeable to the funds of the Association.' He claimed that losses at the Plymouth and Aberdare collieries had become so serious that they had decided all operations must cease unless production costs could be reduced.[37]

Faced by the prospect of losing their jobs altogether, the men first suggested they should work a day a month without pay, and when this was turned down they proposed a five per cent wage cut, but 'ultimately,' said Lewis, 'ten per cent was suggested' − a classic piece of arm-twisting. Lewis claimed that he was not alone in wishing to reduce wages below the minimum, as in his view the coal-owners' association was 'in a most critical condition arising from the increasing dissatisfaction among large owners with the sliding scale basis'.[38] The association actually decided to put back the clock eight years by reintroducing the 69-hour week of 1869 in place of the 54-hour week, which would mean a shift pattern of 7a.m. to 6p.m. on Mondays, 6a.m. to 6p.m. Tuesdays to Fridays and 6a.m. to 4p.m. on Saturdays.[39] To his credit, David Davies refused to impose these hours on his workmen[40] and in 1879 he withdrew his company from the owners' association and introduced a sliding scale of his own at the Ocean collieries;[41] this, however, would not be the end of his troubles.

17 What Price Education?

The settlement of the dispute that closed his collieries was David Davies's prime concern in the first few months of 1875, but he still found time to pursue other of his multifarious interests. He took part in Parliamentary debates, and attended meetings of the council of the University College of Wales. One such took place shortly after the champagne dinner for the miners' leaders at the Royal Hotel, when the college was still short not only of money but of a firm idea of itself. 'Our aim,' Principal Edwards had declared in his report the previous October, 'will be to form such a College as the educational wants of Wales from time to time may demand ... We ask only to be judged by this simple test: is this the sort of thing Wales at present wants? We heartily desire, above all things, to be in entire sympathy with the great mass of our countrymen.'[1] At the meeting of the council in April 1875 Davies, now treasurer of the college, gave his own views on the subject:

> Mr David Davies said that not being a scholar he had an idea of his own, and that was that they must walk before they could run. He had an idea that they were going to have better education throughout the United Kingdom, and he had no doubt that by degrees they would obtain a higher standard in the day schools. There were many clever boys who had gone through the course in the day schools, and wanted to go to universities but could not afford to go a long distance ... They must not expect to do everything at once ... He thought they ought to aim at a university and a high class university too.[2]

He was firmly opposed to the notion that the UCW should be in any way a theological college, especially one training clergy for the Church of England, and he even objected to a proposal to bring religion into the curriculum. In one of those highly distinctive personal letters of his which contrast so sharply with Webb's careful epistles, he bluntly informed Edwards in March 1876 that if he introduced religious teaching at all 'it will be what was not intended by me & I think I can speak for the whole body of nonconformists in Wales.'

> Now you say that the Bishop of St Asaph would ordain young men from this college under certain conditions do you think for one moment that the poor churches of the nonconformist would have collected one shilling towards the support of this College if it was understood that it was to educate young men for the Church

you know as well & better than I can tell you that the persons educated at Lampeter & Ystradmeuric [sic] have surfeited the people of Wales & that they are hated by the majority of people in fact by nearly all nonconformists   I have not that strong feeling against them that the majority of the people have but my own feeling is such that if I believed this College was to promote young men and teach them for the Church I would sooner my money was in the bottom of the sea ... If there is not sufficient young men seeking the advantage offered by the College for Elementary Education it only proves that it is not required or that the people do not realise the value of it. I am perfectly satisfied that it was not intended to educate for the *Church*.[3]

Only two days later, he sent another letter to Edwards from the Hummums Hotel in Covent Garden – his London base – reinforcing the point. Beginning with 'My Dear Sir', his usual way of addressing the Principal, he continued:

I hope to go home tomorrow I have not shown your letter to any one yet . . . I wish you to understand clearly what I have said that is, if it was understood that it was the wish of the Principal or in any way the Intention of the College to promote religious Instruction with a view of bringing up young men for the Church not another £100 would ever be paid by either myself or the Nonconformists of Wales towards the support of the College   I do not wish to say but that plenty of young men will come to the College that will afterwards go to the Church Ministry this we have nothing to do with   Some have gone even from Bala & other Nonconformist Colleges but this Instruction is no part of the duty of the Aberystwith College if I was ever positive on any point it is this[4]

These letters evidently caused a stir in the Edwards family, for within a month Davies was writing from Llandinam to the principal's father, Dr Lewis Edwards of Bala theological college. It contained both a reassurance and further proof that Davies had originally seen the UCW as a commercial college rather than one of academic standing.

You must not take it from any one that your son did say anything to offend me   I know him too well to suppose for a moment that he uttered a single word in favour of his views but from sheer consciousness of what was his duty he stated that he did not believe that any College could ever succeed in Wales that did not take for its studies religious subjects & here where I felt that I was deceived as this College was held out to be a College & be entirely elementary to enable young men from Wales to obtain a

Cheaper Education to assist them in Commercial Persuits [sic], of course there could be no objection to young men intended for the Church or for any other Denomination as Ministers of the Gospel taking up the Elementary part of their training in this College but this College was not intended to be a Theological College on this point I have no doubt, I had paid every farthing of which I had given to the College on this understanding . . .[5]

He thought it 'absurd' to suppose that men could be trained for the 'seven Diferent [sic] Denominations' in one and the same institution.

In the first place there are the Church as bigoted a set as you can find then the Methodists being the best but not much better then the Wesleyans worse than either the Independents full of selfishness ready at any moment to set the Church on fire then comes the Baptist ready to join them the Catholicks [sic] will have nothing to say to either then the Unitarians I do not know much of them but enough to know that they cannot Educate their Ministers in such a College   to put ones money by the thousands to support such a College as this would be an insult to commonsense & I for one will not do it . . . however I have no objection to the Principal making public what he said at the meeting in London that is that he does not think the College will succeed unless it includes those teachings requisite to bring young men up as Ministers of the Gospel perhaps another class of people will do the needfull to support it on those terms . . . from the first I had my fears as to the funds, from the first I had no doubt of its success as a cheaper College to assist men for commercial persuits [sic] but not for a moment did I entertain it as a place to prepare young men for the Ministry of any denomination, however if it will not succeed for the first I have no objection to its being tried for the latter provided it is made public.[6]

Almost a year before this, in the summer of 1875, David Davies had been a member of the deputation that went to London to plead — unsuccessfully — for a Government grant for the college. Led by Lord Aberdare, by then president of the UCW, these emissaries put their case to the Duke of Richmond, who as Lord President of the Council had prime responsibility for education. With supreme cynicism, the duke seized on Davies's passionate plea for support as an argument against any Government grant or subsidy, remarking that his 'untutored eloquence' showed that education was not everything.[7]

Davies made some pragmatic contributions to Commons debates on education, pointing out that for the poor the education of the young was not as simple a matter as it was for the rich. He told how 'a poor woman who had six children, and kept one cow, and whose husband earned 16s. a week on the railway,' had 'come crying to the school board,' saying that if she were compelled to send her eldest girl, aged eleven, to school regularly, 'they must go into the workhouse.'

> Well, what did the school board do? Why, they put it right for the woman, and that was what ought to be done all over the country. The schools were now being built, and the difficulty was to get the children into them without compulsion. There was a certain class of boys who were the masters of their parents, and they could not be got to school unless someone took them by the collar and made them go.[8]

In this same debate of July 1875, Davies said there were four schools in his parish, two denominational and two board schools. 'Let the children be educated for fifteen years, and then the poor rates would probably show a great diminution . . . He himself had, unfortunately, not been properly educated, but he was willing to do his duty in educating the children of the rising generation.'

He returned to the difficulty of getting children to school in a debate on the Elementary Education Bill the following year. There was a district in Wales, he said — without naming it — where there were 13,000 children not attending school. 'Why should the parish or district be put to the expense of providing schools and schoolmasters unless they could get the children there?'[9] This was not an isolated problem, for according to the MP for Sheffield Brightside, Anthony John Mundella, there were places for 3,250,000 children in schools in Britain, but daily attendance was only 1,800,000. The problem, in his view, was the haphazard nature of the provision. Where school boards existed there was compulsory attendance and few absentees, but elsewhere there was no control except that established by the Labour Acts. 'So long as we simply prohibited employment, and did not compel attendance, so long must the result be a failure.'[10]

Although David Davies undoubtedly believed in education, he took what he would have considered a common-sensical view of it. Just as he had originally seen the college at Aberystwyth as a kind of glorified school of commerce, so he viewed the board schools as places where children absorbed the three Rs and other practical lessons. He had no time for anything savouring of the fanciful. So when the Member for Maidstone, Sir John Lubbock, proposed the teaching of 'elementary natural science' in the schools, Davies sounded a note of warning that could have come from the Tory backwoods. He feared the school boards were going 'a little too fast, and making the cause of education unpopular.'

As chairman of a school board, he found that there was a growing difficulty with the parents of children, whom it was difficult to convince that all this education was necessary. Many parents in agricultural districts had an idea that if their children were taught in such subjects as elementary natural science they would never be any good for the farm.[11]

He recalled a 'very respectable farmer' telling him, 'I pay £6 every year for the education of these boys, and here is one of them, 13 years of age, and the first thing he does is to take up a newspaper, and if I tell him to get on with his work, he snubs me by telling me he knows more than I do.' The humour of this was evidently lost on Davies, who declared that the farmers 'objected to the very name elementary natural science', and suggested that 'it would be better to allow the older generation to die off before they pushed education much further.' He might have been Gradgrind himself when he argued that if any board school boys wished for a better education, it should be provided 'by voluntary subscription' and not 'at the expense of the rates.' The motion was, however, carried by sixty-eight votes to thirty-seven, the MP for Falkirk, John Ramsay, dryly observing that the people of Scotland raised no objections to their children being taught those sciences; 'the labouring poor were proud of the education of their children.'[12]

Davies is seen in a far more liberal light when speaking on religious matters. Supporting a Bill to give Nonconformist Ministers the right to conduct burials in churchyards, he claimed to have been the first in his locality to have subscribed towards the restoration of the parish church. The vicar, he declared, was a tenant of his and one of his best friends. 'Anyhow, he had been his friend for 35 years and that was a good deal for a Nonconformist to say.'[13] His mood was expansive enough that day for the Tory MP for North Warwickshire, Charles Newdegate − an elegant figure who was inclined to speak with a blood-red handkerchief in his right hand − to commend with his accustomed gravity 'the bonhomie of the hon gentleman the Member for Cardigan.'

In a debate on education, Davies indignantly read from a Church of England catechism in use in Montgomeryshire to prove his point that religious intolerance had increased since his childhood. Nonconformists had been called an 'unclubbable set' but, he complained, how could it be otherwise when such lessons were taught? Part of the catechism ran:

Q: What are those who separate themselves from the Church of England commonly called?
A: Dissenters.
Q: Are there different sorts of Dissenters?
A: Yes, Baptists, Independents, Quakers and others.

Q: Is it wrong to worship with Dissenters?
A: Yes; we should only attend places of worship which belong to the Church of England.

Hansard records Davies as saying that 'forty years ago when he went to a Church school, no such difficulties of this kind occurred, but somehow the Church has changed ... For himself he wished to see all these separations broken down ... they should all join together as they did in the old times.'[14]

The chapel conscience expressed itself in a broader context when David Davies spoke on a motion calling for the 'total suppression of the slave trade within the dominions of the Sultan of Zanzibar.' After ironically noting that very few were in the House and that the debate lacked the liveliness of the one that had earlier taken place on the blending of Irish whiskey, Davies said he 'trusted we should not be satisfied until we had liberated the last slave.' He realized there were many difficulties in the way, 'but if foreigners perceived that we did not now take some interest in the suppression of the slave traffic as we had many years ago, they would begin to think that we were wrong and they were right with regard to the slave question.' He wished there had been more fiery speeches on the subject that day – 'indeed, had he known it was necessary he would have prepared one himself.'[15]

Forty years had passed since the abolition of slavery in the British Empire, so this hardly qualified as a radical point of view. And when it came to captivity nearer home, Davies – now a magistrate[16] – could sound as reactionary as anyone. 'It should not be forgotten,' he shamelessly observed on one occasion, 'that nobody is obliged to go to prison. If prisons are to be converted into palaces we shall have persons doing mischief in order that they might get there.' More interestingly, he argued that the proposed clause – that prisoners should have the right to call in an outside doctor if they felt dissatisfied with the diagnosis of the prison medical officer – was in his view 'decidedly a class clause' because 'it would afford no relief to the poorer class of prisoners.'[17]

It would have been surprising if a man with so acute an interest in money should have refrained entirely from taking part in major financial debates. His contributions were, however, fewer than one might expect: he was proud to be thought of as a self-made man, but did not set himself up as an authority on the handling of the nation's wealth. Two years after his arrival in Parliament he showed himself to have changed his mind over income tax, which in his election address of 1874 he had wished to see abolished; now he gave his 'hearty support' to the proposal to raise it from twopence to threepence in the pound. 'The constituents of members on his side of the House would have no tax to pay and it was therefore very honourable and the right thing for the right hon Gentleman [the Chancellor] to do.' He was afraid, however, that the Chancellor had been 'over-sanguine' about next year's revenue. 'He thought they were just on the borders of bad times, into which the country would be deeply plunged.'[18]

He showed continued support for this highly unpopular tax — which both Disraeli and Gladstone had hoped to abolish — in the Budget debate of 1878. He then called it a 'very good' tax. 'It was a very ready and handy impost, and it fell on those who had the money to pay it.' There was the threat of war with Russia at the time over the Balkans — the ever-present Eastern Question — and Davies took the opportunity of saying that 'whatever the cost of that war might be, the expense should be paid as we went along, and not impose it as a mortgage on the State.'

> Let the country pay the bill fairly and honestly year by year; if it took £30m or £40m a year to fight the Russians let the money be raised, and let the bulk of it fall on the income tax. If they were to go to war he, for his part, should not be sorry to see a 2s. 6d. income tax.

He saw this not only as good housekeeping but a means of rescuing the country from its war fever. Wherever he went and whoever he saw — 'whether it was a doctor, or a parson, or anybody else — one and all were clamorous for war.' But if you asked them why the war was necessary, they could not tell.

> Now if these people had to pay a 2s. 6d. income tax . . . they would soon find out that they had had enough of it, and they would soon get as heartily sick of the cost to which they were put as they now were eager to rush into the fray.

Having had business dealings with the potential enemy, Davies felt confident in saying that he 'knew a great deal about Russia' and its resources, and that any war would be a long one.

> Those resources were very great, and the Russians could fight at a cheaper rate than the British. They would remain on land, and we on the water, and we could endeavour to starve them; but in doing this we should, to some extent, be starving ourselves. He did not think there would be much bloodshed; we should not attempt to do much with our Army; for supposing we were to land 100,000 men, what would be the use of such a force against the 500,000 they could bring against us? . . . He believed in the principle of calling upon every class to pay its proportion towards the expenses of the country, because he thought every class was thus directly interested in keeping out or getting out of war.[19]

The pacific nature of this speech was in marked contrast to one he would make in the next Parliament, when he would speak lightly of the possibility of 'a bit of a brush with one of those foreign nations' to test the strength of Britain's battleships.[20]

Among the less portentous matters that occupied his attention was the dog licence fee, then known as the 'dog tax'. The Chancellor, Sir Stafford Northcote, had raised it from 5s. to 7s. 6d., but David Davies thought this was still too little. 'He believed that a 10s. tax would produce as much as the 5s. tax did at present; while it would have the effect of ridding the country of something like three-fourths of the dogs.' If his own district were typical, 'there must be hundreds of thousands of dogs which were not only a wretched nuisance to the public, but for which the tax was never paid.'[21] It was, perhaps, the practical farmer speaking, since his possession of a gun dog proved he had no objection to the beasts in principle.

One of his more wayward proposals was that Mr Hansard should be given instructions to curtail his reports of Parliamentary speeches. He believed only those worth preserving should be included in Hansard's Debates, the daily record of proceedings.[22] Fortunately this advice was ignored. On several occasions he gave his opinion of lawyers, once informing the House that he had known them to take 'sometimes four fees in a day,' although he 'had no wish to accuse them of doing this intentionally.' Was his tongue firmly placed in his cheek at the time? 'He had noticed this, that a client who gave £100 was more likely to have the services of a barrister than one who gave £50 so there was something in payment after all.' He noted that he had paid 'many thousands in fees himself, and never had any fees returned to him.' This contrasted with the treatment accorded such as himself, who had pay deducted if the work was not done.[23] Possibly drawing on his experience over Talerddig, when a referee had been called in to adjudicate the amount of earth removed, he confidently declared that 'in his opinion there was nothing worse than going to referees, for counsel always took liberties with them. Barristers arranged matters for their own convenience, and postponed and delayed the trial, by which means those who employed them lost hundreds of pounds.'[24]

Three months before this, in May 1878, he had spoken on a motion seeking to simplify the transfer of land. He recalled being involved in a great deal of compulsory purchase of land for railway companies, so was 'thus acquainted with the difficulty of getting up titles.' Several lots of land purchased fourteen or fifteen years ago had never been conveyed, and on more than one occasion he had bought half an acre for £50 or £60, only to find the legal expenses amounting to over £150 because of the engagement of 'five or six lawyers' in the conveyancing. On the other hand, he could convey 'half an acre of land to a working man for building purposes for 10s.' Something was required to make the transfer of land cheaper.[25]

One of his most vigorous contributions was on the question of limited liability companies. The House had before it in 1878 a motion 'that further provision was required for securing the bona fide character of undertakings,' but David Davies bluntly pointed out that

> Parliament could pass as many measures as there were Members in the House, but it would never cure the evil until the people who invested in trading companies lost every halfpenny they possessed. This arose, not from the wickedness of Parliament, but from the wickedness of those who had the management of such concerns. There was no wonder that people who invested in them lost their money. He did not refer to banks or railway companies; but in iron mines [sic], collieries and manufactories of all descriptions, nothing was easier than to get up a limited liability company. People were anxious to get 10 per cent for their money, and they put it into a limited liability company. The concern got on very well for a year or two, but the directors were not always the best principled men; they did not look to the proper working of the business, but to jobbing in shares. No dividend was paid for the first year or two; the concern came to grief; shares fell from £100, perhaps, to £3; the directors then bought them up, and the result was that people who had invested their all lost everything they had and died of a broken heart. No Act of Parliament, he feared, could prevent this.[26]

This was the kind of contribution David Davies was best suited to make; one in which he spoke from personal knowledge of a subject, in terms that owed nothing to artifice and everything to sincerity. There was a speech towards the close of the 1874–80 Parliament that illustrates this even better. In it he showed, with great effect, how his attitude to drink was reflected in the way in which he viewed his responsibilities as a colliery owner; and in the course of it he rebuked the levity of those MPs who could find humour in the perilous world of the coal miner. After urging that new licences should not be granted without the consent of the majority of people in a district, he went on:

> I will give you a case in point, which is worth 1,000 theories. Take the case of a large colliery where 700 or 800 people are employed. A public house is opened within 100 yards of the pit's mouth. The colliery proprietors would be willing to purchase it at almost any price, in order to get rid of it; but as the law now

stands, if they did purchase it, a new one would be built in its place, and they would be no better off. I know several colliery proprietors who have had to fight the very agent who granted them the lease, because he would insist upon putting a public house close to the pit, for the reason that he could get £50 or £60 a year rent for a public house, when he would only get perhaps £5 for a cottage. I put the case simply and plainly to the Government, and they will be able to put it together in some shape better than I can.

There is an inquiry going on as to the cause of accidents in coal mines, a subject in which I and many others are very much interested. Take the case of one of the South Wales collieries, where 700 men are employed, and work in two shifts, 500 in the day and 200 at night. Two hundred men come to their work at six o'clock in the evening ... A great number of the 200 men having had the day to sleep, and having finished their sleep at about two o'clock in the afternoon, will then come to the pit and lounge about, and call at the public house before they go down. They are good, able men — men who can earn large wages. Many of them are timber men. There is a foreman at the top of the pit; but the question is, when is a man drunk? A man may get in a muddle, and have his senses pretty well gone, yet still be able to walk pretty steady. I know several such. (Laughter). I will explain the work these timber men do, and the House will see that it is no laughing matter ... These men have to take timbers out and put new timbers in, when there is a great squeeze and perhaps 12 or 15 tons of loose rock on the top. Men muddled by drinking for two or three hours at the public house at the top of the pit are in danger in taking the posts out and letting the stones down, and over and over again I have known men killed in that way. Not very long since I was called to my own pit to be told that two men had been killed in taking the posts up, and I had every reason to believe they had been drinking before they went to their work. I was willing to purchase the public house and to pay a large price for it, to get rid of it; but as the law stands a new public house would be opened after I did so, and I should be none the better off. These public houses are many of them in the hands of brewers, and some of them are making £1,000 a year, while the men are half starving. There is no reason in calling upon us to protect the lives of our workpeople, while they are left free to endanger their own lives and the lives of others by getting muddled with drink before they go down the pit. I dread the idea of an explosion. I know what a dreadful thing it is. The collieries with which I am connected are among the most fiery in the whole kingdom, yet the men go drinking about before they go down, and there is no knowing what the consequence may be.[27]

It was small comfort that all the next speaker could say on the subject was that it had not been unusual for their forefathers 'to finish their bottle or two bottles of wine a night,' and that 'a famous resolution had been passed in that House which had been settled by two statesmen over thirteen bottles of claret'.[28] These were not, presumably, forefathers from Llandinam or the Rhondda.

18   The Iron Safe

Although he had spoken of himself as one 'going into the grave' in 1875, David Davies showed no signs of mortality as the decade drew to a close. His vigour and enterprise seemed boundless; whatever he touched turned to gold. His Ocean collieries appeared to have been born under a lucky star[1] and were now five in number, the Western Colliery at Nantymoel in the Ogmore Valley having started production in January 1876 and the Eastern Colliery at Bwllfa in the Rhondda in July 1877.

One who came across him in his prime of life was the historian Charles Wilkins, who recalled him as 'a man of burly frame, with strongly-marked features, careless as to dress, and who might have been a comfortable farmer or a retired publican or trader . . . a man with the courage of his convictions, who . . . was not ashamed to stand amidst hundreds of the most cultured men of England, and tell them his opinion of things.'[2]

David Davies was certainly never afraid to speak his mind, and one of the things about which he had decided views was the best way of running a business. He outlined these in trenchant fashion at the annual meeting of the North and South Wales Bank in 1879, when he seconded the adoption of the annual report and praised the bank's chairman, his old friend and business associate George Rae.

> You have been told that the bank has been making advances, leading you to suppose that the bank has been going in the direction where other banks have been wrecked, and have been told that the Ocean Colliery Company has had large advances from the bank . . . Well, I tell you . . . that the Ocean Colliery Company has not had sixpence from the North and South Wales Bank, neither have they had it from any other bank or anyone else, and I mention this not on behalf of the Ocean Colliery Company. That company stands as well as the Bank of England, and does not owe one shilling to anybody . . . We have got an iron safe, and we put the bills in that and leave them there until they mature, and then send them to the North and South Wales for attention, and the bank gets the usual commission. So much for that wicked device. Well, then, I may say something for myself. People may think it very likely that I have got a large overdraft at the bank. I do not owe the bank one shilling. It is the other way. I could get £20,000 from the bank, but I do not want it.[3]

This was a typical blowing of his own trumpet, yet he had good cause for satisfaction. He had the reputation of being scrupulous in his business methods, and some idea of the self-sufficiency of the company can be

David Davies, the squire of Broneirion.

found in the fact that all the cash needed for the sinking of Western and Eastern collieries in the 1870s, and Garw in the 1880s — £255,280 in all — was raised by calls on the shareholders.[4]

Perhaps it is no coincidence that David Davies saw fit to explain his business methods to the bank's shareholders at the very time he was falling out with the Cambrian Railways, because the essence of this argument was integrity in management. He believed the company, of which he had been a director since 1867, was being fair neither to its employees nor to its passengers. The row blew up early in 1879, and was partly caused by what Davies thought had been the shabby treatment of their locomotive superintendent, Alexander Walker, who appears to have been dismissed after thirteen years in the job — or, at least, forced into retirement. On 22 January, Davies wrote to company secretary George Lewis from Broneirion saying he felt 'awfully ashamed of myself',

> and unless some steps be taken at our next Board to change the present State of things I for one will not continue a Director during the last week I have perused the Balance Sheet of Every co in Wales also the Same of the 5 following English Railways all for the year 1877 ... I find that with the single Exception of the GW [Great Western] Walkers department is the lowest ... Now what have we done sent Walker about his business without giving him a Chance of defending himself there never was a more unenglish act committed by any Set of Men. I feel utterly Ashamed of Myself & this was all done at the dictate of Mr Hadley who knows nothing on Earth about it. as soon as he came to our Board one of the first things he asked was how much notice was required to get rid of the co's officials   this of course frightened the Officials so that the few left are no earthly use, in fact he has been like a Bull in a China shop ... [5]

The very next day saw Davies writing again to Lewis — 'The more I think of what has lately been done ... the more I feel ashamed of myself'[6] — and the quarrel with his fellow-directors, which had obviously been a long time simmering, reached a spectacular climax the following month. On 17 February he sat down at his writing desk in Broneirion and drafted a letter 'to Cambrian Railways Directors' in the bold hand they knew so well. It began uncompromisingly, 'My dear Sir, I will not attend the Board Meeting in London, tomorrow indeed no Board Meeting again of the Cambrian Company, as I am leaving ...' He severely criticized the way the railway was being financed and managed, believing that 'we have been obliged to draw on our Rolling Stock & Road to a very considerable extent' to pay dividends under an arrangement — known simply as The Scheme — devised by a director, E.S. Bolden. When Bolden had realized that his predictions would not be fulfilled, remarked Davies tersely, 'he ran away and left us.' Davies's most damaging accusation is that the track had been neglected to such an extent that it was actually putting passengers in danger.

> During the last ten years we have not renewed more than some 56 miles I believe, I will get the exact figures. We have 120 miles of Road [track] over ten years old. If the road will last any part of it 16 years, we have to renew 18 miles a year for the next 6 years leaving some 14 miles for Branches to be repaired out of old rails.

A considerable part of our Road is now not fit to run fast trains on it, and a large portion of our traffic is from people who need not come on the line if it is considered unsafe. In addition to all this Mr Hadley has brought about a State of things making matters ten times worse, indeed utterly destroying the traffic that we have so carefully nursed for the last ten years. Now we have actually a falling traffic. I have every reason to believe to a much greater extent than is shewn by the weekly returns.[7]

One of these letters went to Captain Robert Davies Pryce – the man who had spoken of Davies as a giant at Edward Davies's coming-of-age celebrations. Davies urged him to 'look at the old rails taken out. No one would ever believe that human lives had been carried over these at any speed. I never saw such rails taken out of an old coal line ... The Engines have been completely wrecked ... I was told, Sir, that the noble chairman and yourself want a quiet meeting; so do I, but we must face the storm before people are killed.'[8]

Before the board meeting, he sent all his fellow-directors copies of a pamphlet bearing the innocuous title, 'Cambrian Railway Workshops.'[9] He had written it himself and had it privately printed in Newtown. Its contents were explosive.

'I have always said that our road is our weak point, but this was not of our creating,' it began.

> When we took charge ten years ago [of the coast section after Savin's failure] we found this state of things – a poor, weak road, with several miles of timber bridges, poor rails, poorer sleepers, and dirt for ballast. If we could raise £200,000 to replace these timber bridges, and lay 140 miles with steel rails and better sleepers and ballast, as well as our £45,000 to improve the Rolling Stock ... we could then work as cheap as any company similarly situated.
>
> But how can a single line in a poor district, beginning with an outlay of £24,000 a mile of a poor, costly road, hope to pay? If the Traffic increase, the Capital must increase. The English Mixed Lines have increased their capital during the last 10 years 46%, and the Scotch 50% – I mean Mixed Lines that is that carry Goods, Passengers, and Minerals in about equal proportions – while the poor Cambrian has increased its receipts 26% without a farthing increase of Capital Account, and then gets nothing but kicks for it from some people who know nothing whatever about it.

He urged anyone who doubted his figures to visit the locomotive workshops and see for himself. 'He will find from 13 to 15 of the company's Locomotives there, or about one in 3 of the whole. When it is considered that each Cambrian locomotive has earned £320 a year more than the North-Western and £537 more than the North-Eastern, these figures prove that we have not one engine to spare. There should not be more than 5 or 6 in the shops at the same time.'

> Those that are in use must be overworked and injured for want of proper time to wash out the boilers and other things necessary to keep them in trim to do the work. If we had not had the four new engines we should have been stopped for want of Locomotives.

He had been a party to putting the men on short time in the workshops, 'but I pointed out at the time that it was wrong in principle to do so, as the men would have a direct interest in doing as little as possible to allow the work to fall behind, so as to be put on full time again. We did this late in 1877 ... to save money to cover guaranteed interest.'

There were none too many men in the workshops, yet 'Mr Hadley said that we had three times the number of men we required to do the work in the shops, and that the best thing for the Company would be that the shops should be destroyed by fire.'

> We have a long single line, difficult to work and poor in traffic, and we are obliged to work passengers, goods and minerals in the same train to a large extent, which is very risky for passengers, unless the Rolling Stock is very good and under a good, practical man of experience as manager.

He was at pains to defend the company's employees, who were 'good, honest, able and faithful' − but several of the 'oldest and best servants have gone, and those that are left are utterly demoralised, expecting every week to have to go.'

> What set of men can work the line with this state of things, and who have the Company to set matters right again? This must be the work of years. Indeed, I expect every day to hear of some terrible accident on the Line. I know the Company is in a false position. There is £2,400,000 of Capital that is not worth the paper it is written upon, and this Stock, if it be worthy of the name, governs and controls the policy of the Company. It is held for the most part by Bankers, in large amounts, handy for voting purposes. These people want to get it off their Books, and some shuffling of the cards is better than good honest working.
>   To shift the value of the Road and the Rolling Stock on to the Balance Sheet may raise the wind, and enable some of these people to sell some of this stuff to some poor dupe, and then leave him and the Company in the mess. This sort of thing has been

done before, and I dare say it may be done again. If it is made out of the Road and Rolling Stock, the Shareholders that really own the Road will have to make it good – perhaps have to pay some years' dividends for heavy accidents . . .

Things are now in a most pitiable condition. If a man is to be a member of this Board he must be a tool to those who sway this large voting power over his head. He must surrender to their dictates, or make way, like myself, for another. The truth is there is not a bit of backbone left in the concern – it is more luck than anything else if it goes right for a month.

His memories of the painful break with Savin surfaced again as he recalled speaking his mind in equally painful fashion in 1860.

See what happened in the following 6 years. How many hundreds of people were ruined in those years by the wicked policy of the Company? My protest then kept my friends clear of loss, and I have no doubt but that they will take warning again. I shall now, as then, be called hard names for taking the course I have taken, but I do not care for that. Truth will prevail in the end, and that will be my reward.

This remarkable document led to bitter recriminations. 'In reply to your telegram to Pryce I and the whole board deprecate your pamphlet entirely,' the company chairman, the Marquess of Londonderry, wired Davies immediately.[10] The marquess claimed to be totally astonished by this assault from a man he had known for years – they had, after all, worked cordially together first on the Newtown & Machynlleth and then on the Van Railway, when the marquess had been Earl Vane. If the track were so defective, he argued, how had they escaped accidents during the last ten years? He 'could not believe his eyes' when he saw the pamphlet, which was nothing less than a stab in the back. 'My acquaintance with Mr Davies does not date from yesterday. I have known him many, many years, and considering that Mr Davies is a friend of mine, and an old acquaintance of mine, it has been most painful to me to speak in the way I have felt it my duty to do,' he told the half-yearly shareholders' meeting at the Assembly Rooms in Crewe on 28 February, with Davies sitting there listening to him. He recalled that at the previous half-yearly meeting, Davies had merely spoken of the need to lay down more steel rails – 'how the line should have become unsafe and the rolling stock wrecked in six months we must leave the proprietors to divine.'

Apparently unperturbed, David Davies rose to say that it was his distrust of Hadley – who in his view had become all-powerful – that had brought matters to a head. 'I never had any difficulty with the Board until Mr Hadley took the whole thing out of our hands.' He repeated that the line was unsafe — 'he should not be at all surprised to see the rails sprinkled with human blood before they were very much older' — suggested that Lord Londonderry had been making a statement prepared for him (presumably by Hadley), and once again claimed that one of the first things Hadley had done on becoming a director was to ask how long it would take to get rid of the company's employees — 'he sent new men all over the line to see how many rogues and dummies we had.'

> His object was to defend himself, to defend his colleagues who had been pushed out of the Board of Directors, and ... to defend the good servants of the company, who had been most villainously turned out as worthless. They had looked perhaps to him more than anybody else, because they knew first that he was honest, and they knew that he had considerable personal knowledge and experience ... The whole concern was being dragged down by one individual, and he was there to protest against it.[11]

'Had you not suddenly left the Room,' Lord Londonderry acidly wrote to him shortly afterwards, 'you would probably have heard the few remarks I made in reply to the violent and personal speech which you thought fit to make ... You appear entirely to forget that after ten years association with the Board you bring before the public direct accusations against your former colleagues. You do not even consult them ... You will I am sure give me credit for feeling grieved that after so long an acquaintance and association the tie has been severed between us, and may I express a hope that in time you may feel a pang of regret that you treated your old Colleagues in the way you have done.'[12]

It is easy to see why the marquess was so hurt, and difficult to understand just why David Davies felt these issues had suddenly become all-important. His personal hatred of Hadley must have played a large part in bringing his anger to a head, and the whole episode is further proof that he was a man of strong passions. In the following weeks the Cambrian directors produced arguments to counter his, and somehow the trains went on running. In one respect at least, though, his arguments were accepted. Four months after he quit the board, the directors ordered an additional 1,000 tons of steel rails and asked the engineer for an estimate of the cost of relaying the whole line.[13]

David Davies never forgave the Cambrian directors, and even went to the lengths of rebooking his journeys to London at Welshpool to deprive the Cambrian of its share of LNWR bookings from there, payable under a secret agreement between the companies. 'This was his way of punishing them,' wrote Davies's grandson, Lord Davies, who was himself the chairman of the Cambrian Railways for many years. The Cambrian 'never flourished — in 1907 it was on the verge of bankruptcy, owing the bank £300,000. For years it paid no dividend on either ordinary or preference stock, and £100 worth of the former could be purchased for £1 or £2. Therefore I imagine my grandfather was right in his condemnation of the general policy pursued by the Board and his insistence upon certain reforms ... was in the long run justified by events.'[14]

19 Wanting All

They say to me 'It is all very well to say that you are on good terms with the men, but it isn't true. All these pleasant gatherings are passing away, and you will see no more of them.' Is this so? [David Davies, 16 June 1873][1]

With the dawn of the 1880s, David Davies remembered his words at Edward's coming-of-age with increasing bitterness. The 'pleasant gatherings' had indeed become a thing of the past. He was at war with his men over the sliding scale, and he bitterly resented what he saw as their ingratitude. By leaving the owners' association and devising his own more generous scale, he had confidently hoped for more settled times, and he lost patience when, after reaffirming their faith in the Ocean sliding scale in 1880, the men demanded its revision only two years later. In an intemperate letter to his son Edward, he wrote:

The men and the scale is what I expected   we made a just scale as between man and man but knowing as we should have done our men it is a very foolish scale and cannot work . . .[2]

There is not much evidence here of Davies the working man, the rich man in a navvy's shirt. It is a coal boss defending his interests − a boss, moreover, who feels thoroughly disenchanted. Where now the comradeship in labour of those railway-making days, the sense of being at one with the men on his payroll? 'You can put me for the master if you like, or for a labourer,' he had said at Edward's coming-of-age. 'I do not call myself capital. I do not like to be called capital.'[3] The cruel logic of the coalfield had deemed otherwise. He was inexorably capital, and the conflict of interest between master and men had divided them as the Severn's banks were divided by its waters.

The fairness of the sliding scale depended on the amount fixed as the standard selling price, for it was the deviations above and below this that settled the miners' pay. Under the Ocean scale the standard was fixed at 10s. a ton, so when the price fell below this, wages were reduced. Conversely, wages rose when the price of coal went up. In March 1882 the Ocean colliers decided at a mass meeting to ask for a lowering of the standard from 10s. to 9s., which meant of course a pay rise under another name. They got nowhere, general manager William Jenkins informing a deputation point-blank that this was unacceptable.[4] Two days later, on 15 March, a furious David Davies wrote that letter to Edward from the House of Commons saying the Ocean scale was 'a very foolish scale':

and it will now cost us five times as much to put it right as it
would have done in 1879 when it was made   we then put ourselves in the wrong on two vital points first and worst to take our
own price as a rule for the scale then make our advance from the
100 Instead of from 85 (this at the Standard gives them 2¼ per
cent above our Neighbours) . . . it is easy to be wise after the
Event but I had as you know my doubts about the whole thing
then your answer was that we certainly should have a strike
   what would a strike cost at the End of 1879 as compared with
now when they can get work Elsewhere and when our competitors
will be delighted to assist them to fights [*sic*] us   in fact we
have been like Chamberlain and Bright with Ireland given them a
good Slice and now they want more than all   the Irish only
want all I will write Jenkins[5]

This curious juxtaposition of the sliding scale and the Irish gives us an
intriguing glimpse into Davies's mind at the time. Before we look closer
at his views on Ireland, however, we must note that the men believed
they had a good case. At a mass meeting on 29 March — made possible
by the decision of general manager William Jenkins to close all the
Ocean collieries for the day expressly to allow them to attend — an
Ogmore delegate said that for the past seven years the sliding scales
operating in the coalfield had 'only been serving to reduce wages.'
Noting that the sliding scale principle had come from the North of
England, he proposed sending it back there — 'or if the North of England
folk won't have it, let it be despatched to the Orkney Islands!' The
chairman, Lewis Meredith — who worked at Eastern Colliery — tried to
smooth things over by saying that their object was to 'bring things to a
close with the best feeling. If Mr Jenkins can show we are wrong, then
we ought to submit.' This gave William Jenkins, who was at the meeting,
his cue to read out a prepared statement notably short on concessions.
Quoting 'one of our company' — undoubtedly David Davies — he said
their proposal

would mean the handing of the collieries over to them absolutely,
if not something more . . . If the men would rather be without the
scale, we will follow the current rate of wages in the district.
Under our scale our men are leading the advance. We are quite
content, instead, to follow the lead of the collieries generally. It is
quite clear we had better stop the works altogether and sell off our
plant and machinery, than attempt to carry them on with the
standard at 9s., because no matter what the price of coal with
wages at that basis, we must be the losers — out of pocket by every
ton of coal raised.[6]

This failed to pacify a Cwmdare miner, Henry Thomas, who said they were being paid starvation wages and ringingly declared, 'The three sliding scales are nothing but a blank for the workmen — they are all for the masters. Every honest man looks to his master to give him what is fair.'[7] Next day the Tory *Western Mail*, no friend either of the miners or of David Davies, sneered that by separating themselves from their 'brother owners' and giving their men an 'exceptionally liberal rate', the Ocean collieries had imagined they were doing 'a very clever thing, and securing the goodwill, if not the gratitude, of their employees.'

> What has been the result? They have been the very first firm of colliery owners to be attacked. And their workmen know that at the present moment they have got them in a cleft stick — that, powerful as the Ocean company is, it will, in the long run, be compelled to accept one of two alternatives, either to submit to the most rigorous terms employed by the workmen, or to abandon the ostentatious position of isolation adopted in 1880. The company must, in fact, either knuckle under to their workmen or retrace their steps and make common cause again with the Associated Masters ... experience has shown that no firm of coalowners single-handed can successfully contend against a well-directed strike of its work people.[8]

In the event, the Ocean company neither knuckled under nor rushed to rejoin the masters' association. After giving six months' notice of their intention to end the sliding scale agreement, the men eventually decided to stick by it after all, the Liberal *South Wales Daily News* recording with satisfaction that

> the individual rancour which of old made bitter and revolutionary a dispute of this kind was, at the Ocean, conspicuous by its absence. The men fought for a principle and not against a person ...[9]

They fought with a sense of rightness in their cause, and capitulated only after a last appeal to the Ocean management for a change of heart. William Jenkins, however, would not budge, refusing to lower the standard even to 9s. 6d.[10] He could do little else, with his chief in such a sour mood with his workmen.

The Irish continued to 'want all', in the opinion of the master of the Ocean collieries. 'Home Rule for Ireland!' was the cry, and Gladstone — Premier for the second time after the Liberal landslide of 1880 — lent it a sympathetic ear. He believed the return of sixty-three MPs fighting under the Home Rule banner meant the Irish had unmistakably declared in favour of self-government, and he was prepared to let them have it.

His Home Rule Bill, however, led to a devastating split in his party and the fall of his government.

David Davies, who appears never to have contemplated seriously the possibility of home rule for Wales, had little sympathy with this cause. He was prepared eventually to support a 'moderate measure' of Irish home rule,[11] but only reluctantly. He was as fervent a believer in Empire as any Tory, and was proud of the contribution Wales made to the 'greatness' of England. This did not mean, however, that he was unsympathetic to the Irish claims of injustice. He believed there were wrongs in Ireland that should be redressed, but as a constitutionalist he was against illegal acts and became increasingly impatient with Gladstone for what he saw as his haste to bend over backwards to conciliate the nationalists.

Curiously, one of Davies's first pronouncements on Ireland in the Commons had contained the remarkable suggestion that in some circumstances he might himself have been a Fenian. This was in 1876, during a debate on the borough franchise. After noting that an objection had been made to the Irish members bringing forward questions of home rule, he said they ought not to give them reasons for doing so. 'It was complained that the Irish were Fenians; but he was not sure if he were treated as they were that he would not be a Fenian himself. Therefore when the Irish brought a fair case before the House, it ought to be fairly considered.'[12] In the context of later events, this can be seen as pure hyperbole. The previous year, Davies had spoken of the Irish in friendly but patronizing terms in a debate on the Science and Art Department in Dublin.

> The Irish people he had in his employ always seemed to him to be suitable for something better than they were doing. They were very witty, ready and faithful, and he felt that if they had a little more assistance to enable them to study art and science they would become a very happy and useful people. It always seemed to him that Ireland was like a child which they were responsible for, and ought to educate in every possible way.

He added that a good many of the Irish in his employ could neither read nor write, 'but the best workman he ever had was an Irishman, who on one occasion had broken down a strike, and ever since he had had a great respect for the Irish people.'[13] The naïveté of the expression must have made some fellow-Liberals squirm.

He was on safer ground in 1878, when supporting the motion that 'laws under which destitute poor were subject to removal in England and Scotland inflicted many wrongs and cause great suffering' — the word 'England' again embracing Wales. Davies argued strongly against the sending of any poor Irish back to Ireland against their will, employing impeccably Liberal arguments which curiously anticipated those which would be heard in a different context a century later.

He could remember many occasions on which he had employed Irishmen to go to Ireland to seek labour. These Irishmen did not come to this country of their own accord, but on pressure when their labour was required ... England had had that labour, and what was any country without labour? ... It certainly would be most cruel that, having had it, England should send them back to Ireland when they became incapacitated. In his opinion it would be very unjust, and a reflection on a civilised nation, that they compel poor Irish men and women to go back to Ireland against their will when unable to keep themselves.[14]

An earlier speaker had disapprovingly observed that there were 76,000 Irish on parish relief in mainland Britain, a statistic which did not impress David Davies. This only showed the vast number of Irish people here, he countered. They had 'formed the wealth of this great country ... Wealth was only an accumulation of labour.'[15]

He became increasingly irritated, however, with the behaviour of the Parnellite MPs, who systematically obstructed the business of the House, as the administration of Disraeli – now aggrandized to Earl of Beaconsfield – drew to a close. When Frank O'Donnell of Dungarven claimed that the Royal Irish Constabulary had 'used their bayonets against women and children,' and 'struck them with the butt end of their rifles,' Davies reprimanded him. He did not believe the police would be guilty of such violence, but 'if there was much excitement ... the poor people might rush against the bayonet and so get hurt' – a remark which surprisingly escaped immediate mockery.

He took the opportunity to add – with more than a hint of paternalism – that he found the Irish 'a very good class of men, provided that care was taken not to excite them. They generally kept together, and sometimes some among them might say very strong things, and then there was a row.'[16] As he blandly made such statements, he was not to know that Ireland would be the cross on which his political life would be crucified.

The general election of April 1880 saw David Davies returned unopposed for the constituency he had represented for six years. In his bilingual election address he espoused the causes of 'Religious Freedom, Peace and Justice, and sound and useful Reform', and spoke of the 'honest and friendly services' he had rendered the county.[17] He took his place in a Commons in which there were 352 Liberal MPs, 237 Conservatives and 63 Home Rulers. A sign of the times was the great fuss over whether the atheist Charles Bradlaugh, who had been returned for Northampton, should be allowed to sit in the House after refusing to take the oath.[18]

Wales had declared for radicalism more emphatically than ever, returning twenty-nine Liberal MPs and only four Tories. One of the newcomers was Stuart Rendel, who had succeeding in breaking the eighty-year Wynnstay stranglehold in Montgomery to become the Liberal MP for the county.[19] Rendel, an Englishman with an educational background of Eton and Oriel College, Oxford, had considered farming as a career but on being rebuked by his mother for this 'objectionable' plan, had taken up arms manufacturing,[20] a career regarded in the family as thoroughly satisfactory.

David Davies at first enthusiastically welcomed Rendel's appearance in the county, but in time an antipathy developed between the two men. They were of different temperaments, Rendel's cool self-possession contrasting with Davies's volatility. There is little doubt, too, that Rendel considered himself both the intellectual and the social superior of Davies, the avowedly 'self-made man'. His Liberalism was more consistent and conventional than Davies's; over Ireland he supported Gladstone wholeheartedly, and despised what he saw as Davies's shameless self-interest in refusing to support reforms that might have affected his interests as a landowner and industrialist.

'We travelled to Abermule with D. Davies and his son' that later grandee of the Liberal Party in Montgomeryshire, A.C. Humphreys-Owen, wrote to Rendel in October 1879. 'D.D. was emphatic about your speech. "It was the speech of a gentleman," and he predicted your success in the House.'[21] Rendel was, however, already suspicious of Davies. 'D.D. is *very* shrewd,' he wrote back to Humphreys-Owen the very next day. 'I noticed his regard of me to be just a little altered. In his speech too I became "my friend" instead of as before "our friend." It is better that I should stand over him than he over me … The self esteem of the selfmade man is beyond gauging.'[22] Nine months later, he was lamenting 'the apparent want of public spirit in Liberal members whose private interests appear affected by great measures,'[23] and there is no doubt that he classed Davies among these.

Between 1880 and 1886, David Davies was to come increasingly under fire for his ambiguous Liberalism. He claimed himself to be in favour of 'useful' reforms, but exactly which reforms did he find useful? Those which did not hit him in the pocket, cynics said. Even without the Irish issue, he would have found himself at loggerheads with the new generation of Liberals symbolized by T.E. (Tom) Ellis of Cymru Fydd,[24] who categorized him as one who 'has been buying landed estates and sinking deeper into Whiggism after each transaction.'[25] Doubts about him were also growing in the constituency, where it was felt that his attitude to land reform was, to say the least, questionable.

His last speech in the Disraeli Parliament of 1874–80 was an ominous hint of things to come, for he then opposed a motion that because of the dangers incurred by 'railway servants' they should be paid 'adequate compensation in all cases of injury to which they had not personally contributed.' He said his sympathies were with railway servants – he 'owed his position, to a great extent, to railwaymen' – but they might be the losers from legislation of this kind.

> It was well known some Railway Companies were very liberal; but if companies had to pay compensation when they were found to be at fault, there would be so much litigation and expense that the Companies would not, in other cases, give so much voluntarily as they did at present.[26]

The fact is, however, that the number of railway accidents was startlingly high – in 1875 alone, 765 railwaymen were killed and 3,618 injured – and the excessive hours worked on the railways were a national scandal. Engine drivers on the Rhymney line in south Wales were working up to eighteen hours a day, and goods guards on the Taff Vale Railway sometimes had to endure twenty hours on duty at a stretch.[27] In spite of this evidence, David Davies defended the Taff Vale – 'one of the best-worked lines in the country' – and blandly declared that 'as a rule the men did not work more than ten or twelve hours at a stretch.'[28]

His social position as one of the landed gentry of Montgomeryshire left him wide open to gibes such as Tom Ellis's, and he did nothing to allay the doubts about his radicalism by his attitude to land reform measures. In May 1881 an Irish member, Rowland Blennerhassett of Kerry, proposed that tenants of agricultural holdings in England, Wales and Ireland should no longer be subject to the law of distress when they fell behind with their rent. He complained that the very day after the rent fell due, the landlord was allowed to send any 'dissolute ruffian out of the streets to run riot on the tenant's premises,' and that the amount of goods taken was often 'out of proportion to the debt incurred.' The landlord, in his view, should be put on the same footing as other creditors.[29]

Davies argued rather obscurely that the law of distress was a protection for small farmers,[30] and expanded his views when the proposal came again before Parliament the following year.

> When he took a farm in 1848 the rent was £214, the land was in a bad condition and he was ashamed to tell the House that he had not enough money to stock it properly. And had it not been for this old friend they were now prepared to abolish [the law of

distress] he would not have had the farm. His landlord knew him, but would not have trusted him were it not for that protection.[31]

This comfortable view of landlords would have come better from one who was not a landlord himself, and in time such sentiments would be ammunition in the hands of his enemies.

20 A Funny Dog

Needy members! clear your thoughts; study speeches, discount votes.
Lawyers hasten! here are fees! Navvies! here are bread and cheese.
    Bare the quarry,
    Rend the rock.
    Delve and hurry,
    Barry Dock.

George Fardo did not write the greatest of poetry, but he captured a
mood, and his verses on *The Building of Barry Dock*, published in his
Poetical and Humorous Works in 1903, remind us of the enthusiasm
aroused by one of David Davies's greatest achievements — the creation
of the port of Barry.

To appreciate the scale and splendour of this, we must remember that
when he embarked on the enterprise he was an old man by Victorian
standards, well into the seventh decade of his extraordinarily busy life —
a man, moreover, who was beginning to feel his age. His determination
to see the project succeed shows that however questionable his
judgement was becoming politically, he still had the imagination to
fashion great ventures in his mind and the courage to carry them
through. 'In the Barry dock scheme,' wrote John Gibson, 'his confidence
was not the confidence of hope, but the certainty of vision.'[1]

The Barry Docks project was conceived out of anger and frustration.
The Rhondda coalowners were desperate for more dock accommodation
for their exports and the third Marquess of Bute, owner of Cardiff docks,
was reluctant to provide it. A languid young aristocrat whose
Catholicism fed his absorption in medievalism, such passion as he
possessed was going into the restoration of Cardiff Castle in highly
romantic style in collaboration with the architect William Burges, and
he regarded business as a frightful bore. His indifference was such that
having obtained permission for building Roath Dock in 1874 he did
nothing at all about it,[2] while the coalowners fumed and fretted and the
coal wagons queued up for miles on the Taff Vale line between Cardiff
and Pontypridd.

The coalowners, however, did not rush into the Barry project, and for
a long time they clung to hopes of persuading the marquess to enlarge
his docks. There was also talk of transferring ownership of the docks to
a harbour trust,[3] an idea to which he seemed at first amenable. The
gates of the castle, however, were closed to commonsense, and behind

them he dreamily wove his fantasies, deaf to the clamorous and dirty world that had been the making of his fortune.

A complication was his decision to put William Thomas Lewis in charge of his docks in 1881. As a coalowner himself Lewis understood the need for expansion, but he pandered to Bute's greed by going along with a scheme to levy higher charges at the new Roath Dock.[4] David Davies was scandalized by this, and Lewis's betrayal of the interests of his fellow colliery proprietors played an appreciable part in ensuring that the dream of Barry became reality. The first Lord Davies even went so far as to say that had it not been for Lewis's opposition, the Barry scheme would probably never have materialized: 'He was the irritant.' According to Lord Davies, Lewis — who was knighted in 1885, made a baronet in 1896 and raised to the peerage as Baron Merthyr of Senghenydd in 1911 — was 'a domineering old devil, who treated my grandfather with scant courtesy, ridiculing his projects, and by his obstinate opposition and refusal to entertain any compromise goaded my grandfather on in his efforts to secure a new dock.'[5]

Other projects were considered before Davies and his associates fixed on Barry — then an unimportant parish with a tiny population — as the site of a new port. Davies had first turned his attention to Newport, putting forward a plan in the 1870s which would have made it a second Liverpool. Serious thought was also given to the construction of docks at the mouth of the River Ogmore before the die was finally cast in favour of Barry.[6] Once the location was decided, however, the scene was set for a battle royal between the Bute interests on the one hand and the Barry promoters on the other.

This epic legal contest fattened the purses of lawyers and provided marvellous copy for reporters. It took up weeks of Parliamentary time and the records of the proceedings run into several volumes. The names of the witnesses virtually amount to a cast-list of everyone of importance in the business life of Cardiff and Rhondda, and the evidence painstakingly transcribed by the shorthand writers contains marvellous cameos and unexpected humour. The leading role in this real-life drama was played by the man whose pre-eminence was acknowledged by the siting of his statue outside the Docks Office in Barry — David Davies the Ocean.

The best description of him as a witness comes, ironically, from a hostile force — the *Western Mail*, which was so much a mouthpiece of Lord Bute that the paper had at one time felt compelled to deny that he was its proprietor.[7]

> This, the eighth day of the enquiry, has seen the case for the promoters advocated with his customary volubility by Mr 'Ocean' Davies, MP, who led Mr Matthews, the examining counsel, a

A postcard of Barry Docks in the early twentieth century.

pretty race, and gave him all his work to prevent him — to use his own favourite simile — from 'running off the line.' Mr Davies' notion of giving evidence has certainly the merit of originality. He does not understand answering questions with a laconic 'Yes' or 'No,' or explaining an opinion in a crisp sentence, but he dashes off like an express locomotive with a succession of tremendous speeches. Thus it was that his examination-in-chief was a long business, the facts being extracted under circumstances of unusual difficulty to all concerned. Mr Davies' admirers profess to regard him as a kind of vessel, crammed to the brim with racy humour, which bubbles over at short intervals, but the impartial observer must have found it difficult to trace this supposed attribute in anything that the member for Cardigan condescended to say today. Like a good many reputations, that of Mr Davies, as a 'funny dog,' is to be taken on trust, and on that flimsy foundation it may perhaps be allowed to rest.[8]

These sour reflections came during the first of the Parliamentary hearings, the proceedings of the Select Committee on the Barry Dock and Railways Bill having opened on 10 April 1883. One of the two QCs leading the Barry promoters' legal team, Henry Matthews, claimed that 'all the great landowners whose land will be affected' supported the scheme, the foremost of these being Lord Windsor and Lord Romilly, 'whose land will be taken for the construction of the dock itself and the dock approaches.' Moreover, 'almost all the colliery proprietors in the Rhondda Valley are supporters and those shipowners who now use Cardiff and Penarth.'

The Taff Vale Railway Company and Lord Bute's trustees are our chief opponents ... though of course we are competing with the Bute Docks, and want a competitor to the Bute Docks in the interests of the trade, yet in reality this South Wales trade is a trade of such gigantic growth that there will be enough of it for the Bute Docks, the Newport Docks, the Swansea Docks, the Barry Docks, and every one of these docks will require enlargement almost before they are made ... Our belief is that the trade will always outstrip the docks in an enormous proportion; and what we submit to the Committee is a question of public policy. It is this, that it is the docks that ought to wait upon the trade, and not the trade upon the docks. We say that the dock accommodation ought to be in advance of the trade, instead of always being behind it.[9]

Witness after witness testified to the mineral wealth of the Rhondda and its neigbouring valleys, and the difficulties caused by the congestion at Cardiff and Penarth. There had been no fewer than thirty-seven collisions in the roadstead between 1878 and 1882, causing the sinking of five vessels.[10] A businessman spoke of the time it took to get a vessel to a tip for the loading of coal, because so many other ships had to move out of the way. Registered tonnage per acre in Cardiff was nearly three times that of Liverpool.

Times were changing, and new inventions were altering fundamental concepts. 'You say you think the position of Barry is a favourable one. Is not the distance of the port from the coalfield a very important consideration?' Mr Bompas QC, for the Rhymney Railway Company – a Bute ally – craftily asked. 'Not at all,' replied the splendidly-named Willoughby Legay Hawkins, of Cardiff Chamber of Commerce. 'In these days of telephonic communication I think eight miles a very little, either here or there.'

David Davies MP was sworn as a witness on Thursday 19 April. 'We know you are Member for Cardigan, and you are also largely interested in the Ocean Collieries?' Matthews put it to him expansively.

'I am,' replied Davies, 'and I am also a tenant of the noble lord, the Marquess of Bute, and I am very sorry to appear to be in opposition here to the Marquess of Bute. My feeling is entirely with the Marquess of Bute. I am obliged to be here because I feel that things have not been done in accordance with the interests of the Marquess of Bute, nor in accordance with the interest of the large colliery proprietors.'

Unhappily, we do not know how William Thomas Lewis, sitting in the committee room with a Primrose Day flower in his buttonhole,[11] reacted to this shaft of criticism.

The record of David Davies's evidence – those *Western Mail* strictures notwithstanding – makes lively reading. He said the Ocean Collieries had between 5,000 and 6,000 acres of mineral property, 'and I may also mention that the company is a young company. It has only commenced 15 years ago, and the quantity that we now raise is 1,200,000 tons of steam coal. In fact, we are much the largest of any in South Wales. We have about 4,000 workmen and a very large population there.'

The delays on the Taff Vale line meant they could no longer do the work in a practical manner. 'Our wagons used to make three journeys a week to and from Cardiff. Last year it was 2½. Now the average is 1½.' The line was so clogged that engine drivers were stuck in queues for hours – 'that ridiculous business of the men having to stand on the engines all night,' Davies called it. The drivers and brakesmen were claiming £15,000 a year overtime because the railway was so overburdened.

When he maintained that Cardiff was at present 'the only practical outlet' for Rhondda coal, he was reminded of a scheme to take a line to Swansea from the top of the valley at Treherbert.

'What is the name of that line, the Swansea Bay, I think?' he was asked.

'I think it is,' he dismissively replied. 'I do not know the name, I never took the trouble of ascertaining it, it is of no use'.

'That is the sort of suggestion that has been made on the other side as an alternative to the Taff?' — 'We have been greenhorns so long that they thought we would swallow anything; that is the truth ... I may mention this to the Committee, that I am the proprietor of the one-half of this immense Ocean Colliery, I and my family and two managers and a few friends own the whole.'

'You necessarily, therefore, have a very large personal and pecuniary interest at stake, and you are bound to consider the best means of serving the district?' — 'In fact it is a matter of life and death to us. If we do not get some relief in some direction, we cannot carry our works on, possibly.'

He and other members of his company had undertaken to subscribe £100,000 towards the line, 'but if £200,000 or £300,000 more is required we are prepared to find it, rather than have any difficulty about it.' Unsolicited subscriptions totalled £616,040. 'We could get the money all in one day; there is no difficulty about the money'.

There was a hint of the ill-health that was to dog him henceforth when he was asked if the new line that would carry the coal to Barry had been effectively planned. 'The engineers will be paid for doing this [i.e. submitting evidence] and I am not very well, or I could do it as well as the engineers; but I don't see why I should,' he replied. 'No doubt it is well laid out, because I laid it out myself.'

He was not so unwell, however, as to resist the temptation to be discursive on this very point. He had gone 'all the way up from Hafod ... with the engineer and solicitor to lay the line out in the best possible way to accommodate the different pits.'

> The different colliery proprietors had more faith in me, for some
> reason or other, than they had in the engineer and solicitor, and I
> remember going to Moses Rowlands' place there, and I was very
> hungry; we wanted to go on to Mr Hood's place for our lunch,[12]
> but Mr Moses Rowlands wanted to show me where he could sink a
> new pit; and he could speak Welsh better than English, so I had
> to explain it to him in Welsh and then repeat it in English to the
> solicitor and engineer, to lay it on the map; by the time I had
> done so he altered his mind again, and I had to explain it over
> again to him and put in some additions.

So it went on, a virtuoso display of reasoned argument spiced with garrulous irrelevance and vivid metaphor. They were 'asking for the crumbs that fall from the Taff Vale Company's table; simply for what they cannot carry.' The coal was 'huddled together all in a heap' in

Cardiff because of the failure to build the new dock sanctioned in 1874. They had enough steam coal in the Ocean collieries in Rhondda to raise a million tons for 300 years.

'How much of that is best coal?' Bompas asked.

'I have not measured it,' replied Davies. 'It will always be the best, because when the best is gone the second best will be the best there, and those who are alive will get a better price for their best than we get for ours.'

'You have made no calculation about when the best coal will come to an end?' Bompas persisted.

'No, because you and I will be gone to a better place than this, I hope, long before then.'

The select committee approved the Bill after a 24-day hearing during which 17,000 questions were asked,[13] but the winning of the first battle did not constitute victory in the war. The Lords had to be convinced as well, and the hearing there began on 5 July. It was remarkable chiefly for the bizarre evidence of Crawshay Bailey, son of the man from whom David Davies had obtained his lease in the Rhondda in 1864.[14] He was speaking in favour of Barry, but turned out to be the kind of ally who gives aid and comfort to the enemy. First he claimed that the output in his collieries had gone up from 932,000 tons to 1,900,00 tons in a year, then agreed that the increase had in fact not been a million tons but merely 77,000 − the figure in question was not 1,900,000 but 1,000,900. 'Excuse me,' he said, 'it was a little mistake.' It was certainly little in comparison with his next blunder, which was to confuse the Rhondda Fach − which he thought meant 'the big Rhondda' − with the Rhondda Fawr.

'Do you reside there?' asked an amazed Mr Bidder QC, cross-examining him.

'No, I do not.'
'Do you often go there?'
'No, very seldom.'
'How often, once a year?'
'Not once a year.'
'When were you there last?'
'At the opening of the new church.'

All his colliery business, he explained later, was done upon his private estate in Monmouthshire.

No doubt there were other considerations in their lordships' minds than the evidence of Crawshay Bailey when they threw out the Bill on 26 July. Disappointing though this was, it did not crush the spirits of the promoters. David Davies went home to Llandinam to attend the funeral of an old chapel deacon who had lived all his life on the mountains three miles from the village,[15] and was in Cardiff a week later for the meeting which would decide whether the fight should go on. On 10 August he wrote to his son Edward jauntily informing him that

> the meeting were [sic] unanimous and very Enthusiastic [for] going on with Barry Except our Riche [J.Osborne Riches, Ocean commercial manager] he was like usual queer no one knew what he meant . . . we propose changing the Site of the Dock altogether leaving the old channel open at both Ends . . . bringing the Dock a mile nearer Cardiff . . . Forrest is gone to see Lord Windsor to try to arrange the land.[16]

A new Bill was prepared, and the hearing began on 30 April 1884. After thirty-three days the preamble of the Bill was passed and the issue again went before the Lords. Once more the old arguments were trundled out, for and against. It was all becoming very tiresome. The chief interest in this last round of evidence is in the appearance of a small Rhondda coalowner as a hostile witness. He was Alfred Tylor, after whom Tylorstown was named. He had opened Tylor's Colliery in 1872, and differed drastically from David Davies in his estimate of the amount of coal in the Rhondda. In his opinion, they would have exhausted all the best coal in the valley within forty-two years — a remarkably precise figure. He also believed that they would have all the dock accommodation they required when the Roath Dock opened and new docks were provided at Penarth.

When it was suggested that he was in a tiny minority of Rhondda coalowners in opposing the scheme, he launched into a violent assault on 'great capitalists like Mr David Davies, who are so very prosperous.'

> 'They have had all the plums, and the people at the north end [of the Rhondda] have had all the discomfort and the loss. I can inform the Committee of this — I truly believe that if you excepted the promoters, the average profits of the people to the north and middle have not been more than 5 per cent for their money with all their risks. That is why I come here, really. I know I am in a prosperous district now, but having suffered before, I do entreat that the Committee will not consider only these very rich people, and give them this great concession, which would be worth no end of money to them, but really injure us dreadfully . . .'
>
> The Chairman [the Marquess of Waterford]: 'How would it make a difference . . . whether this railway was granted or not?' — 'The whole of the trade will be put into the hands of two or three people. If you were kind enough to give them the Bill you would give them an engine by which they could work the Bute Docks

and the Taff Vale Railway, and we should not be able to get our coal shipped for anything. It will be a great monopoly if they get it.'

'Then you say that the whole object of the promoters is merely to get hold of the Bute Docks?' — 'No, it is to make an immense mass of money, that is what it is. They have made so much now. It is what our ancestors used to say — nobody used to like to feed their lean cattle, it was always the fat cattle they wanted to feed, and it is the opposite to Pharaoh's dream. It is the thin ears of corn being eaten up by the full ears, or it will be if you give them this Bill.'[17]

His fears of a monopoly were never realized, but they remind us of the suspicion that existed not only between employer and employed but between the 'large' and 'small' capitalists in the coal-rich valleys.

This time the Lords approved the Bill, and the sanctioning of Barry was greeted as 'the greatest event which has happened in Wales for half a century.'[18] There was intense excitement in Cardiff, and the *South Wales Daily News* saw this as an opportunity for the town to throw off the 'incubus' of Bute and become 'an independent borough.'[19] The contract for building the docks and the southern part of the railway was awarded to Thomas Walker, who was already engaged on another gigantic task — the construction of the Severn Tunnel. At the first meeting of the directors of the new company on 4 September Lord Windsor, who owned Barry Island, was elected chairman and David Davies vice-chairman.[20]

The ceremony of cutting the first sod took place on 14 November at Castleland Point, near the site of the present Dock Offices. David Davies was in his element, spitting on his hands before digging a load of turf 'in true workmanlike manner' and loading the wheelbarrow — a real navvy's barrow, it was noted, not a decorative one. One of the promoters, Richard Cory, said Davies had been the backbone of the whole affair: 'If the Lords had cast the bill out a third time he would have been game enough to go on with it again, and even a fifth time.' And Davies himself said: 'We have had to fight great giants with unlimited money and power — the Marquess of Bute and the Taff Vale Railway Company. Today we have begun a great work.'[21]

The transformation of Barry had begun.

21 Votiwch Dros David Davies!

In retrospect, we can see the triumph of 1884 as the final summit in the life of David Davies before the descent into anti-climax. Within two years, the hero of Barry would suffer humiliation at the polls and find himself spurned as one of yesterday's men. Ironically, some of the cruellest blows of all during the 1886 election campaign came from a section of society which owed him an irreparable debt — the students of Aberystwyth.

Davies had continued his strong support of the college during a crucial period. Its very survival was in doubt after a Government report declared in favour of one college for north Wales and one for south Wales, each institution receiving a £4,000 annual grant. Aberystwyth would qualify as the north Wales college, or not at all. The trouble is that north Wales did not want Aberystwyth, its representatives making this perfectly clear at a conference in Chester on 23 January 1883. Here they decided that the college must be sited in one of the north Wales counties, which were listed — in the spelling of the time — as Anglesey, Caernarvonshire, Denbighshire, Flintshire, Merionethshire and Montgomeryshire. An incensed David Davies, one of a number of MPs at the meeting, wanted to know — 'as a North Welshman' — what Cardiganshire had done to be excluded. It had contributed £8,611 alone towards the college in Aberystwyth since 1863, compared with £8,692 from all six north Wales counties put together.[1]

Davies's anger was increased by the fact that the chairman of the departmental committee which drew up the report was the president of the college, Lord Aberdare. He felt the president had betrayed them, and said so when responding to the toast of 'The University College of Wales' at a dinner in Aberystwyth later that year. He even suggested that the report had been drawn up 'purposely to take the college away from Aberystwyth.'

> It was a shame, an abominable shame, for the president of the college to do such a thing, one to whom the college was entrusted, who should have nursed and looked after it. He could hear the cheers of the young students now ringing in his ears when they celebrated the appointment of president, thinking that they had got a learned man, and now see what they had got. It was an abominable shame the way the trust had been carried out. Now the college had done such good work, and when the number of students was increasing, it was a great shame, in fact it was a great

cruelty in removing the college. Indeed, it was like taking the bread out of another man's mouth, for if it had not been for what Aberystwyth had done, Wales would not have had the Government grant towards higher education.[2]

Principal Edwards feared the college would 'languish and die slowly',[3] but as E.L. Ellis explains in his history of the UCW, an extraordinary eleventh-hour battle was fought to save it from extinction. It was the townspeople who led the fight, with the doughty campaigning editor of the *Cambrian News*, John Gibson, prominent among them.[4] There were meetings of support throughout Wales, and Stuart Rendel became the chief Parliamentary voice for Aberystwyth. In March 1884 the battle was won, the Government offering a grant of £2,000 a year, although by this time Bangor had been chosen as the site of a north Wales college. Characteristically, David Davies immediately said he would hold to his promise of £500 a year if the Government gave £2,500.[5]

This failed to impress Lord Aberdare, who according to Rendel was saying openly at this time that 'DD has wanted to get the credit of being generous without putting his hands in his pocket' – an outrageous accusation made out of pique. He further – and, perhaps, more justifiably – charged him with inconsistency, saying that he had spoken 'most strongly at one time against Abth [*sic*] as a complete failure.'[6]

Rendel would eventually become the acknowledged leader of Welsh Liberals,[7] but at this time he was still feeling his way. He took a poor view of David Davies's Liberalism, but was careful not to offend him openly. 'Wales returns a compact body of Liberal members but with singularly small results,' he confided in a letter written in October 1884. 'We are in desperate want of a voice in the Cabinet and a powerful leader.' He even doubted whether Nonconformists would remain solidly Liberal after their grievances were redressed. 'Wales is very open to bribery and the Tories are adept at political bribery.'[8]

Rendel must have listened with disbelief to some of David Davies's speeches in the 1880–85 Parliament. One was on the proposal to pay candidates their election expenses, a Liberal measure. It was argued that this would mean the return of more working men, but Davies – who all his life had been so proud of being one himself – rose to oppose it 'body and soul.'

The ratepayers had enough to pay, and did not want to be further burdened. There were plenty of candidates willing to pay their own expenses, and they were a better class of candidates than those who would go upon the rates. [If the Bill became law] There would be a contest at every General Election in every constituency ... He should therefore stand on his guns, although he voted against the Government.[9]

In fairness to Davies, it must be said that there is no knowing what his attitude might have been had it been proposed to pay the expenses out of central funds rather than local rates. There are few excuses to be found, however, for a blimpish speech on the Navy Estimates which show the devout chapel-goer eager for war simply to test the strength of British battleships.

> In the old time their Navy was built of old English or Welsh oak; and if a bullet went through it, the hole could be easily caulked up again; while the timber of foreign nations tore up and went into splinters. But now all nations were similarly provided. There was a sort of sameness in the ironclad everywhere ... There was this difference also. In the old time, if they were turned out of the sea altogether, they could live at home; but now they were dependent on foreigners for their very bread. If that supply were stopped they would be done for — they would starve ... He would not mind a bit of a brush with one of those foreign nations, just to gain a little experience; they did not really know what they could do. (Laughter) That was no laughing matter at all. They might, at the moment, have a brush between their ironclads and those of a foreign nation. It would be a very serious matter if four or five of their ironclads were sunk. Where would be the rest of their Navy then?[10]

Half a century later, Lord Davies found this speech hard to reconcile with a boyhood memory of his grandfather. He recalled 'arousing his wrath' by telling him he intended to become a soldier. 'He told me that he would cut me off without a penny, and that soldiers were the scum of the earth.'[11] It is hard to resist the conclusion that the Squire of Broneirion now drew a sharp distinction between what was good for his own family and what was good for other people's.

He was certainly forgetting the sins of his youth — those happy days in the woods and fields around the village when he was as crafty a poacher as any. As a landowner he took a different view, and when he found that the grandson of one of his old workmen was setting rabbit traps on his land he angrily declared, 'Thee must send that boy o'thine away, send him to the South as he is poaching here.'

'No,' was the stout reply, 'I wonna send my boy away, thee wast once a great poacher thyself and besides, I think as much of my boy as thee dost of thine!'

David Davies was big enough to take the point, and close the matter with a laugh.[12]

The poacher turned squire spent all the time he could in Llandinam. He was as rooted in its soil as any Montgomeryshire oak, stepping into the clean morning air with his gun dog at his heels with the look of a man who had known no other life but this. He took to the ownership of large estates as if he had come from generations of gentry, and was proud to be considered a good landlord, improving the land and treating his tenants fairly. The village owed much to him, and the wealth inherited by his descendants would provide even more benefits in future. The names of Davies and Llandinam were now inextricably intertwined.

It was as well that he had so deep a love for his native hearth, for when the lightning struck, he would find a solace in Llandinam that ensured him a quiet end.

The storm clouds gathered distantly but unmistakably. David Davies chose to ignore them, buoyed up by his confidence in himself and in his concerns. He spoke in Parliament as he had always spoken, with a directness and homeliness of expression that was like a breath of country air in a foggy London street. 'The Bill is like a locomotive when it runs off a line — no-one can say when it will stop,' he said of a measure of which he disapproved in 1882.[13] We have a picture of him restlessly moving around an uncrowded chamber from the parliamentary writer Henry W. Lucy, who had a soft spot for this unconventional and unpretentious member. For an hour 'Mr David Davies . . . had been excitedly moving about, trying various benches, as if he were prospecting for a lime rock, and leaving them one after another, as if each turned out to be mud or gravel'.[14] After eight years in the House, however, he was seriously considering whether to stand again for election. He lacked the energy of former years, and was disillusioned with his party leader — 'it does not do to lecture people these days,' he wrote to A.C. Humphreys-Owen after a Government defeat in 1882. 'Mr Gladstone I have always thought is not a good leader of his party this rebuff I hope will do him good'.[15]

The openness that had always characterized Davies's dealings worked eventually to his disadvantage in politics. He spoke his mind where the shrewder if less honest course would have been to remain silent, and his enemies rejoiced. In the nature of things, the deadlier enemies were within his own party. 'I consider Cardiganshire the most helpless County in Wales,' the Radical Henry P. Cobb wrote from Stanmore to Stuart Rendel. 'The Liberal party has been kept under by a clique of incapable Whigs'.[16]

Resentment of David Davies and the sense that he represented the Liberalism of a bygone age were fuelled by his antagonism towards agricultural reforms. He was vehement in his opposition to Jesse Colling's Bill of 1883, which proposed State aid for agricultural workers and tenant farmers wishing to own land — an idea popularized as 'three acres and a cow.' Davies railed against it as if the peasantry were poised to storm the gates of Broneirion, calling it 'simply ridiculous' and arguing the impracticality of it. What was the use of paying 5 per cent interest on money borrowed to buy land that would only yield 2½ per cent? he asked. Moreover, the men who lived on their own farms in Wales 'were not fit to be in the same parish as the tenant farmers; the owners were the worst farmers in the country.'

This brought the retort from fellow-Liberal Henry Broadhurst that the people who would benefit were 'those poor creatures who were perpetually flocking into the towns from the country, and who lived in a chronic state of poverty, and were a constant source of danger to the State.' He sardonically added that as he was no landowner he could not speak on the subject with the authority of the Hon. Member for Cardiganshire, 'but he had had some experience of small allotment holdings, and with the care and labour that were devoted to them they were made remarkably productive and successful.'[17]

Davies was unconvinced, but whatever the logic of his arguments he undoubtedly damaged himself politically by laying himself open to the charge of putting self-interest before progress.

Having twice been returned unopposed to Parliament, David Davies faced a fight in the general election of November 1885. This followed a brief period of Tory rule under Lord Salisbury, Gladstone's administration having fallen in June when a meretricious alliance of Tories and Irish nationalists brought about his defeat on a major vote of confidence.

Significant changes had taken place since 1880. The extension of the franchise in 1884 meant that there were between 5,000 and 6,000 more voters in Cardiganshire, many of the new electors being tenant farmers and farm labourers. Moreover, there was now only one MP for the entire county, the two constituencies having been merged into one under the Redistribution Act.[18]

Davies's opponent was Vaughan Davies, a Tory landowner who later turned Liberal and ended up as Lord Ystwyth, having been granted a peerage by Lloyd George. In the view of the first Lord Davies he was 'one of the greatest humbugs . . . a dreadful fellow' whose speeches could rarely be reported fully because of his 'command of unparliamentary language.'[19]

Intriguingly, there had been talk earlier in the year of David Davies being offered the Montgomeryshire seat to allow Rendel into Cardiganshire. The suggested deal was that the Tory candidate should stand down in Montgomery to allow Davies to be returned unopposed —

a clear indication that in his native county Davies was regarded as so tame a Liberal as to rank with the Tories. Speculating on Davies's reaction to this, Rendel wrote:

It is hard upon him that he should have to fight Vaughan Davies (though I don't believe the fight is genuine) for himself and help to fight Wynne for me and after all sit for a county where he is rather bullied instead of for one where he lives and would be at peace. I should like to know his mind on the matter. He is very straight but he is shrewd and has a clear view of his own interests and no abstract ideas to encumber him.[20]

We do not know if the proposal was ever put to David Davies himself, Rendel's knowledge of it coming from letters he had received from unspecified correspondents. Significantly, though, Davies reacted angrily the following year to charges that he had canvassed for Rendel's Tory opponent in Montgomery.[21] In the run-up to the 1885 election Davies was protective towards Rendel when he feared he might run foul of the Corrupt Practices Act of 1883, which had placed more effective curbs on bribery. It had come to Davies's notice that Rendel had promised a £15 subscription to a British School and he warned:

Do you not think that you are running considerable risk in doing this if you have not been in the habit of giving to this school a Judge may consider that this £15 would have some Influence on Voters   If so you would be unseated if the Tories take advantage of this as they would be most likely to do. I was asked to give a subscription to assist the people of Borth to stop the Water the Sea invading on the Place   I was told by my agent a solicitor at Aberystwyth that if I did I would certainly be liable to be unseated if I got in and advantage taken of it, your case is so near this is why I call your attention to it   it is too bad that people ask in this way just before the Election.[22]

The Land Question, on which he was so vulnerable, played a prominent part in David Davies's election address. He claimed to 'know the requirements of all the three classes interested in the land, namely the owners, the farmers and the labourers.' He would 'do justice to all without injury to any.' He also promised to support any 'fair and just' scheme for the disestablishment and disendowment of the Church.[23]

'The Tories have tried to make out that Mr David Davies is not a Radical on land questions, but he has declared in the most emphatic way that he is in favour of the most advanced Land Law Reform,' ran a *Cambrian News* leader, John Gibson still being prepared at that stage to give Davies wholehearted support.

He is in favour of giving all the ground game to tenants; he will support Mr Broadhurst's Leasehold Enfranchisement Bill ... There is, in short, no point in land law reform which Mr David Davies is not prepared to support, and it is to be hoped that the tenant farmers will not be so unwise as to vote for the Tory candidate, who is sure to oppose every Liberal reform.[24]

The farmers were, however, said to be losing faith in David Davies,[25] the old argument of Protection v. Free Trade having seduced some into joining the Tory camp. In spite of pleas that the siren voices of the Tories on this subject were no more than a 'delusion' and a 'most dangerous charm', farmers were prepared to listen even in the Liberal heartland of Tregaron. 'Protection is fully preached in this neighbourhood by the tories and a great many of the farmers of the district believe in it as the only gap out of the present depression now prevailing amongst them. Therefore Mr Davies ought to have good speakers to riddle this political scare out of the electors of liberal tendencies,' the county registration agent for the Liberals, H.C. Fryer, was warned by a supporter.[26]

The argument was heard on another front as well, the case for protection of the county's struggling lead mine industry being put by the vicar of Llanfihangel-y-Creuddyn, the Revd Benjamin Edwards, at a lively meeting in Cnwch Coch. Ships taking coal to Spain were returning with lead ore as ballast, and he appealed: 'As raw material is brought in cheaper than we can raise it, will you not protect us?'

> Davies: You cannot protect the miner without protecting everybody else ... That is against the principles of Free Trade and I cannot support it.
> Vicar: As raw material is brought in cheaper than we can raise it, will you not protect us?
> Davies: No.
> Vicar: My friends, do not vote for David Davies.
> Davies: Oh yes they will (Loud laughter and cheers.)
> Vicar: Will you go in for Disestablishment?
> Davies: Yes, and for Disendowment to get back from the Church what does not belong to it.
> Vicar: What do you mean?
> Davies: I mean that whenever such a bill is brought in by the Government I will support it.
> Vicar: Does the Church receive anything not her property?
> Davies: She receives the tithes and they belong to the people (Applause). The Church only represents one out of every five in Wales, and it is not right that the Church should have all these rates. The Church has been indolent and has lost the people, so she ought now to lose the tithes (Loud applause).

Vicar: Perhaps you want a share of the money yourself.
Davies: No I do not, but I would apply the money to better
purposes such as educating the people.
Vicar: If the Government pay men for their services they should
receive the payment.
Davies: The Government are the people, who pay tithes to you.
You do not do any work, and we want to pay you off and get rid
of you.[27]

At a public meeting in the Assembly Rooms in Aberystwyth, Davies
encountered some persistent heckling when defending his record as a
landlord.

I allege in the first place that there is no better landlord in
England and Wales than myself. The second point is that I treat
my tenants as members of my own family. (A voice: Does that
refer to the collieries, Mr Davies?) My first consideration is my
tenants' comfort. (A voice: Does that include the collieries?) I am
not a very old landlord, but I never raise the rents however cheap
the farm may be ... The next point is, I have never sent a tenant
away however badly he may farm ... The one consideration is
that they pay the rent, and this they do most regularly.[28]

In Borth, he spoke in favour of votes for women − or, as he put it, 'the
power of voting to the ladies.' There was, however, an important
qualification. 'I do not mean the wives whose husbands are working, but
widows and unmarried women.' In the issue containing this report,
Gibson noted in his *Cambrian News* that the Tories had been trying to
persuade people that Davies was more Conservative than his opponent,
but warned that the Tory candidate's Liberalism was 'a very weak
concoction indeed.'[29]

Davies was in poor health (he had been suffering from quinsy) but
responded to requests for meetings in all parts of the county. 'I do hope
that you will arrange to be at Bethania and Penuwch as these places is
[sic] very important places,' urged a Llanon shopkeeper, John Davies.
'We are here at Bethania over Seventy Voters and I do not think that
they are all in your favour.'[30] He warned Fryer that on polling day
Major Price Lewis of Tyglyn Aeron may 'try to frighten some weak voters
so I hope that one of the Officers on our Side will be Sharp enough to
keep him out of the Booth'[31] − proof that the Screw was still being
applied even in the days of the secret ballot.

Coercion was also to be found in the Tregaron area.

Mr Evan Rowlands Ystrad has told several persons (mostly poor
people) Unless they vote for Vaughan Davies they must not expect

EXCURSION TICKETS

Will be issued by the Railway Companies on
THURSDAY, the 26th instant from Merthyr by the
12 o'clock (Noon) Train. and probably also from the
Stations on the Taff Vale Line

TO ABERYSTWYTH AND BACK,

available till WEDNESDAY, DECEMBER 2nd.

VOTE FOR DAVID DAVIES,

THE WORKING MAN'S FRIEND.

TOCYNAU EXCURSION.

Ceir Tocynau Rhad gan Gwmniau y Rheilffyrdd
DDYDD IAU nesaf, y 26ain, gyda'r *Train* o Merthyr
am 12 o'r gloch haner dydd, ac hefyd, yn ol pob tebyg,
yn Stations y Taff Vale Railway

I ABERYSTWYTH AC YN OL.

Gellir dychwelyd gyda'r Tocynau hyn gan unrhyw
Drain hyd DDYDD MERCHER, RHAGFYR 2ail.

VOTIWCH DROS DAVID DAVIES,

CYFAILL Y GWEITHIWR.

R. G. BENNETT, ARGRAFFYDD, ABERYSTWYTH.

A handbill issued by Davies and his supporters during the 1885 election, when special trains were laid on from south Wales.

anything in the shape of assistance from him . . ., Also Rees
Morgans Cattle & Horse Dealer is canvassing and telling farmers
that unless they vote for V. Davies they must not expect him to
buy any more of their animals. Threats of this sort according to my
opinion is right down corruption.[32]

There were fears that David Davies may have contravened the Corrupt
Practices Act by giving a sovereign to a boy who had been hurt while
helping to draw his wagon to an election meeting,[33] and protests at the
appointment of known Tories as presiding officers. Some electors were
said to have votes in two or three different districts,[34] and the fact that
both candidates were named Davies was causing confusion. There were
fears that some of the new voters may vote for the wrong Davies — 'you
have no idea how ignorant people in the country are,' Fryer was warned
by a well-to-do Liberal living near Llandysul.[35] (There were, in fact,
5,521 illiterate voters in Wales at this time.)[36] Writing from the Liberal
Committee Rooms in Aberaeron, John M. Howell even thought it
advisable for canvassers 'to instruct each voter how to place the X on the
voting paper, and not to leave the house until every one is able to make
it right himself in his presence.' His letter to Fryer continued:

This I deem important *from the testimony* of a gentleman whose
vocation leads him to the working men's cottages of about one half
of the county, and he feels from his personal experience that this
is the great danger of our losing the election. If the working men
are rightly to record their votes, we shall have 8 out of every 10 of
them. Our hope for a majority is not from the farmer at all, but
from the working class.[37]

Every attempt was made to persuade Cardiganshire men working in the
industrial areas of South Wales to return home to record their votes.
Many of them received copies of a printed letter saying that while the
candidate was not allowed to pay their rail fares, their support was
urgently required. Excursion tickets were eventually made available by
the railway companies for travel to Aberystwyth between 26 November
and 2 December, polling day conveniently falling on 27 November. The
printed handbills announcing this carried the legend: 'Vote For David
Davies, The Working Man's Friend,' followed by the Welsh version:
'Votiwch [sic] Dros David Davies. Cyfaill y Gweithiwr.'[38]

David Davies, who was often accompanied by his son Edward, was
received with elation in many areas. At Tan-y-groes, his horses were
removed from the shaft and his carriage pulled to the chapel where the
election meeting was being held by supporters shouting 'Llandinam for
ever!'[39] When his opponents staged a torchlit procession in Cardigan,

the Liberals were said to have wrested the flaring torches from the hands of the Tory 'roughs'.[40]

Davies held a trump card in this election — the support of the Nonconformist ministers, which was denied him the following year. The *Aberystwyth Observer*, Tory rival of the *Cambrian News*, accused them of 'neglecting their most sacred calling' to sit on election platforms and sneered at the fact that the Liberal candidate and his wife had 'actually taken apartments on the Terrace at Aberystwyth . . . Mr and Mrs David Davies generally spend a week or two in the summer at one of the genial resorts in Merionethshire or North Wales.'[41]

On polling day, however, the voters declared emphatically for David Davies, who polled 5,967 votes to his opponent's 3,634, a majority of 2,333. The *Aberystwyth Observer* saw it as 'another proof of the great power of wealth,'[42] whereas at the rival paper Gibson rejoiced in the victory of a man whose 'sympathies are all with the people.'[43]

Within a year, the little world of Cardiganshire would be turned topsy-turvy and the editors calling a different tune.

22 The Bogs of Whiggism

The election was not the only excitement in Aberystwyth in 1885: on a summer night in July a disastrous fire swept through the College by the Sea, gutting the north wing and raising fresh doubts about its future. The *Western Mail* openly rejoiced, saying Aberystwyth's misfortune was Swansea's opportunity — 'a long pull, and a strong pull, and a pull together and the College is theirs.'[1]

Once more David Davies played a leading role in the fight for survival, addressing a public meeting a few weeks later and saying that 'by giving sixpence you can get another penny out of me, and every penny will help the work forward.'[2] (During the election in the autumn he was reported to have given £5,000 to the college, against Vaughan Davies's £5.)[3] Ironically, public sympathy aroused by the fire swayed the Government more than reasoned argument ever had, and within a matter of weeks they had agreed to increase their grant to £4,000, putting Aberystwyth on the same footing as Cardiff and Bangor.[4]

David Davies was in favour of rebuilding the college on a new site — 'one better sheltered, together with a better building for the same money'[5] — but sentimental attachment to Savin's folly delayed the move for another fifty years. The suggestion that his defeat on this issue was the reason for his severing all ties with the college a year later, however, is mistaken: he made it perfectly clear that this was due to his rejection by the Cardiganshire electorate, and to some extent to his treatment by students during election meetings.[6]

The return of eighty-five Home Rule MPs for Irish seats in 1885, the other sixteen being filled by Conservatives, convinced Gladstone that he had to press on with all speed with his mission of pacifying Ireland. He became 'an old man in a hurry', earning the displeasure of Queen Victoria and failing to carry his party with him. There were many Liberals like David Davies, who for one reason or another voted against the party on this issue. He felt so strongly about it that were it not for Home Rule, he would almost certainly have resigned before facing another election.

Davies was, by now, thoroughly out of patience with the Irish. He felt they were twisting the arm of government, and did not think concessions should be made under duress. The obstructionist tactics of her MPs wearied him, physically and mentally. In the 1885 campaign he had complained of being 'in the House for forty-eight hours at a stretch when

the Tories and Home Rulers did all they could to hinder legislation,' adding
that a large number of Liberal MPs were 'old men tired out by such
treatment.'[7] He declared himself in favour of 'some moderate measure of
Home Rule' to 'make the Irish respect the law like other people'[8] but was
Unionist by instinct. What he failed — or refused — to recognize, however,
was the extent to which pro-Irish sentiment was growing in his
constituency, especially among the very people who had done so much to
ensure his victory at the polls: the Nonconformist ministers.

The dawn of the new year of 1886 found him feeling the weight of his
sixty-seven years. The euphoria that had followed his crushing defeat of
Vaughan Davies had quickly passed, and in the rural tranquillity of
Llandinam the endless rail journeys to London and tedious nights at
Hummums Hotel in Covent Garden looked increasingly unattractive.
He spent more time gazing reflectively down the long avenue of the
years, and — inevitably — wondering how many years were still left him.
His close bond with Margaret, the wife who had given him such steady
support while never aspiring to the limelight herself, made him begrudge
more and more the time spent away from her.

Politics had become a curse, and he had little sympathy with the new
movements gathering force in his party. Irish Home Rule was one,
agrarian reform another. He viewed the land question as a practical
farmer, and was suspicious of any redistribution of ownership based
merely on theories of equality. He had flourished as a tenant farmer
himself, and knew that a landlord would have to be foolish to the point
of idiocy to evict a tenant who farmed effectively. Therefore the system
worked; why meddle with it? His feeling of revulsion against both the
Irish lobby and the zeal of land reformers such as the urban dweller Jesse
Collings surfaced in a letter he sent Edward from the loneliness of
London one January day:

> It was a queer sight in the House last night the Government
> beaten by 79 led by Gladstone   I voted as I said I would
> against Collins [sic] but the order of the day is to give all to the
> Labourer for he has the power   take the Land compulsory from
> its present Owner and hand it over to the agricultural labourer
>   the next stroke of business is to give Ireland to the Rebels for
> the home Rule votes   anything for place and office   I shall
> give the whole thing up at the next general Election   I feel
> disgusted with the thing it is no good to belong to a party you
> cannot support   I am curious to see what sort of a government
> Gladstone can put together   I am going to see a Doctor now.[9]

Those more devious than David Davies were assessing how best to
benefit politically from the fact that the humble agricultural labourer, the

allegedly slow-witted 'Hodge' beloved of *Punch* cartoonists, now had the
vote. It had been assumed that Hodge had brains of straw, but his
detractors had learned otherwise. In the election of 1885, squire and
parson had been 'amazed to see the labourer, of whose stagnant
indifference to politics they had been so confident, trudging four or five
miles to a political meeting, listening without asking for a glass of beer
to political speeches, following point upon point, and then trudging back
again . . .'[10] A.C. Humphreys-Owen discussed the question of 'Land
Agitation' in a letter to Edward Davies in February 1886:

> The labourers have the votes and what is more important they and
> not the farmers have the sympathy of the town voters. If the
> landowners make it clear that they are ready and willing to
> concede the reasonable demands of the labourer that will go a long
> way in their favour when the matter is being seriously discussed in
> Parliament . . .

He added that 'it is to the success of the Irish agitation that the Welsh
agitation is due and I hope that if there is the least sign of overt violence
or boycotting in Wales the law will be vigorously enforced.'[11]

Ireland presented no difficulties of conscience for the Montgomery
MP, Stuart Rendel. With remarkable prescience, he put forward
arguments which would have a familiar ring a century later.

> I see no alternative but to give in. Do you? Does any one? . . .
> What is the good of another see-saw of parties? Or of a coalition
> against Ireland? I am not prepared within to abandon democratic
> institutions or to deluge Ireland with troops for the sake of resisting
> a measure which will make the Irish responsible to Ireland for its
> order and prosperity.
>   To talk of an Irish Parliament disintegrating the Empire is silly.
> To talk of the danger to the Empire of such a Parliament is idle:
> for we have to consider the present danger to the Empire resulting
> from no Parliament.[12]

In this letter of 1 February 1886, Rendel went on to say that he was
distressed to hear of the state of David Davies's health — 'his friends have
certainly been anxious about him.' He revealed that Margaret's health
had also been declining, and that Davies was worried by this and her
failing eyesight. 'Keep me informed if you can,' he concluded, with a rare
revelation of his private feelings. 'I am fond of the old man.'[13]

Edward Davies shared the same views on Ireland as his father, seeing
the creation of a 'very serious split' that would take years to close. 'Let
us hope,' he added piously, 'the Almighty will guide the statesmen of this
country in the great crisis through which we are passing.'[14]

Gladstone was so convinced of the ultimate success of his plans that he was unperturbed by the Irish MPs' refusal to seek office at Westminster, taking the view that they would need all the talent at their disposal for their own parliament. He had long talks with the Irish leader Parnell about financial arrangements between the new assembly and the imperial parliament, and introduced his Bill in a three and a half hour speech on 8 April.[15]

By now David Davies's future was being intensely debated in Cardiganshire. The rift between himself and his constituents widened as Gladstone's radical solution took a hold on people's imaginations. He was rapidly losing the support of Gibson of the *Cambrian News*, who admitted to having 'changed his mind on the Irish question during the past nine months,'[16] and his health was also causing concern. By the beginning of May his retirement was being confidently predicted, although Gibson was assuring him privately that nobody wanted him to resign – 'absolutely nobody.'[17] There was obviously an exchange of letters between them, but only Gibson's survive. On 7 May he wrote to Davies again:

> That you are festered [*sic*] with begging letters I know. I have been asked to write to you for subscriptions to replace dead cows and to get men situations. I have now before me a prospectus in which you are a director in a Spanish Railway Company. This prospectus was given to me by a man who wants a situation as manager. When I contemplated repaying you the money kindly lent to me [for the purchase of the *Cambrian News* in 1880] everybody said I was a fool, and that it was absurd to repay you. The fact is that you are believed to be so fabulously wealthy that a few thousands are less than nothing to you, and that it is rather a charity than otherwise to get money from you. If you were to give half a million to something few people would be surprised at the amount as they believe you possess millions . . .
>
> In reference to your position on the Irish Bills I will say nothing. You are a man of business and you know your own mind. I think you are mistaken just as you think I am mistaken . . . I have not shown any of your letters as I have a sort of hope that you might see your way to not giving up the seat. The Mines' Bill, the Leasehold Enfranchisement Bill, and other Bills in which you differ from your constituents, are important. The argument is one that can scarcely be entered into as you know so much better than I can know what you think will lead to national disaster . . . We have no candidate ready. I do not think that anybody anticipated your retirement . . . We do not even know of a lawyer who, as you suggest, could make money out of the seat.

The feeling here grows every day in favour of Home Rule. I am very much tempted to argue with you, but I suppose neither of us could be convinced.

I suppose you mean to retire from Parliament altogether. I am sorry for the whole thing, very sorry. You have great interests to carry out in South Wales and perhaps the course events have taken is inevitable. I wish that course had been otherwise.[18]

The emotions of David Davies were always volatile, and he now felt that he was being hustled off the stage to make way for a younger, more radical candidate. He virtually said so in a letter he despatched to the Press, which brought the retort from Gibson that the Liberals of Cardiganshire had been 'far truer than you seem to believe.'

You throw down an uncalled-for challenge to the people who have done nothing but support you and who on your retirement have no candidate to bring forward ... I am accused of cowardice because I do not write savagely about you, for I believe you are altogether mistaken in the views you hold about the people down here. They are not against you individually, but you are aggravating them. They feel strongly on the Irish question and they do not understand you sending first one letter and then another containing hints that you will fight them. Politically they differ from you, and they think you ought to vote for the second reading of the Bill under protest, but they fully recognize your inability to think as they do.

It is not often that I plead for peace and unanimity, but I do feel strongly that it would be a great calamity if anything but the greatest friendliness existed between you and the Liberals of Cardiganshire.[19]

Gibson reminded Davies that far from being pushed out, he had spoken of resigning the seat — 'And it was your health and not your political opinions that was deemed to be the cause.'

Events were now moving fast, and Davies's publicly-voiced suspicions of his constituency party had caused opinion to shift decisively against him. A delegate meeting of Cardiganshire Liberals at Aberaeron voted 110 to 3 for Home Rule for Ireland, the spirit of the meeting being 'out-and-out in favour of pronounced Radicalism.'[20] This was manna from heaven to such as Tom Ellis, who in a letter to the *Cambrian News* had dismissed Welsh MPs as a set of 'easy-going and respectable folk, fearful of giving offence and anxious to stand well in the opinions of their little world.' Always strong on rhetoric, he had longed for the appearance of one 'ready to lead forlorn hopes for Wales, to be if necessary a scarecrow of violence to the political warblers of whose tune the Welsh people are getting so sick.'[21]

If Home Rule for Ireland, why not Home Rule for Wales? The question was being asked, and not only by Liberal 'red guards' like Tom Ellis. By the end of May, Gibson was one of those who had come round to the idea that 'this controversy will never cease until the whole country has been provided with local Parliaments.'[22]

Ellis, then twenty-seven and about to become MP for Merioneth, saw the interests of the Irish and Welsh as identical. 'Their past history is very similar, their present oppressors are the same, and their immediate wants are the same — riddance from landlordism and ampler opportunities for developing their own genius and their own powers.'[23]

On 8 June, David Davies was one of ninety-three Liberals who voted against Gladstone's Home Rule Bill, which was lost by 343 to 313. The Premier — 'composed though pallid' at the Cabinet meeting next day[24] — asked the Queen for a dissolution, and the way was clear for a general election.

Cardiganshire thus became Looking-Glass Land. People formerly on one side were now on the other, and Davies became a new breed of man — a Liberal Unionist. His political friends fell away from him, as from an untouchable. He was branded a Tory, a traitor, a 'paper Unionist'.[25]

For the admirers of a man who had been so lately a hero in the county, the contrast with the previous year's election was painful. There was no triumphal progress now, only a faltering campaign that inspired derision. The sight of David Davies on the same platform as the Tory squires he had hitherto condemned made people doubt the evidence of their eyes. Was it for this they had sent him to Parliament?

The anguish of one supporter, D.J. Jones of Lampeter, spilled over in a letter he sent Edward Davies warning him that his 'dear father' would be 'certainly defeated at the polls.'

> I can speak of this town and neighbourhood, they are Gladstonians to the core. I am not able to form anything like a working committee. They have all joined our opponents. Mr Davies' Address has been pulled down as soon as they had been [sic] put up. I never witnessed such a feeling as there is here at a parliamentary election.[26]

That address unconvincingly stated that he had decided to stand after all because he now felt 'in better health.' He believed an 'overwhelming majority' of his constituents agreed with him on the Irish question. They knew his views on other important matters, so it was unnecessary to repeat them.[27]

It all sounded very perfunctory.

Bowen Rowlands QC appeared in the county not as the 'young man imbued with the new spirit' for whom Tom Ellis yearned,[28] but as just the kind of middle-aged lawyer whom David Davies had believed might make money out of the seat. A product of Jesus College, Oxford, he had first been a cleric and then headmaster of Haverfordwest Grammar School. Now, at fifty, he was a practising barrister, a man fluent of speech and imbued — declared Gibson — with 'aggressive unadulerated Liberalism.'[29] He was adopted as the Gladstonian Liberal candidate on 21 June, and assured the voters in his election address — sent from his home in Broad Haven, Pembrokeshire — that he was 'a warm supporter of Mr Gladstone's Irish policy, believing that the Real Unity of the Empire will thus best be maintained.' Loyalty to his leader was his main theme, for he declared himself 'content to fight with you this battle of the people for the people under the leadership of our veteran captain, Mr Gladstone.'[30]

The excitable Gibson now cast aside any lingering sense of obligation he might have felt to the man whose loan of £400 had helped him purchase the *Cambrian News* six years before. Throwing his weight wholly behind Rowlands, he promised David Davies 'one of the sternest fights he ever took part in,'[31] and true to his word penned a vitriolic leading article early in July.

> Mr David Davies has gone over to the enemy, and trusts the Tory votes for victory … To see the poor, proud squireens of Cardiganshire dancing attendance upon Mr David Davies, whom we have rejected and whom they pretended to despise, is one of those pieces of satire which we accept with delight. We know his contempt for them, and we know also that the contempt is mutual … Mr David Davies … has stuck fast in the bogs of Whiggism.[32]

Pro-Irish feeling was such that the nationalist Michael Davitt was invited to Aberystwyth, where on a hot July day he addressed a huge open-air rally in the castle grounds. He said that if a federal scheme went ahead with local parliaments for England, Scotland and Ireland, Wales should have one too. It would not mean the end of empire but a closer unity and 'an end to the racial disputes that have existed for so many hundred years.'[33]

David Davies put his case before a meeting at the Assembly Rooms in Aberystwyth on 28 June. The Irish must 'obey the law as they did in Wales.' There was talk of coercion in Ireland, but were they not coerced in Wales if they disobeyed the law? Moreover, in his view the Home Rule Bill could not become law without the Land Purchase Bill, which would place an additional £11m a year burden on the taxpayers. He was quite prepared to take the voice of his constituents on the question; if they told him to vote for Home Rule he would do so. He never went to Parliament with a view to making money; he went there as their representative, and having done so for many years, were they going to turn him out now?[34]

The answer came on Friday 9 July, when Bowen Rowlands polled 4,252 votes to David Davies's 4,243.

23 Why?

David Davies went home to Llandinam to lick his wounds, and the inquests began. How had a man who had done so much for the county, and who had won the seat hands down only seven months before, come to lose it to one who was — as had been said once of Davies himself — 'a perfect stranger'?

There were many factors at work. One was that there was strong popular support in Wales for Gladstone — a man whose sympathy with Welsh causes such as Sunday closing and higher education had been amply demonstrated. Cardiganshire Liberals could not easily bring themselves to go against the Grand Old Man, even if they may not themselves feel strongly on the Home Rule issue.

There were also considerable doubts about David Davies's judgement and motives. Why did he change his mind about standing for the seat again after saying he intended to resign? How could he bring himself to sit on the same platform as the Tories? These seemed to many to be the actions of a proud man who believed his personal standing in the county was such that he could get away with anything. He had undoubtedly done great things for Cardiganshire with his money, but generosity is a two-edged sword which can wound those who exercise it.

The legendary wealth of David Davies had become, in some respects, his greatest problem. When a man has so much to give, the act of giving is diminished, and arouses resentment among the beneficiaries. And when people are made to feel they are under an obligation to the giver, they are likely to assert their independence in unexpected ways.

There were many who spoke of the 'ingratitude' of the electors, but this is to suggest that by his railway making and his donations David Davies had virtually bought the county, that it had become a kind of pocket borough. But as a columnist in the *Cambrian News* pointed out after his defeat:

> The men of Cardigan are stubborn as he; as proud as he; as independent as he. There are scores who found it far harder to go against him than it would have been to go with him, but they went against him, for they were as honest as he. He did not know the feeling of the county, and he overestimated his personal influence.[1]

The editor-proprietor, John Gibson, put it another way. 'Rich men seldom hear the truth, and still more seldom are prepared to accept it.'[2]

The Llandinam Papers contain letters to Edward Davies which are touching in their expression of remorse at his father's defeat. One from 'T. Davies, Treorky' runs:

> I blame myself for not doing more for Mr Davies this time . . . I had no idea that the ministers were against him as I afterwards found out rather too late . . . if we had a day or two more Mr Davies would have been in with a good majority. There was a strong feeling in his favour on the increase every day . . .
> I did not know that there was a canvassing going on in the Rhonda [sic] in favour of Mr Davies. If I knew I should certainly do all I could to stop it. It was a great mistake this time . . . I was told that 60 or 70 went up and Mabon travelling with them. The greater number of these voters I am almost certain voted against us. However Mr Davies deserved better treatment in Cardiganshire . . . There was no rejoicing in the Valley on Saturday. I passed through crowds of people from the station − I was afraid they would shout, but they did not. It makes me sick to think of it − the less I think of Cardiganshire the better it is for me.[3]

Another letter came from one who felt they had been 'defeated honorably' [sic] and had the consolation of knowing they were 'still on the right side of the question. Poor Mr Gladstone has found out that he has made a sad blunder, the nation collectively will have nothing of his Home Rule.'[4]

Gladstone had indeed been defeated, the Conservatives and Liberal Unionists winning 393 seats to the Liberals' 192 and the Home Rulers' 85. Lord Salisbury again became Premier, and Parnell's involvement in a divorce case a few years later helped to ensure that the problem of Ireland was bequeathed to the tender mercies of the twentieth century.

The Nonconformist ministers had certainly turned against David Davies with a vengeance. His benefactions meant little when set against their convictions that history was on William Ewart Gladstone's side, and that he must be supported. The power they exercised over their flocks puzzled the editor of the Tory *Aberystwyth Observer*, who felt obliged to write a leading article about this curious phenomenon.

> We have no special love for Nonconformist ministers as such, but their existence and their influence must be acknowledged, and it will be well to consider for what reasons the people accept them in preference to the clergy and the landlords as their leaders. It cannot be for their wealth, for they are poor. It is not for high social positions, for they are socially humble. It is not because of

their education and culture, for their advantages in these respects are slight, and not to be compared with those of the clergy. Possibly, and probably, it is because they are trained extempore speakers, and associate more with their congregations than the clergy do. These two influences go a long way.[5]

Back in Llandinam, David Davies felt worried enough by the accusations that had been made against him to call a public meeting in the schoolroom. He had been called 'a turncoat and a Tory', but he wanted his neighbours to know that he 'hadn't changed at all, he was a good Liberal still.' Mr Gladstone may be the greatest man in the world, but he was a 'very proud and haughty man, and he thought that would carry him through everything.'[6]

Perfectly at home among people he had known all his life, Davies relaxed and expanded his views on Ireland. He had evidently given the subject careful thought, realizing − as history would make perfectly clear − that the divisions between Catholic and Protestant did not make for an easy solution.

Whatever was done for Ireland it must be two Irelands in one, and did they think that the English people were to shed blood and treasure to compel the loyal people of Ireland to submit because the rebels wanted it? They would never do it. He himself did not object to Home Rule for Ireland, but it must be of a certain sort which they would have control over, and they would have no control over the Home Rule now proposed.[7]

In spite of these explanations, ugly rumours persisted. It was whispered that David Davies had actually told his servants at Broneirion to vote Tory, and had sent his carriage to the Tory candidate to enable him to canvass in Llandinam. All that had happened, Davies assured Stuart Rendel, was that his daughter-in-law had gone to visit Mrs Rendel in the carriage. There had been 'considerable unpleasantness' between himself and the rumour-monger, 'this stupid Station Master at Llandinam . . . I felt so angry that before 40 or 50 people I told him that if I had been as young as I once was I would kick him from the platform into the River.'[8]

Rendel had sent him a present to soften the defeat in Cardiganshire, which Davies said he appreciated very much 'especially at a time when silly people think that you and I have a quarrel.'[9] The good feeling between them on a personal level did not prevent Rendel from denouncing Davies's stand on Ireland in an article in the *Oswestry Advertizer* written under the pseudonym 'A True Unionist'.[10] This appeared in the paper's Open Column, which allowed 'the freest expression of opinion on every side of any public question . . . so long as it is consistent with good taste,' a careful qualification by the proprietor, E. Woodall.

In effect, Rendel's case was that David Davies should have supported the Home Rule Bill because Gladstone had made a closer study of Ireland than he had: 'We do not uphold servile subserviency, but it is plain that busy men must upon all matters beyond their power of study accept freely the judgment of chosen leaders' — peculiar advice from one who presumably upheld the sovereignty of individual conscience.

The article was not entirely unsympathetic, however, praising Davies's 'sincerity and sagacity', the 'shrewdness of humour and unstudied frankness' of his speeches and acknowledging him to be 'at bottom, a genuine friend of civil and religious liberty.' Any slackness in accepting Liberal reforms, he added, could be put down to Davies's 'burden and impediment of wealth.'[11]

Davies appears not to have publicly replied to this, although he may well have said a word or two privately to Rendel. We do know, though, how he responded to the way he was treated by his erstwhile supporters during the election campaign. 'I have made up my mind to never again go to Aberystwyth,' he told Principal Edwards's father by letter.

> I cannot therefore support a College in a place where I cannot see it. At the last Election I had to be protected by the Police or I should have been kicked perhaps to death & all this after all I have done for the place in years past ... there is not a Church or Chapel in the place but that I have given large sums too [sic] besides what I have done for the College   I can only show my contempt for the place by doing no more.'[12]

It was noted that Principal Edwards had not even bothered to go home to vote for Davies; but perhaps this too was an example of the Liberal conscience at work.[13]

24   The Consecration of Wealth

With his political career over and his work for Aberystwyth at an end, David Davies's horizons narrowed considerably, but his business concerns provided occupation enough for a man whose health was failing. There were now seven Ocean collieries, Garw having come into production in July 1885 and Lady Windsor in December 1886.[1] The new company of Davies, Scott and Co. had been formed in 1884 to develop the latter at Ynysybwl, but in 1887 this firm had combined with David Davies and Co. to form the public limited company of Ocean Coal Co. Ltd.[2] Barry Docks, too, were approaching completion, and Davies regularly travelled south to attend company meetings in Cardiff.

Presiding at the seventh half-yearly meeting in February 1888, he contended that he 'did not suppose that there had ever been such a gigantic concern in any part of the world which has gone on so rapidly.' He also advised shareholders not to sell out because they might fear the competition from Cardiff: 'There will be plenty of traffic for everyone,' he assured them.[3]

The creation of the new port was an engineering feat of some magnitude, involving the excavation of five million tons of soil[4] and the construction of breakwaters 200 feet wide at the base and forty-six feet high.[5] The steep rise and fall of the tides in the Bristol Channel added to the difficulties of the task.[6] The company had its own railway running nearly nineteen miles to Trehafod in the Rhondda and linking with the Great Western Railway by means of a branch line to Peterston-super-Ely. It was to be known as a buccaneer of a railway, shamelessly raiding the territory of other companies and drawing its coal traffic from the Taff Vale, the Rhymney, and the Brecon and Merthyr railways, as well as from the GWR.

Water was let into the dock on 29 June 1889[7] and the port was formally opened less than three weeks later, on 18 July. The day began at 7.15 a.m. with an inspection of the dock gates by the principal engineer, John Wolfe Barry (who in time became Sir John) and the resident engineer, John Robinson. The company was proud of the fact that these 'were absolutely the first dock gates erected to be opened and shut by means of hydraulic rams'.[8] Two special trains brought more than 2,000 invited guests to Barry and at twenty-past twelve David Davies, as vice-chairman of the company, escorted Mrs Lewis Davies of Ferndale into the dock enclosure so that she might perform the ceremony of cutting the ribbon.[9] At a banquet the following day Davies emphasized that he had told his fellow-promoters firmly at the outset that once committed to the project, there must be no turning back.

> When the construction of a dock at Barry was first talked about they met on the island to inspect the place, but he felt suspicious of some of the promoters and told them they were not going to frighten the Cardiff people into a reduction of rates, and then give the matter up. If the question of making a new dock was to be taken up at all, it must be carried out.[10]

He added that they did not intend to work in opposition to any other dock — 'they did not wish to starve the people of Cardiff and Penarth ... The promoters of Barry Dock must be moderate, and take their share of the trade.' The fact is, however, that the trade at Barry grew so rapidly that by 1901 its coal and coke exports exceeded those of Cardiff, Barry exporting 7,844,464 tons against the Bute Docks' 7,216,311 tons. Thus Barry became the premier coal exporting port in the Bristol Channel, reaching its high-water mark with the export of more than eleven million tons of coal and coke in 1913, a year before the outbreak of the First World War.[11] David Davies, however, did not live to see this.

There was further evidence of his far-sightedness in his speech at the banquet celebrating Barry's opening, as he spoke of the town's potential as a resort.

> Provision could be made on the island for visitors, and with a little spirit of enterprise it could be made a popular watering place. Houses should be built, and every accommodation provided for excursionists. He was a total abstainer himself but they must not think of starving those who liked a drop of drink. He was more liberal than some people. He had been a total abstainer all his life, but he did not believe in withholding a glass of beer from those who wished it. He was not narrow-minded.[12].

Thus did he anticipate the galloping horses and coconut shies and scenic railway of Barry Island.

He acknowledged that this would 'doubtless be the last great undertaking he would have anything to do with.'[13] He was feeling his age. At last he had more time for his family, which now included his grandchildren David, Gwendoline and Margaret.[14] David, at six, was the eldest of these and there was an affinity between the old man and this robust boy whose love of the outdoors equalled his own. There is a touching story of how the grandparents would summon the children to tea by hanging a large white towel out of an upstairs window at Broneirion so that it might be seen from Plas Dinam, across the valley.[15] This was the kind of homely delight that brought solace to an

The statue at Llandinam, showing David Davies studying a map of Barry Docks.

old man who was now perceptively loosening his hold on worldly matters. Slightly bow-legged and with spectacles perched low on his nose,[16] he took a proprietorial interest in the affairs of Llandinam. He would occasionally visit the local board school he had paid for out of his own pocket and every Sunday saw him in chapel alongside such trusty servants as Abraham Thomas, who had been with him since those far-off days at Gwernerin. He rejoiced in the role of benefactor, reducing the rents of indigent tenants and insisting that an improvident old miner who called at Broneirion should be given a free meal and two sovereigns.[17] There were many reminders that he had changed life in Montgomeryshire not only by introducing railways but by providing jobs in south Wales. Family after family uprooted themselves to move south: the census returns for the Ystradyfodwg district of the Rhondda in 1871 and 1881 provide ample evidence of this. There is no way of telling whether the pride David Davies felt in opening new doors of opportunity was counterbalanced by some regret at being the means of emptying cottages in the surrounding countryside.

In the winter of 1889–90, David Davies was taken seriously ill. His health had been a cause for concern for some time and about three years before this he had received treatment for diabetes. An attack of influenza in February 1890 seriously weakened him and according to a newspaper report he was 'more or less an invalid' after that, 'his usual robust health failing and strength gradually diminishing.'[18] His regular physician, Dr Ferguson of Caersws, became so alarmed by his condition that he brought in Dr Burd of Shrewsbury, and together the two men saw him four times between March and June 1890. During April a third physician was consulted, Sir William Roberts, 'late of Manchester and now of London', for by this time Davies was said to be 'suffering from derangement of the digestive organs.'[19] Towards the end of June a Harley Street consultant was called to his bedside and advice was sought from three more doctors, one of whom was the patient's brother-in-law. This desperate search for a cure yielded no results and the two London specialists, Sir Andrew Clark and Sir William Roberts, 'held out no hope of ultimate recovery' after a visit early in July.[20] He gradually became weaker and was often heard to say at night that he wished to meet his Saviour by morning.[21] He died on the evening of Sunday 20 July, 1890.

The one-time sawyer was given a polished oak coffin with brass mountings, which lay in a bedroom at Broneirion overlooking the front terrace.[22] He was buried on a stiflingly hot day when the mourners, four abreast, made a coal-black scar on the landscape as they stretched half a mile from Broneirion to the churchyard. At the funeral service the Revd J. Cynddylan Jones said that in the life of David Davies they had seen 'the grand idea of the consecration of wealth realized in practical life. This is a new idea to our country, a practical idea.'[23] Not everyone was impressed. As the fulsome tributes poured forth, a north Wales paper brusquely observed:

> Mr Davies' Liberalism was that peculiar kind of middle-class Liberalism which in reality contains even more elements of Conservatism than much of which goes openly by that name. Prosperous men of business who have built up their fortunes with their own hands, and have watched the growth and expansion of their material interests, cannot in the majority of cases be expected to be true and steadfast Liberals. There are many glorious exceptions it is true; but as a general rule it may be said that if you scratch a man of huge financial interests, whatever he outwardly professes to be you will find a Tory.[24]

The *Barry Dock News* naturally took a different view, seeing David Davies as a man who had 'worked his way up from the saw-pit to the Senate House, and had never forgotten his people or deserted the place of his birth.'[25]

With the self-made squire in his grave, Llandinam had somehow to learn to live without him. So did the Ocean collieries, which expanded still further with the purchase of the Deep Navigation Colliery at Treharris in 1893.[26] It then had the biggest coal output of any firm in south Wales, producing one million tons more than its nearest rival.[27] Its failure to sink any new collieries after 1894, however, has been seen as evidence that it never recovered from the loss of its dynamic founder.[28]

David Davies's widow, Margaret, survived him by only four years. She died on 4 October 1894, at the age of eighty. A few days before her death she had a 'spiritual conversation' with the Revd Edward Griffiths of Meifod in which she said that she 'would not wish to die triumphantly, just confidently.' There is something at once touching and pathetic in her confession that she had forgotten many of the old Welsh hymns 'because of spending so many years in English circles.'[29] It also says much about the period of Welsh history spanned by the life of David Davies, when Welsh was the tongue of the poor cottager but English was the language to make money by.

Postscript

The life of David Davies can be seen as falling into three phases: the period up to his first railway contract, the brief but hectic decade of his railway making, and his years as a colliery proprietor. The first phase was by far the longest: he was thirty-seven years old when he became a railway contractor and it is tempting to speculate on the difference it might have made to events had he decided to remain a farmer. Perhaps most if not all of his railways would have been made by others, although with less of the calculated daring that characterized his enterprises: there is unlikely to have been a Talerddig or a line across Tregaron Bog. The steam coal seams of upper Rhondda would have been exploited eventually, possibly by capitalists with a flimsier social conscience than his: in spite of his collaboration in the lock-out of 1875 his concern for the welfare of his colliers and their families was in advance of his time. His insistence that safety must come before profit helped to keep the Ocean collieries free of major disasters and he was always a friend of improvement: Dare was the first pit in the Rhondda to have a ventilating fan and Cwmparc the first village in the Rhondda to have electric light. In 1915, twenty-five years after his death, the first pit-head bath in Wales was installed at the Ocean's Deep Navigation Colliery. Scores of the sturdy stone cottages he built for his workmen were still providing comfortable accommodation in 1990, having been improved over the years by means of block grants from the local authority.

In the dangerous game of hypothesis, some calculations are more difficult. Would a sizeable port have been built at Barry without his panache and determination? Probably not, for although denigrating voices have been heard in recent years playing down his part in the project, there was no doubt in the minds of his contemporaries that his role was crucially important. Time, of course, makes a mockery of all things human, and by the final decade of the twentieth century most of Davies's railway lines had been torn up, the pits he sank had closed and Barry was but a shadow of the port of former days. Yet his legacy was a lasting one. His philanthropy gave higher education in Wales a firm basis and the way he used his wealth inspired his grandchildren to prodigious acts of patronage which enriched the life of the entire Welsh nation. Perhaps their greatest achievement was the creation of the King Edward VII Welsh National Memorial Association for the prevention and treatment of tuberculosis: a shining example of how the wealth of a few can further the happiness of many. Lord Davies's crusade for a new world order, an ideal enshrined in the Temple of Peace in Cardiff, bears further witness to the vision of this remarkable family.

All these things came about because of David Davies of Llandinam. Yet did he bequeath us something more, a gift so elusive that we have yet to grasp it? He stood above all for courage and self-reliance, urging his countrymen to have faith in themselves and to take command of their destinies. Perhaps this is the principal lesson he taught us, and the way it is applied will shape not only individual lives but the future of Wales itself.

Notes

The style I have adopted is to spell out author, title, place and date of publication first time, but simply to mention the author thereafter: hence C.P. Gasquoine, *The Story of The Cambrian*, Llandybïe, 1922, becomes C.P. Gasquoine.

NLW denotes the National Library of Wales, Aberystwyth, and PRO the Public Record Office, Kew, London. Research into newspaper files was conducted at the Newspaper Library, Colindale, London, the National Library of Wales and Cardiff Central Library of South Glamorgan Libraries.

1   The Navvy's Shirt

1. *Cambrian News*, Aberystwyth, 16 July 1886.
2. Ibid.
3. Mrs Eleonora Bowen Davies, Whitland, in conversation with the author, October 1987.
4. Somerset House: Will of David Davies, proved 11 October 1890, at Principal Registry.
5. *Cambrian News*, 13 February 1874.
6. Goronwy Jones: 'David Davies (1818–1890) Llandinam'; typescript in Box E1/6, Lord Davies Papers, National Library of Wales, Aberystwyth. This work was published in Welsh under the same title in Wrexham, 1913.
7. The *Star*, London, 23 July 1890.
8. *The Times*, London, 22 July 1890.
9. Goronwy Jones.
10. Dorothy P.H. Wrenn, *Welsh History Makers*, Wakefield 1976, pp 65–72.
11. Lord Davies's correspondence with Ivor Thomas, author of *Top Sawyer*, 1937. Box E1/1, Lord Davies. NLW.
12. *Barry Dock News*, 25 July 1890.
13. Edwin Jones recollections, Box E1/1, Lord Davies. NLW.
14. *The Welshman*, Carmarthen, 25 July 1890.
15. Goronwy Jones.
16. *The Welshman*, 7 September 1866.
17. Ivor Thomas: *Top Sawyer*, London 1938, reprinted Carmarthen 1988, p 78.
18. *Liverpool Daily Courier*, quoted in *Cambrian News*, 1 May 1874.
19. *Liverpool Daily Post*, quoted in Cambrian News, same date.
20. Ibid.
21. Alfred Tylor, in evidence to House of Lords Select Committee on the Barry Dock & Railways Bill, 29 July 1883.
22. Alexander Macdonald, MP for Stafford and president of the National Association of Miners, quoted in *Colliery Guardian*, 26 February 1875.
23. Report of coalfield conference, *Colliery Guardian*, 16 April 1875.

2   Peasants of the Better Class

1. A.C. Humphreys-Owen to Lord Rendel, 12 January 1898, Rendel Papers, NLW 19466C685.
2. Somerset House: Will of Edward Davies, probate London, 31 October 1890.
3. Edward Davies to A.C. Humphreys-Owen, 5 July 1896, Glansevern Papers. Vol 1/5681. NLW.

4. David Davies, speaking at Penllwyn, Cardiganshire, quoted *Cambrian News*, 13 November 1885.
5. Report on National Eisteddfod of Wales, *Aberystwyth Observer*, 30 September 1865.
6. In the first of five articles in *Y Brython Cymreig*, 7 July 1893, Matthew Humphreys says that ten children were born to David and Elizabeth Davies: David, Thomas, Edward, John, Richard, Joseph, Mary, Sarah, Elizabeth and Jane, 'and of this large family only two survive'. One of these would have been Joseph. Llandinam Papers D277, NLW, translated for author by Aled Llyr. The christening of Thomas on 28 October 1821 is recorded in the International Genealogical Index for Montgomeryshire. NLW.
7. Bishop Basil Tickell Jones, 1886, quoted in *Rebirth of a Nation: Wales 1880–1980*, by Kenneth O. Morgan, Oxford, 1981, p 3.
8. Goronwy Jones.
9. Bishop's Transcripts for 1818, Llandinam Parish. NLW.
10. 1841 Census. Parish of Llandinam. NLW.
11. 1851 Census. Newtown District. Llanwnog Sub-district. Parish of Llandinam. NLW.
12. 1861 Census. Newtown District. Llanwnog Sub-district. Parish of Llandinam. NLW.
13. Matthew Humphreys, *Y Brython Cymreig*, 7 July 1893. Llandinam Papers D277 NLW.
14. 1861 Census.
15. Ivor Thomas, p 2.
16. Ivor Thomas to Lord Davies, 26 October 1937. Box E1/2, Lord Davies. NLW.
17. Lord Davies to Ivor Thomas, 28 October 1937. Box E1/2, Lord Davies. NLW.
18. Edwin Jones recollections, Box 1/1 and Box 1/3, Lord Davies. NLW.
19. Bishop's Transcripts for 1788, Llandinam Parish. NLW.
20. Bishop's Transcripts for 1818, Llandinam Parish. NLW.
21. Ibid.
22. T. Mervyn Jones, Cardiff, typescript in author's possession.
23. Reg Francis, in conversation with author, 1987. (At the opening of the Llanidloes and Newtown Railway, David Davies referred to his birthplace of Draintewion as 'a little thatched cottage.' *Llanidloes and Newtown Telegraph*, 10 September 1859.)
24. C.E.Vaughan Owen, Llanidloes: Pamphlet, 'Presbyterian Church of Wales, Llandinam, Centenary 1873–1973'.
25. David Davies to Revd Kilsby Jones, quoted *Barry Dock News*, 25 July 1890.
26. Goronwy Jones.
27. David Davies, speaking at Penllwyn, see note 4.
28. 'The Gleaner: In Days of Old', 22 May 1915. Cutting from unidentified newspaper preserved in scrapbook in possession of Miss Lucy Waite, Llandinam.
29. Dr David Jenkins, Welsh Industrial and Maritime Museum, writing to author, 26 February 1990.
30. Harold Carter and J. Gareth Thomas: *Gregynog — The Regional Setting*, p 6. Contribution to *Gregynog*, edited by Glyn Tegai Hughes, Prys Morgan and J. Gareth Thomas, Cardiff 1977.
31. Dr David Jenkins.
32. Goronwy Jones.
33. The *Montgomeryshire Echo*, 26 July 1890.
34. Daniel Rowlands, *Y Traethodydd*, November 1890, translation from the original Welsh, Box E1/4, Lord Davies. NLW.
35. Ivor Thomas, p 178.
36. Death certificate of David Davies senior, 30 September, 1846. Register of deaths, Llanwnog Sub-district, Newtown registration district, 1846.

37. *Hansard's Parliamentary Debates*, Vol 225, 1 July 1875.
38. Goronwy Jones.
39. Ibid.
40. Ibid.
41. Recollections of Matthew Humphreys, Box E1/1, Lord Davies. NLW.
42. Various entries in Diary 1 January–27 July 1854 of William Richard Jones (1837–c.1912) of Pullan Cottage, Llandinam, afterwards Vicar of Hyssington. NLW Minor Deposit 1366A.
43. International Genealogical Index gives the date of Thomas's birth as 3 October 1821. NLW.
44. The details relating to John, Edward, Mary, Joseph and Sarah are to be found in the International Genealogical Index. NLW.
45. Anonymous note in Box 1/1, Lord Davies. NLW. This was almost certainly written by Edwin Jones, headmaster of Llandinam Board School, 1889–1907.
46. *Barry Dock News*, 19 July 1889.
47. Matthew Humphreys, *Y Brython Cymreig*, 14 July 1893. Translated for author by Dafydd Ifans.
48. A. Howell, Rhiewport, Montgomeryshire: *Roads, Bridges, Canals and Railways in Montgomeryshire*, Montgomeryshire Collections, Vol. 15 (London, 1882). Howell says Penson was appointed first to Montgomeryshire, becoming 'also surveyor of Denbighshire'.
49. Goronwy Jones.
50. Matthew Humphreys.
51. *Civil Engineering Heritage: Wales & Western England*, edited by W.J. Sivewright, London, 1986.
52. Goronwy Jones.
53. See note 36.
54. Certificate of marriage of David Davies and Margaret Jones, Capel Isaf, Llanfair, in the Llanfyllin district of the counties of Montgomery and Denbigh, 7 May 1851.
55. Register of deaths, Llanwnog Sub-district, 23 November, 1846. X appears as the mark of David Davies as witness of this death also.
56. Letter from Dr John Cule, University of Wales College of Medicine, to author, 21 October 1988.
57. The register of deaths shows that John died on 16 April 1847.
58. Glynne R. Jones: 'The King Edward VII Welsh National Memorial Association, 1912–48', in *Wales and Medicine*, edited by John Cule, Llandyssul, 1975.
59. Ibid.
60. Ivor Thomas, p 19.
61. Matthew Humphreys, *Y Brython Cymreig*, 14 July 1893.
62. Ibid.
63. Tithe maps, Montgomeryshire. Parish of Llandinam. 29 November 1845. NLW.
64. Matthew Humphreys, *Y Brython Cymreig*, 7 July 1893.
65. Ibid.
66. Matthew Humphreys, *Y Brython Cymreig*, 14 July 1893.
67. Anonymous note, Box 1/1 Lord Davies. NLW. Probable author Edwin Jones.
68. Goronwy Jones.
69. Matthew Humphreys, *Y Brython Cymreig*, 14 July 1893.
70. 1851 Census, see note 11.
71. Goronwy Jones.
72. Matthew Humphreys and Goronwy Jones.
73. See note 54.
74. Goronwy Jones.
75. Ibid.

76. Edwin Jones, Box 1/1, Lord Davies. NLW. He recalls that after relating the tale of the 'five-minute contract' in the *Barry Dock News*, David Davies gave him the facts but refused to allow him to make a correction as 'the story was such a good one.'
77. C.P. Gasquoine: *The Story of The Cambrian*, Llandybïe 1922, reprinted 1973, pp 6/7.
78. Advertisement in the *Oswestry Advertiser*, 12 December 1855.
79. C.P. Gasquoine, p 6.
80. Charles E. Howell: *The Montgomeryshire Collections*, Vol. 30. London, 1898.

3   Contract Won

1. David Kinsey: Scrap-album/Diary. NLW 22344F. NLW.
2. Cutting from unidentified newspaper in Kinsey Scrap-album; the views are attributed to the Revd Morgan Jones, vicar of Llandinam, 1893.
3. Kinsey, 6 April 1852.
4. Ibid., 25 February 1855.
5. William Richard Jones Diary, 3 May 1855.
6. Ibid., 28 February. Jones records that on the night of 17 February the frost was so intense that the 'animal water froze under people's beds'.
7. *The Times*, 25 August 1855; *Shrewsbury Chronicle*, 24 August 1855.
8. Minutes of directors' meetings, Llanidloes & Newtown Railway Co., RAIL 379/2. Public Record Office, Kew, London.
9. *The Times*, 5 October 1855.
10. *Shrewsbury Chronicle*, 5 October 1855.
11. Goronwy Jones.
12. *Barry Dock News*, 19 July 1889. Articles on Davies in this newspaper at this time were the work of Edwin Jones.
13. *Shrewsbury Chronicle*, 5 October 1855.
14. Ibid.
15. David Hamer, Box E1/5, Lord Davies. NLW.
16. Matthew Humphreys, Box E1/5, Lord Davies. NLW.
17. George Brace to Ann Warburton Owen, 29 April 1853, Glansevern. Vol 4/6395. NLW.
18. Ibid., 7 May 1853, Glansevern Vol 4/6396. NLW.
19. Ibid., 13 May 1853.
20. David Hamer.
21. Minutes of L&N directors' meeting, 19 September 1855. RAIL 379/2. PRO. At that stage, the land involved in the negotiations was valued at £6,600. The previous month, 200 shares with a total value of £2,000 had been taken up; altogether £15,000 in shares had to be raised for the works to proceed.
22. Matthew Humphreys.
23. Probably Edwin Jones.
24. Johnny Griffiths, Llandinam, in conversation with author, 1986. The story had come down from his grandfather, who was one of David Davies's employees on the Talerddig cutting.
25. Goronwy Jones.
26. Frederic Kerr to Ann Warburton Owen, 17 November 1855, Glansevern, Vol. 4/6694. NLW.
27. Rex Christiansen and R.W. Miller, *The Cambrian Railways*: Vol. 1, 1852–1888, Newton Abbot, 1967, p 23.
28. David Hamer.
29. Goronwy Jones.
30. Census returns of 1851 and 1861.
31. Kinsey, 19 August 1856.
32. Ibid., 3 February 1856.

33. Jones Diary, 17 March 1855.
34. L&N company minutes, 13 February 1857. PRO.
35. Ibid.
36. Ibid., 28 February 1856.
37. Matthew Humphreys, *Y Brython Cymreig*, 21 July 1893. Translated by Dafydd Ifans.
38. Shrewsbury Journal, 27 May 1857.
39. Box 1/1, Lord Davies, NLW, contains a report of the meeting.

4   Well Now We've Got a Railway!

1. Kinsey, 4 August 1857.
2. These advertisements appeared in the *Oswestry Advertiser*; Goronwy Jones tells the tale of Savin at the livestock sale.
3. Llandinam Papers. A: Group 1/1. NLW.
4. The notice was printed in Denbigh and signed Martin Smith Junr, Hon. Secretary. RAIL 92/ 132. PRO.
5. Gasquoine, p 38.
6. Peter E. Baughan: *A Regional History of the Railways of Great Britain*. Vol. Eleven; North and Mid Wales; Newton Abbott, 1980. Baughan, p 150, says the *Dove* was an 1839 Sharp, Roberts ex-Birmingham & Derby Junction locomotive.
7. David Hamer.
8. Ibid.
9. Ibid.
10. Kinsey, 23 December 1857.
11. General Proctor is mentioned by David Hamer and his name also appears in the L&N company minutes of 3 February 1858 and 28 August 1858. PRO. He apparently lived in the Penstrowed area.
12. According to David Hamer, the locomotive 'turned out to be quite useless'.
13. Kinsey, 23 December 1857.
14. Christiansen & Miller, p 21.
15. L&N company records, 3 February 1858. PRO.
16. Ibid., 31 December 1857.
17. Ibid., 3 February 1858.
18. Ibid., 6 February 1858.
19. Ibid., 25 February 1858.
20. Ibid., 27 May 1858.
21. Ibid., 27 August 1858.
22. Lord Davies to Ivor Thomas, 1937.
23. Richard Williams: *Montgomeryshire Worthies*, Newtown, 1894.
24. Ivor Thomas, p 38.
25. Richard Williams.
26. Baughan, p 66.
27. Ivor Thomas, p 41.
28. Goronwy Jones.
29. *Baner Cymru*, 1 September 1858. Translated by Howell and Iona Edwards.
30. David A. Robertson, letter to *Carnarvon Herald*, 4 September 1858.
31. *Chester Courant*, 20 October 1858.
32. Ibid.
33. Ibid.
34. Ibid.
35. *Eddowes' Shrewsbury Journal*, 1 December 1858.
36. Ibid.
37. Ibid.
38. Kinsey, 30 November 1858.

39. Ibid., 26 January 1859.
40. David Hamer.
41. Kinsey, 1 February 1859.
42. Ibid., 5 April 1859.
43. Ibid., 20 May 1859.
44. Ibid., 26 January, 31 March, 5 April 1859.
45. L&N records, 25 August 1858. PRO.
46. Ibid., 9 December 1858.
47. Ibid., 5 January 1859.
48. Ibid., 3 May 1859.
49. Ibid., 30 June 1859.
50. *Shrewsbury Chronicle*, 27 May 1859, and the *Aberystwyth Observer*, 28 May 1859, both give his age as 69, but in Kinsey's diary entry of 20 May 1859 it appears as 68.
51. *Oswestry Advertiser*, 22 June 1859.
52. Ibid., 17 August 1859.
53. *Shrewsbury Chronicle*, 2 September 1859.
54. Ibid; *Llanidloes and Newtown Telegraph*, 10 September 1859.
55. *Llanidloes and Newtown Telegraph*, 10 September 1859.
56. Gasquoine, pp 23–25.
57. Kinsey. The acrostic is dated 'Llandinam, August 31 1859', and was printed by 'Cliff, Printer, Newtown.'

5   The Little Urchin

1. *Carnarvon Herald*, 3 September 1859.
2. Ibid., 27 July 1859.
3. Ibid., 3 September 1859.
4. *Dictionary of National Biography*, Vol. 20, Oxford, 1921/22.
5. Henry W. Lucy: *A Diary of Two Parliaments: The Disraeli Parliament 1874–80*, London, 1885, p 91.
6. See note 4.
7. Ivor Thomas, p 46.
8. *Eddowes' Shrewsbury Journal*, 7 September 1859.
9. Notice: Llanidloes & Newtown Railway, September 1859. RAIL 92/132. PRO.
10. Ibid.
11. Ivor Thomas, p 48.
12. *Oswestry Advertiser*, 7 September 1859.
13. Leading article in unidentified newspaper. RAIL 92/132. PRO.

6   Large Sceams With Great Risk

1. Edwin Jones, Box E1/1, Lord Davies. NLW; *Barry Dock News* 19 July 1889.
2. 1861 Census.
3. Edwin Jones; also Ivor Thomas, p 50.
4. Edwin Jones.
5. 1861 Census.
6. *Eddowes' Shrewsbury Journal*, 7 September 1859.
7. Christiansen & Miller: *The Cambrian Railways*, p 30.
8. Cutting from unidentified newspaper, RAIL 92/132. PRO.
9. Ibid.
10. Christiansen & Miller, p 31.
11. Gasquoine, p 41.
12. Christiansen & Miller, p 31.
13. *The Times*, 18 August 1865.

14. Christiansen & Miller, p 31.
15. Baughan, p 151, says the Montgomery was one of six Sharp, Stewart 0—4—2 mixed-traffic tender engines built in 1859—60 which in time came to work the entire length of track between Oswestry and Machynlleth, under a joint committee of the O&N and L&N companies.
16. Gasquoine, p 44.
17. Gasquoine, p 46.
18. Oswestry & Newtown Railway Co. records, 2 August 1860. RAIL 1110/55. PRO.
19. Baughan, p 151.
20. Richard Williams.
21. Baughan, p 151.
22. Richard Williams.
23. David Davies to Ann Warburton Owen, 27 November 1860. Glansevern Vol. 4/6462. NLW.
24. *Cambrian News*, 25 July 1890.
25. *Montgomeryshire Echo*, 26 July 1890.
26. Goronwy Jones.
27. See particularly David Davies to Ann Warburton Owen, 27 November 1860, Glansevern Vol. 4/6462 and 26 August 1861, Glansevern Vol. 4/6463. NLW.
28. Christiansen & Miller, p 32.
29. Oswestry Advertiser, 25 September 1861.
30. Terry Coleman: *The Railway Navvies*, London, 1965, pp 49—50.
31. *Oswestry Advertiser*, 17 August 1859.
32. *Shrewsbury Chronicle*, 27 September 1861.
33. Ibid.
34. Ibid.
35. Ibid.
36. Ivor Thomas, p 64.
37. Llandinam Papers. A: Group 1/5. NLW. The dispute was with George Symonds of Newtown and the referee was John Wilkes Poundley, county surveyor of Montgomeryshire.
38. The partnership was dissolved on 12 February 1861, according to Llandinam Papers. A: Group 1/4. NLW.
39. *Shrewsbury Chronicle*, 6 September 1861.
40. Ibid; also supplement to the *Railway Times*, 7 September 1861.
41. The *Railway Times*, as above.
42. *Shrewsbury Chronicle*, 20 September 1861.
43. Ibid.
44. The House of Commons, presumably.
45. David Davies to Ann Warburton Owen, 26 August 1861, Glansevern Vol 4/6463. NLW.
46. Ivor Thomas, p 60.
47. Goronwy Jones.
48. See note 40.
49. Christiansen & Miller, p 33.

7   Comradeship in Labour

1. Kinsey, 8 January 1861.
2. Ibid., 8 April 1861.
3. Ibid., 25 October 1860.
4. Ibid., 17 November 1860.
5. Ibid., 25 December 1860.

6. David Davies, 'An Essay on Llanidloes 1861.' This translation from his Welsh appears in *The Montgomeryshire Collections*, Vol. 61, 1969–70.
7. Kinsey, 30 December 1860.
8. Ibid., 14 May 1861.
9. Ibid., 12 May 1861.
10. Ibid., 15 May 1861.
11. Gasquoine, p 51.
12. Ibid., p 52.
13. David Davies letter to *Shrewsbury Chronicle*, 22 September 1861.
14. The *Railway Times*, 28 September 1861.
15. *Shrewsbury Chronicle*, 27 September 1861.
16. Ibid.
17. *Oswestry Advertiser*, 10 September 1862.
18. *Barry Dock News*, 19 July 1889.
19. Johnny Griffiths, Llandinam. See note 24, chapter 3.
20. Goronwy Jones.
21. Edwin Jones, Box E1/1, Lord Davies. NLW.
22. See the recollections of Matthew Humphreys and the notes of Edwin Jones, Box 1, Lord Davies. NLW.
23. R. Williams, Montgomeryshire Dialect (Newtown), *The Montgomeryshire Collections*, Vol. 24, London, 1890.
24. *Shrewsbury Chronicle*, 27 September 1861.
25. *Oswestry Advertiser*, 5 March 1862.
26. The *County Times* (Montgomeryshire), 14 April 1923.
27. The *Railway Times*, 16 November 1861.
28. *Oswestry Advertiser*, 30 April 1862.
29. Goronwy Jones.
30. *Oswestry Advertiser*, 30 April 1862.
31. Ibid., 13 August 1862.
32. Ibid., 6 May 1862.
33. Ibid.
34. Ibid., 10 September 1862.
35. *Oswestry Advertiser*, 7 January 1863; *Montgomeryshire Mercury*, 24 June 1863; *Oswestry Advertiser*, 24 October 1863.
36. Christiansen & Miller, p 45.
37. *Oswestry Advertiser*, 1 October 1862.
38. Ibid., 22 October 1862.
39. Ibid., 12 February 1862.
40. Ibid., 3 December 1862.
41. Newtown and Machynlleth Railway Co records. PRO.
42. Kinsey, 22 June 1862.
43. Ibid., 15 October, 1862.

8   One of the Gentry

1. 1851 Census.
2. Lord Davies to Ivor Thomas, see note 11, Chapter 1.
3. David Davies's involvement in the Sardinian project is described by Ivor Thomas, pp 71–72. Curiously, in his detailed description of Piercy's work in Sardinia in *Montgomeryshire Worthies*, Richard Williams does not mention Davies at all.
4. Richard Williams, *Montgomeryshire Worthies*.
5. Ivor Thomas, p 135.
6. 1851 Census and 1861 Census.
7. 1871 Census.

8. Matthew Humphreys, *Y Brython Cymreig*, 28 July 1893. Translated for author by Dafydd Ifans.
9. *Montgomeryshire Express*, 17 April 1923.
10. *Montgomeryshire Express*, 10 April and 17 April 1923; *County Times*, 14 April 1923.
11. C.E. Vaughan Owen, Llanidloes: Pamphlet, Llandinam Parish Church.
12. Kinsey, 20 May 1864.
13. Ibid.
14. Register of deaths, Llanwnog Sub-district.

9 The Cross-way

1. J.H. Morris and L.J. Williams: *The South Wales Coal Industry 1841–1875*, Cardiff, 1958, p 77.
2. Ibid.; William Rees: *An Historical Atlas of Wales*, London, 1959, p 70.
3. John Coke Fowler: *Collieries and Colliers*, London, 1861. Fowler, barrister and stipendiary magistrate for Merthyr Tydfil and Aberdare, notes on p 1: 'It is a general maxim of the common law, that whatever is in a direct line between the surface of any land and the centre of the earth belongs to the owner of the surface.'
4. Ivor Thomas, p 144.
5. Hon. Society of Cymmrodorion: *The Dictionary of Welsh Biography*, London, 1959.
6. Charles Wilkins: *The History of the Iron, Steel and Tinplate Trade*, Merthyr Tydfil, 1903, p 69.
7. E.D. Lewis: *The Rhondda Valleys*, Cardiff, 1958, p 69. Lewis notes on p 68 that in 1850 the Taff Vale Railway Co offered a premium of £500 to anyone sinking a pit 120 yards below the river bed in the upper Rhondda Fawr. Clark advised the Bute Trustees to accept the challenge and the Upper Four Feet seam of steam coal at Cwm-Saerbren was proved at a depth of 125 yards.
8. Thomas Roscoe: *Wanderings Through South Wales*, Part 33, p 244.
9. Lady Charlotte Guest: *Extracts from her Journal 1833–1852*; edited by the Earl of Bessborough, London, 1950, p 117.
10. Ivor Thomas, p 145.
11. Llandinam Papers B. Group 1/87. NLW.
12. *North Wales Chronicle*, 3 August 1861.
13. *The Welshman*, 7 September 1866.
14. Ledger showing expenses incurred by Messrs Davies & Roberts, Railway Contractors, Pembroke, August 1862– December 1867 in connection with the Tenby & Pembroke Railroad. Llandinam Papers A: Group 1/6. NLW.
15. *The Welshman*, 7 September 1866.
16. Ibid.
17. Ibid.
18. Llandinam Papers B. Group 1/87. NLW.
19. Ibid.
20. Ivor Thomas, p 147. E.D. Lewis, pp 80 and 81, says the six-foot seam was struck at 253 yards at Maindy and 189 yards at Park: 'much deeper collieries than any others in Rhondda Fawr at that time.'
21. The Ocean Coal Co. was incorporated in 1887, with David Davies controlling the main portion of the capital.
22. John Gibson to David Davies, 7 May 1886. Llandinam E303. NLW.
23. A.P. Barnett & D. Willson-Lloyd (editors): *The South Wales Coalfield*, Cardiff, 1921.
24. *Cambrian News*, 25 July 1890. Leading article written by the editor/proprietor John Gibson.
25. Christiansen & Miller, p 74.
26. Edwin Jones, Box E1/1, Lord Davies. NLW.
27. Llandinam Papers B. Group 1/87. NLW.

28. *Cardiff Times*, 30 March 1866.
29. Ibid., 6 April 1866.
30. 31 August 1866.
31. Ibid., 14 September 1866.
32. Ibid., 2 November 1866.
33. Ibid., 21 December 1866.
34. Ibid., 10 October 1866.
35. Morris and Williams, p 148.
36. Ocean and United National Collieries Ltd: *A Tribute*, Cardiff, 1946, p 7.
37. 14 December 1866.
38. Ibid., 21 December 1866.
39. Ibid., 19 January 1867.
40. Ibid., 30 March 1867.

10   A Fightable Man

1. *Aberystwyth Observer*, 30 September 1865.
2. Ibid.
3. Ibid.
4. Ibid.
5. Ibid.
6. Ieuan Gwynedd Jones: 'The Elections of 1865 and 1868 in Wales,' *The Transactions of the Hon. Society of Cymmrodorion*, Part 1, London, 1964.
7. The *Chester Courant*, 20 October 1858.
8. *The Times*, 8 September 1866.
9. Census returns (see chapter 2).
10. Manchester & Milford Railway Co. records, 14 May 1860. RAIL 456/1. PRO.
11. Ibid., 2 February 1864.
12. Ibid. The report was signed by the company chairman, John Barrow.
13. Ibid., 7 April 1864.
14. Ibid., 17 May, 10 June, 30 August 1864.
15. Election address dated 'Llandinam, July 5th, 1865.'
16. *Aberystwyth Observer*, 22 July 1865.
17. Ibid.
18. Herbert M. Vaughan: *The South Wales Squires*, London, 1926, reprinted Carmarthen 1988, p 152.
19. See note 6.
20. *Aberystwyth Observer*, 8 July 1865.
21. *The Dictionary of Welsh Biography*.
22. John Matthews to John Matthews Jr, 22 July 1865. Letters to John Matthews. Matthews 1 Collection. NLW 8321E. NLW.
23. Ibid.
24. Ibid.
25. Ibid.
26. Ibid.
27. Henry Richard letter to *Merthyr Telegraph*, 9 November 1867.
28. *Cambrian News*, 25 July 1890.
29. Lord Davies to Ivor Thomas, 1937.
30. The *Montgomeryshire Guardian and Cardiganshire Advertiser*, 26 July 1865.
31. Extract from 'A New Song of Cardiganshire Patriots', pre-1865, quoted by Francis Jones in *Cardiganshire Election Songs*, Ceredigion, Vol 5, 1964–67. NLW.
32. Lord Davies to Ivor Thomas, 1937.
33. *Aberystwyth Observer*, 22 July 1865.

34. Thomas Harris, Llechryd, quoted in letter from 'Iddhon Goch' to Aberdare Times, 4 January 1868.
35. *Aberystwyth Observer*, 22 July 1865.
36. Ibid.
37. Ibid.
38. See ref 15.
39. *Aberystwyth Observer*, 22 July 1865.
40. Ibid.
41. Ibid.
42. *The Times*, 24 July 1865.
43. Extract from contemporary leaflet in sundry notes in Box 1/3, Lord Davies. NLW.
44. *Aberystwyth Observer*, 22 July 1865.
45. See note 22.
46. *Aberystwyth Observer*, 29 July 1865.
47. Broadsheet, 'The Conservatives of Cardiganshire', 1865, in scrap-book kept in Llandinam Church.

11   Across Cors Caron

1. Matthew Humphreys, *Y Brython Cymreig*, 28 July 1893.
2. *The Times*, 14 August 1865.
3. *The Dictionary of Welsh Biography*.
4. See note 2.
5. *The Times*, 22 August 1865.
6. Herbert Spencer: 'Railway Morals and Railway Policy', reprinted from *The Edinburgh Review*, London, 1855.
7. *The Welshman*, 16 August 1867.
8. Ibid., 31 August 1866.
9. David Davies a William T. Hughes: *Atgofion Dau Grefftwr*, Aberystwyth, 1963. Translated for author by Lilian M. Williams.
10. Terry Coleman, pp 39–40.
11. *Aberystwyth Observer*, 17 August 1867.
12. Ibid., 6 January 1866.
13. Ibid.
14. Manchester & Milford Railway Co. records, 6 February 1866. RAIL 456/1. PRO.
15. Ibid., 12 October 1866.
16. *The Welshman*, 31 August 1866.
17. Ibid.
18. David Davies, quoted in *The Welshman*, 16 August 1867.
19. *The Welshman*, 7 September 1866.
20. Ibid., 16 August 1867.
21. Ibid., 31 August 1866.
22. *Aberystwyth Observer*, 7 September 1867.
23. Defunct Companies files: David Davies and Co., Davies, Scott and Co., Ocean Coal Co., BT 31, PRO.
24. *The Welshman*, 31 August 1866.
25. *Aberystwyth Observer*, 17 August 1867.
26. *The Welshman*, 16 August 1867.
27. Ibid.
28. Ibid.
29. Ibid.

12 Strangers in the Valley

1. Confession of Faith of the Calvinistic Methodists, adopted at the Associations of Aberystwyth and Bala in 1823; pp 54–60 of the translation from the Welsh, printed in Conway, 1900.
2. Revd Professor S.I. Enoch of Aberystwyth in conversation with the author, 20 March 1990. Also Professor Ronald Feuerhahn of Concordia Seminary, St Louis, Missouri, USA, writing to the author on 26 February 1990: 'There has been in Calvinistic communities almost a doctrine of success — the Elect are bound to be successful. That shows the glory of God by the fact that He so often blesses His Elect. Today in North America there is even a discussion of "Success Theology."'
3. E.T. Davies: *Religion in the Industrial Revolution in South Wales*, Cardiff, 1965, p 53.
4. Confession of Faith, note 1, pp 24, 25, 26, 28.
5. The relevant details are in extracts from reports on the ordinary half-yearly meetings of David Davies and Co. held in Cardiff on 15 August 1872 and 13 February 1874, contained in Box 1/5, Lord Davies. NLW.
6. W.J. Thomas, Ocean Collieries, Treorchy, to V.J. Lewis, Aberystwyth, 9 September 1933. Box 1/5, Lord Davies. NLW.
7. *South Wales Coal Annual*, 1922.
8. William Rees: *Cardiff: A History of the City*, Cardiff 1969, pp 271, 273.
9. *Barry Dock News*, 25 July 1890.
10. David Davies to William Jenkins, 15 March 1882. W.J. Lewis notes in Box 1/3, Lord Davies. NLW.
11. Ibid.
12. D.J. Williams: *Capitalist Combination in the Coal Industry*, London, 1924, p 58.
13. A.P. Barnett & D.Willson-Lloyd: *The South Wales Coalfield*.
14. *Western Mail*, 20 July 1871.
15. Alexander Dalziel: *The Colliers' Strike in South Wales*, Cardiff, 1871. Although unashamedly an employer's view of the 1871 strike, this gives detailed information on its progress.
16. Ibid.
17. Ibid.
18. Ibid.
19. *Western Mail*, 28 July 1871.
20. Ibid., 1 August 1871.
21. Dalziel.
22. *Western Mail*, 14 August 1871.
23. Dalziel.
24. Ibid.
25. *Western Mail*, 7 August 1871.
26. Ibid., 10 August 1871.
27. Ibid., 11 August 1871.
28. Ibid., 15 August 1871.
29. Ibid., 1 February 1872.
30. Ibid., 29 January 1872.
31. Ibid., 11 August 1871.

13 A Ghost at the Feast

1. 'Letters of Administration of all and singular the personal estate and effects of Elizabeth Davies late of Nyoddfach [*sic*] in the parish of Llandinam ... were granted by Her Majesty's Court of Probate to David Davies one of the natural and lawful children and one of the next of kin ...' Box 1/8, Lord Davies. NLW.
2. Mainly About People, unsigned column in the *Star*, London, 23 July 1890.

3. Eirene White. *The Ladies of Gregynog*, Newtown, 1984, pp 12–13.
4. The *Montgomeryshire Express*, 4 January 1898, says Edward Davies obtained his early education at a school in Chester and the Holt Academy, Wrexham, where he passed the Oxford and Cambridge examination in senior mathematics and Scripture.
5. *Western Mail*, 4 January 1873.
6. Ibid., 27 January 1873.
7. Ivor Thomas, p 163.
8. See ref 2.
9. This account of the day's events is based on the reports in *The Welshman*, 20 June 1873, and the *Newtown and Welshpool Express*, 16 June 1873. *The Welshman* fully reports the speeches, but the words of the song for Edward appear only in the *Express*.
10. If one excludes the iron manufacturers, the largest coal producer in south Wales at this time was the Powell Duffryn Steam Coal Co.

14   Where Are The Rich Men?

1. *Barry Dock News*, 25 July 1890.
2. Ibid.
3. Gibson to Stuart Rendel, 13 March 1894. He notes how David Davies 'practically sulked with me because I paid him £400 he had lent me to purchase the paper (*Cambrian News*). He never forgave me for repaying him. He thought the money was lent to me by some of his opponents to repay him. And when I fought him in 1886 he had no doubt about it!' NLW 20571D.
4. *Cambrian News*, 25 July 1890.
5. Goronwy Jones.
6. E.L. Ellis: *The University College of Wales, Aberystwyth, 1872–1972*, Cardiff, 1972, p 6.
7. Ibid., p 11.
8. Ibid., p 13.
9. Ibid., p 14.
10. Ibid., p 14.
11. Ibid., p 19.
12. Ibid., p 20.
13. Ibid., pp 20–24.
14. *Cardiff Times*, 4 May 1867.
15. David Davies to T.C.Edwards, 29 March 1876. T.I. Ellis (editor), *Thomas Charles Edwards Letters*, Aberystwyth, 1952.
16. E.L.Ellis, p 50.
17. *Barry Dock News*, 25 July 1890.
18. E.L.Ellis, p 91.
19. David Davies to Lewis Edwards, 19 October 1886. *T.C. Edwards Letters*.
20. *Cambrian News*, 18 October 1872.
21. Hughes Jones notes, Box E1/7, Lord Davies. NLW; E.L. Ellis, pp 8, 14, 34.
22. *Cambrian News*, 18 October 1872.
23. Ibid.
24. Ibid.
25. Ibid. 'Spare ribs' appears in the report, but Davies is more likely to have said 'bare ribs' – an understandable error, perhaps, by the hard-pressed reporter making a verbatim note of the speech.
26. Ibid.
27. VJL notes, Box E1/4, Lord Davies. NLW.
28. Ibid.; Ivor Thomas, p 172.

29. *Newtown and Welshpool Express*, 1 February 1870.
30. Edwin Jones notes, Box E1/1, Lord Davies. NLW.
31. Goronwy Jones.
32. Cambrian Railways Co. Board Minute Book No 1, 21 February 1867, RAIL 92/17 pt 2. PRO.
33. Christiansen & Miller, p 71.
34. Cambrian Minute Book 1, 8 March 1867. PRO.
35. Ibid., 22 March 1867.
36. Ibid., 6 April 1867.
37. Cambrian Railways Co. Board Minute Book No 2, 6 August 1869. RAIL 92/1. PRO.
38. Ibid., 17 September 1869.
39. VJL notes, Box E1/4. NLW.
40. *Cambrian News*, 16 July 1870.
41. Pauline Phillips: *A View of Montgomeryshire*, Swansea, 1977, p 133.
42. Lewis Cozens: *The Van and Kerry Railways*, London, 1953, p 9.
43. Llandinam Papers. A: Group 1/4. Van Railway General Cash Account 1870–1877. NLW.
44. Richard Williams; Lewis Cozens, p 12.
45. Lewis Cozens.
46. Lord Davies to Ivor Thomas, Box E1/1, Lord Davies. NLW.
47. Kinsey, 5 July 1870.
48. Ibid., 26 October 1865.
49. Ibid., 13–15 March 1867.
50. Ibid., 24 January 1868.
51. Ibid., 2 June 1869.
52. See especially *Slater's Directory*, Manchester, 1868.

15   Into Parliament He Shall Go!

1. *Aberystwyth Observer*, 8 August 1868.
2. David Davies to John Matthews, 1 August 1868, NLW 8321E.
3. Thomas Harris to John Matthews, 19 June 1868, NLW 8321E.
4. Lord Davies to Ivor Thomas, Box E1/1, Lord Davies. NLW.
5. Ivor Thomas to Lord Davies, 23 October 1937, Box E1/2, Lord Davies. NLW.
6. *Merionethshire Standard*, 28 November 1868.
7. See note 4.
8. Kenneth O. Morgan: *Wales In British Politics 1868–1922*, Cardiff, 1963, p 22.
9. *Merionethshire Standard*, 5 December 1868.
10. Fragment of letter, author and date unknown, to E.M. Richards, NLW 8321E.
11. Robert Blake: *Disraeli*, London, 1966, p 538.
12. *Cambrian News*, 30 January 1874.
13. Ibid.
14. Ibid.
15. Herbert M. Vaughan, p 125.
16. *Cambrian News*, 13 February 1874.
17. Ibid., 20 February 1874.
18. F.W.S.Craig (editor): *British Electoral Facts*, London, 1881.
19. Henry W. Lucy: *A Diary of Two Parliaments. The Disraeli Parliament of 1874–1880*, London, 1885. See especially pp 267 and 286.
20. Ibid.
21. Ibid., p 91.
22. Kinsey, 23 April 1874.
23. Hansard, Vol. 218, 23 April 1874.

24. Ibid.
25. Quoted in *Cambrian News*, 1 May 1874.
26. Hansard, Vol. 218, 27 April 1874.
27. Ibid., 28 April 1874.
28. Ibid., Vol. 219, 11 June 1874.
29. Ibid., Vol. 220, 17 June 1874.
30. Lucy, p 267.
31. *South Wales Daily News*, 15 December 1875.
32. Ibid.
33. Ibid.
34. Blake, p 553.

16 Despots and Poltroons

1. Trevor Boyns: 'Growth in the Coal Industry: the Cases of Powell Duffryn and the Ocean Coal Co, 1864–1913', p 166. This is a contribution to *Modern South Wales: Essays in Economic History*, edited by Colin Baber and L.J. Williams, Cardiff, 1986.
2. Aled Eames: *Ventures in Sail*, London, 1987, p 20. 'A Note on Comparative Values (1840–1982)' is based on tables compiled by E. Barry Bowyer in the *Sunday Telegraph*, 5 September 1985.
3. Boyns, p 165.
4. *Ocean and United National Collieries Ltd: A Tribute*, Cardiff, 1946, p 7.
5. R.H. Walters: *The Economic and Business History of the South Wales Steam Coal Industry 1840–1914*, New York, 1977, p 100.
6. Walters, p 163.
7. *Ocean Tribute*, p 15.
8. Ibid., p 9.
9. *The Ocean and National Magazine*, vol 2, no 4, April 1929, p 101.
10. *Post Office Directory of Monmouthshire and South Wales*, 1871, p 19.
11. *History of the Barry Railway Co, 1884–1921*, Cardiff, 1923, p 123.
12. Ibid.
13. Walters p 302.
14. Walters p 164.
15. *The Ocean and National Magazine*, vol 6, no 4, April 1933, p 126.
16. Hansard, Vol. 218, 23 April 1874.
17. See note 15.
18. *Colliery Guardian*, 1 January 1875.
19. Ibid., 22 January 1875.
20. Ibid., 29 January 1875.
21. Ibid., 12 February 1875.
22. Ibid.
23. *The Times*, 17 March 1875.
24. E. Page Arnot: *The Miners*, London, 1949, p 45.
25. See note 23.
26. *The Times*, 24 March 1875.
27. *Colliery Guardian*, 26 February 1875.
28. *The Times*, 29 March 1875.
29. *Colliery Guardian*, 16 April 1875.
30. Ibid.
31. Ibid.
32. Ibid., 28 May 1875.
33. Ibid., 4 June 1875.
34. *South Wales Daily News*, 12 May 1875.
35. *Colliery Guardian*, 22 January 1875.

36. Sir Thomas Hughes: *Great Welshmen of Modern Days*, Cardiff, 1931, p 17. See also Barnett and Willson-Lloyd.
37. W.T. Lewis to David Davies, 31 May 1877, Coalowners' Scrap-book, NLW CC10.
38. L.J. Williams: 'The Coalowners of South Wales 1873–80'. *Welsh History Review*, Vol. 8, June 1876.
39. *South Wales Daily News*, 25 May 1877.
40. Ibid., 14 June 1877.
41. Ivor Thomas, pp 164–165.

17   What Price Education?

1. E.L. Ellis, p 44.
2. *South Wales Daily News*, 16 April, 1875.
3. David Davies to T.C. Edwards, 29 March 1876, *Thomas Charles Edwards Letters*.
4. Ibid., 31 March 1876.
5. Ibid., 22 April 1876.
6. Ibid.
7. E.L.Ellis, p 47.
8. Hansard, Vol. 225, 1 July 1875.
9. Ibid., Vol. 229, 15 June 1876.
10. Ibid.
11. Ibid., Vol. 241.
12. Ibid.
13. Ibid., Vol. 223, 21 April 1875.
14. Ibid., Vol. 229, 15 June 1876.
15. Ibid., Vol. 228, 4 April 1876.
16. Goronwy Jones states in his biography that Davies became a county magistrate in 1873.
17. Hansard, Vol. 234, 7 June 1877.
18. Ibid., Vol. 228, 3 April 1876.
19. Ibid., Vol. 234, 11 April 1878.
20. Ibid., Vol. 297, 20 April 1883.
21. Ibid., Vol. 234, 11 April 1878.
22. Ibid., Vol. 234, 13 May 1878.
23. Ibid., Vol. 238, 21 February 1878.
24. Ibid., Vol. 240, 30 May 1878.
25. Ibid., Vol. 234, 14 May 1878.
26. Ibid., Vol. 234, 10 May 1878.
27. Ibid., Vol. 244, 11 March 1879.
28. Ibid. This was A. Pell, Conservative MP for Leicestershire Southern.

18   The Iron Safe

1. Barnett and Willson-Lloyd, p 28.
2. Charles Wilkins: *The South Wales Coal Trade*, Cardiff, 1888.
3. 43rd Annual Report, North and South Wales Bank, January 1879, Llandinam Papers D282. NLW.
4. Rhodri Walters: 'Capital Formation in the South Wales Coal Industry, 1840–1914', *Welsh History Review*, Vol. 10, June 1980.
5. David Davies to George Lewis, 22 January 1879, Llandinam Papers A: Group 3/39. NLW.
6. Ibid., 23 January 1879.
7. David Davies to Cambrian Railways Directors, 17 February 1879, Llandinam Papers, Box 1/8. NLW.

8.   David Davies to R.D. Pryce, 17 February 1879, Llandinam Papers A: Group 3/39. NLW.
9.   Llandinam Papers A: Group 3/39. NLW.
10. Ibid. The telegram was sent on 19 February 1879.
11. *Oswestry Advertiser*, 5 March 1879.
12. Marquess of Londonderry to David Davies, 6 March 1879, Llandinam, Box 1/8. NLW.
13. Llandinam, Box 1/8, 18 June 1879. NLW.
14. Lord Davies to Ivor Thomas, 27 September 1937, Box E1/2, Lord Davies. NLW.

19   Wanting All

1.   *The Welshman*, 20 June 1873.
2.   David Davies to Edward Davies, 15 March 1882, Llandinam Papers E 290/20. NLW.
3.   See note 1.
4.   *Western Mail*, 14 March 1882.
5.   See note 2.
6.   *Western Mail*, 30 March 1882.
7.   Ibid.
8.   Ibid.
9.   *South Wales Daily News*, 7 August 1882.
10. Ibid., 5 August 1882.
11. David Davies to Stuart Rendel, 22 July 1886, NLW 19449D.
12. Hansard, Vol. 228, 28 March 1876.
13. Ibid., Vol. 225, 13 July 1875.
14. Ibid., Vol. 241, 2 July 1878.
15. Ibid.
16. Ibid., Vol. 251, 4 March 1880.
17. *Cambrian News*, 19 March 1880.
18. Henry W. Lucy: *A Diary of Two Parliaments: The Gladstone Parliament 1880–1885*, London, 1886, p 7.
19. *The Dictionary of Welsh Biography*.
20. Biographical note in Vol. 4, Rendel Papers. NLW.
21. A.C. Humphreys-Owen to Stuart Rendel, 1 October 1879, Rendel Papers, NLW 19459C32.
22. Stuart Rendel to A.C. Humphreys-Owen, 2 October 1879, Glansevern Papers Vol. 1/35. NLW.
23. Stuart Rendel to A.C. Humphreys-Owen, 22 July 1880, Glansevern Papers Vol. 1/52. NLW.
24. Thomas Edward Ellis (1859–99) entered the UCW, Aberystwyth, in 1875 and matriculated at New College, Oxford, in 1880. He was Liberal MP for Merioneth, 1886–99. A nationalist, he was a founder of the Cymru Fydd (New Wales) movement.
25. T.I. Ellis: *Thomas Edward Ellis Cofiant*, Liverpool, 1944.
26. Hansard, Vol. 251, 9 March 1880.
27. Ibid. C.H. Raikes, MP for Chester, provided these statistics during the debate, quoting Board of Trade returns and evidence to the Royal Commission on Railway Accidents, 1877.
28. Ibid.
29. Ibid., Vol. 260, 3 May 1881.
30. Ibid.
31. Ibid., Vol. 281, 1 March 1882.

20   A Funny Dog

1.   *Cambrian News*, 25 July 1890.
2.   Harold Pollins, 'The Development of Transport 1750–1914', in *Glamorgan County History*, Vol. 5, p 453.
3.   *Western Mail* 13, 21, 23 October 1882, *South Wales Daily News* 23, 24 October 1882.
4.   See note 2, p 479.
5.   Lord Davies to Ivor Thomas, Box E1/1, Lord Davies. NLW.
6.   *South Wales Daily News*, 7 October 1882; also Western Mail, same date.
7.   *Cardiff Times*, 1 March 1873.
8.   *Western Mail*, 20 April 1883.
9.   Barry Dock and Railways Bill. Minutes of Proceedings, 10 April 1883.
10. Ibid. Evidence of Joseph Laing Bourne, secretary to the Cardiff Mutual Iron Steamship Insurance Association.
11. *Western Mail*, 20 April 1883.
12. Archibald Hood was one of the promoters of the Barry scheme.
13. R.J. Rimell: *History of the Barry Railway Company, 1884–1921*, Cardiff, 1923, p 28.
14. Crawshay Bailey gave evidence on 12 July 1883.
15. Translation of article by Revd D. Lloyd Jones, Llandinam, in *Y Drysorfa*, September 1880. Box E1/4, Lord Davies Papers. NLW.
16. David Davies to Edward Davies, 10 August 1883, Llandinam Papers E293. NLW.
17. Tylor gave evidence on the fourteenth day of the hearing, 29 July 1884.
18. *South Wales Daily News*, 1 August 1884.
19. Ibid.
20. See note 13, p 35.
21. *South Wales Daily News*, 15 November 1884.

21   Votiwch Dros David Davies!

1.   *Western Mail*, 24 January 1883.
2.   *South Wales Daily News*, 3 August 1883.
3.   E.L. Ellis, p 75.
4.   Ibid., p 77.
5.   Ibid., p 82.
6.   Stuart Rendel to A.C. Humphreys-Owen, 18 March 1884, Glansevern Papers, Vol. 1/141. NLW.
7.   David R. Howell: 'Stuart Rendel and Welsh Liberal Political Organization in the Late 19th Century', *Welsh History Review*, Vol. 9 No 4, December 1979.
8.   Rendel to M.E. Grant-Duff, 7 October 1884, Rendel Papers, NLW 20572D.
9.   Hansard, Vol. 268, 19 April 1882.
10. Ibid., Vol. 297, 20 April 1883.
11. Lord Davies to Ivor Thomas, 1937.
12. Edwin Jones: Box E1/1, Lord Davies Papers. NLW.
13. Hansard, Vol. 272, 20 July 1882.
14. Henry W. Lucy, p 221.
15. David Davies to A.C. Humphreys-Owen, 8 July 1882, Glansevern Papers, Vol 1/5669. NLW.
16. Henry P. Cobb to Rendel, 27 January 1885, Rendel Papers, NLW 19449D.
17. Hansard, Vol. 282, 20 July 1883.
18. J.O. Morgan: *Cardiganshire Politics: The Liberal Ascendancy 1885–1923*, Ceredigion, Vol. 5 No 4, 1967.
19. Lord Davies to Ivor Thomas, 1937.
20. Rendel to Humphreys-Owen, 4 February 1885, Glansevern Papers, Vol 1/194. NLW.

21. David Davies to Rendel, 22 July 1886, Rendel, NLW 194449D29.
22. Davies to Rendel, 1 August 1885, Rendel, NLW 194449D27.
23. *Cambrian News*, 27 November 1885.
24. Ibid.
25. *Western Mail*, 17 November 1885.
26. John Davies, Tregaron, to H.C. Fryer, 20 October 1885, NLW 19643B15a.
27. *Cambrian News*, 6 November 1885.
28. Ibid., 16 October 1885.
29. Ibid., 23 October 1885.
30. John Davies, Llanon, to Fryer, 17 October 1885, NLW 19643B9.
31. Davies to Fryer, 19 November 1885, NLW 19643B10.
32. John Davies, Tregaron, to Fryer, 19 November 1885, NLW 19643B17.
33. John M. Howell, Aberaeron, to Fryer, 21 November 1885, NLW 19643B66.
34. See especially NLW 19643B18/27/30/65a/69/71.
35. O.S. Owen, Sarnau, to Fryer, 10 November 1885, NLW 19643B112.
36. F.W.S. Craig, quoting Home Office Returns of Illiterate Voters.
37. John M. Howell to Fryer, 17 November 1885, NLW 19643B62.
38. NLW 19643B2.
39. *Cambrian News*, 27 November 1885.
40. O. Beynon Evans, Cardigan, to Fryer, 29 October 1885, NLW 19643B52.
41. *Aberystwyth Observer*, 28 November 1885.
42. Ibid., 5 December 1885.
43. *Cambrian News*, 4 December 1885.

22   The Bogs of Whiggism

1. *Western Mail*, 10 July 1885.
2. Ivor Thomas, p 265.
3. *Cambrian News*, 27 November 1885.
4. Ivor Thomas, p 265.
5. Ibid p 263.
6. David Davies to Lewis Edwards, 19 October 1886, *Thomas Charles Edwards Letters*; J. Cynddylan Jones to Edward Davies, 26 October 1886, Llandinam E303. NLW.
7. *Cambrian News*, 6 November 1885.
8. David Davies to Stuart Rendel, 22 July 1886, Rendel, NLW 19449D29.
9. David Davies to Edward Davies, 27 January 1886, Llandinam E301. NLW.
10. John Morley: *Life of Gladstone*, Vol 2, London, 1908, p 367.
11. A.C. Humphreys-Owen to Edward Davies, 20 February 1886, Llandinam E301. NLW.
12. Stuart Rendel to Humphreys-Owen, 1 February 1886, Glansevern Papers Vol 1/231. NLW.
13. Ibid.
14. Edward Davies letter from 'Ocean Collieries, Treorky', dated 13 April 1886, Llandinam E302, NLW. The recipient was probably C.M. Williams, who on 9 April had invited him to become an honorary member of the Rheidol Lodge of Odd Fellows Friendly Society. Other honorary members, wrote Mr Williams, included 'your much respected father.'
15. Morley, Vol 2, pp 408–412.
16. John Gibson to David Davies, 1 May 1886, Llandinam E303. NLW.
17. Ibid.
18. Gibson to Davies, 7 May 1886, Llandinam E303. NLW.
19. Ibid., 19 May 1886.
20. Ibid., 29 May 1886.
21. *Cambrian News*, 7 May 1886. Ellis wrote under the pseudonym 'Cymro.'

22. See note 20.
23. T.E.Ellis to David Daniel, 17 February 1886, quoted in T.I. Ellis, *Thomas Edward Ellis Cofiant.*
24. Morley, Vol 2, p 436.
25. *Cambrian News*, 25 June 1886.
26. D.J. Jones to Edward Davies (undated), Llandinam E302. NLW.
27. *Cambrian News*, 25 June 1886.
28. See note 21.
29. *Cambrian News*, 23 July 1886.
30. Ibid., 2 July 1886.
31. Ibid., 25 June 1886.
32. Ibid., 2 July 1886.
33. Ibid., 9 July 1886.
34. *Aberystwyth Observer*, 3 July 1886.

23   Why?

1. P.W., Up and Down the Coast, *Cambrian News*, 16 July 1886.
2. *Cambrian News*, 30 July 1886.
3. T. Davies to Edward Davies, 16 July 1886, Llandinam E302. NLW.
4. John Williams, Aberystwyth, to Edward Davies, 13 July 1886, Llandinam E302. NLW.
5. *Aberystwyth Observer*, 17 May 1886.
6. *Montgomeryshire Express*, 27 July 1886.
7. Ibid.
8. David Davies to Stuart Rendel, 22 July 1886, Rendel NLW 19449D29.
9. Ibid.
10. Rendel is identified as the author from Woodall's letter to him on 1 August 1886, NLW 19456D583.
11. *Oswestry Advertizer*, 4 August 1886.
12. David Davies to Lewis Edwards, 19 October 1886, *T.C. Edwards Letters.*
13. J. Cynddylan Jones, Whitchurch, nr Cardiff, to Edward Davies, 26 October 1886. Llandinam E303. NLW.

24   The Consecration of Wealth

1. W.J. Thomas, Ocean Collieries, Treorchy, to V.J. Lewis, 9 September, 1933. Box E1/5, Lord Davies. NLW.
2. Boyns, p 163.
3. *South Wales Daily News*, 18 February 1888.
4. *History of Barry Railway Co.*, p 39.
5. Ibid., p 40.
6. Ibid., p 37.
7. Ibid., p 42.
8. Ibid., p 45.
9. Ibid., p 47.
10. *Barry Dock News*, 26 July 1889.
11. *History of Barry Railway Co.*, p 61.
12. *Barry Dock News*, 26 July 1889.
13. Ibid.
14. They were the offspring of the marriage of Edward Davies and his cousin Mary Jones, who married in 1877.
15. Ian Parrott: *The Spiritual Pilgrims*, Narberth, 1964.
16. Sir Thomas Hughes, writing in the *Western Mail*, 26 November 1930.

17. Edwin Jones: Box E1/1, Lord Davies. NLW.
18. *Barry Dock News*, 25 July 1890.
19. Ibid.
20. Ibid.
21. Daniel Rowlands in *Y Traethodydd*, November 1890. Box E1/4, Lord Davies. NLW.
22. *Montgomeryshire Express*, 29 July 1890.
23. See especially the *Montgomeryshire Express*, 29 July 1890 and *Montgomeryshire Echo*, 26 July 1890.
24. *North Wales Observer and Express*, quoted in the *Barry Dock News*, 1 August 1890.
25. *Barry Dock News*, 25 July 1890.
26. *Ocean and United National Collieries: A Tribute*, p 9.
27. Boyns, p 165.
28. Ibid, p 168.
29. This 'spiritual conversation' is recorded in the D. Teifigar Davies collection in NLW. I am indebted to Dafydd Ifans for his translation.

Select Bibliography

Colin Baber and L.J. Williams (editors): *Modern South Wales: Essays in Economic History*; Cardiff, 1986.

Robert Blake: *Disraeli*; London, 1966.

Rex Christiansen & R.W. Miller: *The Cambrian Railways*, Vol. 1: 1852–1888; Newton Abbot, 1967.

G.D.H. Cole & Raymond Postgate: *The Common People 1746–1946*; London, 1938.

Terry Coleman: *The Railway Navvies*; London, 1965.

E.T. Davies: *Religion in the Industrial Revolution in South Wales*; Cardiff, 1965.

E.L. Ellis: *The University College of Wales, Aberystwyth 1872–1972*; Cardiff, 1972.

Glyn Tegai Hughes, Prys Morgan and J. Gareth Thomas (editors): *Gregynog*; Cardiff, 1977.

Philip N. Jones: *Colliery Settlement in the South Wales Coalfield, 1850 to 1926*; Hull, 1969.

T. Mervyn Jones: *Going Public*; Cowbridge, 1987.

E.D. Lewis: *The Rhondda Valleys*; Cardiff, 1959.

W.J. Lewis: *Born on a Perilous Rock: Aberystwyth Past and Present*; Aberystwyth, 1980.

Philip Magnus: *Gladstone*; London, 1954.

Donald Moore (editor): *Barry: The Centenary Year Book*; Barry, 1984.

Kenneth O. Morgan: *Wales in British Politics 1868–1922*; Cardiff, 1963. Also *Rebirth of a Nation: Wales 1880–1980*; Oxford, 1981.

Prys Morgan and David Thomas: *Wales: The Shaping of a Nation*; Newton Abbot, 1984.

John Morley: *The Life of William Ewart Gladstone* (2 vols); London, 1908.

J.H. Morris and L.J. Williams: *The South Wales Coal Industry 1841–1875*; Cardiff, 1958.

William Rees: *Cardiff: A History of the City*; Cardiff, 1969.

Dai Smith: *Wales! Wales?*; London, 1984.

Ivor Thomas: *Top Sawyer*; London 1938, reprinted Carmarthen, 1988.

R.H. Walters: *The Economic and Business History of the South Wales Steam Coal Industry 1840–1914*; New York, 1977.

Eirene White: *The Ladies of Gregynog*; Newtown, 1984.

David Williams: *A Short History of Modern Wales*; London, 1961.

Gwyn A. Williams: *When Was Wales?*; London, 1985.

Herbert Williams: *Railways In Wales*; Swansea, 1981.

Index